In Their Presence

In Their Presence

Untold Stories of Women and Children During the AIDS Epidemic

by Dale Napolin Bratter

MIANUS RIVER PRESS • COS COB, CONNECTICUT • 2023

Published by Mianus River Press, mianusriverpress.com

ISBN: 979-8-9880002-0-4 trade paperback
       979-8-9880002-1-1 electronic book

Some identifying information has been changed, such as times and locations of events. Some conversations are verbatim from telephone or in-person interviews or were taken from the videotapes the author produced while at Birch Family Camp. Many conversations have been reconstructed from memory. All the clients' names have been changed.

"A Dream Is a Wish Your Heart Makes"
from *Cinderella*
Music by Mack David and Al Hoffman
Lyrics by Jerry Livingston
© 1948 Walt Disney Music Company
Copyright Renewed.
All Rights Reserved. Used by Permission.
Reprinted by Permission of Hal Leonard LLC

Design and composition: dmargulis.com

First printing

MANUFACTURED IN THE UNITED STATES OF AMERICA

A mi Warren, el marido más querido y solidario del mundo

and

to Susan Widmayer,
who gave me the opportunity to fulfill a long-held dream
of working with women and children with HIV and AIDS

Contents

Acknowledgments

MY LUCK IN LIFE STARTED by being born to my fifty-two- and forty-four-year-old parents, Morris and Dorothy Napolin. They were overjoyed to have a baby at their "advanced" ages and worked hard to step outside their comfort zones so I could pursue things that sometimes scared them. I will forever be grateful to my parents for teaching me to work hard and be kind and inclusive, and for encouraging me to see the humanity in all of us. Having these character traits helped enrich the satisfaction I experienced while working with children and adults with developmental and cognitive disabilities, women with addictions, women experiencing domestic violence, and women and children with HIV and AIDS. I was good at every job I held because my parents' values were always guiding me.

My heartfelt thanks to Susan M. Widmayer, PhD, founder and executive director for thirty years at Children's Diagnostic & Treatment Center in Fort Lauderdale, Florida. Dr. Widmayer gave me the opportunity to fulfill a long-held dream of working with women and children with HIV and AIDS. Her trust and support throughout my decade of employment with CDTC helped contribute to making it the most meaningful professional experience of my life

I am indebted to the women and children in the Comprehensive Family AIDS Program whom I had the honor of knowing and serving. By welcoming me so familiarly into their homes and lives, they taught me more about the world and about myself than I could have ever imagined.

And my gratitude as well to my inspirational colleagues in the Comprehensive Family AIDS Program and the pediatricians and nurses in the clinics. Sharing such an important mission with you made the darkest days brighter and the brighter days more joyous.

I was fortunate to know and work periodically with the late Phyllis Susser. Of her many professional accomplishments, Phyllis established one of the first camp programs for families living with HIV/AIDS. Meeting these people at Birch Family Camp while I was producing the fundraising videotapes lit a flame in me to find a way to work with this population. Five years later I was doing social work in the Comprehensive Family AIDS Program at Children's Diagnostic & Treatment Center. That job was the catalyst for me to write this book. This journey started with Phyllis Susser.

I'm going to change the proverb "It takes a village to raise a child" to "It takes a village to make a book." I am deeply indebted to the following people for working on my manuscript in hands-on ways, as well as providing other forms of deeply meaningful support.

I hit the jackpot with my editor, Philip Bashe. His decades of experience as a book editor and author, coupled with his encouragement and generous compliments, helped this first-time author feel relaxed and confident. I am so privileged to have had the experience of working with Phil.

I am deeply grateful to Barbara Murphy, my more-than-a-sister-in-law, who read and edited the early drafts of my book. As an author of several books and a PhD educator of advanced placement language and other college-level courses for twenty-three years, Barbara guided me with love and generosity of spirit, always presenting new ways for me to think about writing.

Dick Margulis copyedited *In Their Presence* and designed and produced the book. I am very grateful for his comprehensive knowledge and experience, and I appreciated being in his competent hands.

A deep sense of gratitude goes to Carol Vogt, my cherished friend of forty-six years, for her thoroughness in reading my manuscript and helping make it better with her intelligent comments and suggestions.

Special appreciation goes to my Florida friends Eva Axel and Mollie Newman for their encouragement and enthusiasm throughout the years I was writing. Not having lived in Broward County for eighteen years, my recollections about its geography, certain names and locations of organizations, etc., was sometimes hazy. They always filled in the blanks, just as having them in my life always fills me with joy.

Thanks also go to the professionals who assisted me with AIDS research: Pauline Thomas, MD, FAAP, professor, director, Residency in Public Health and Preventive Medicine, Department of Medicine, Rutgers New Jersey Medical School, and General Pediatrics, Summit Health Pediatrics, New Jersey; Murli Purswani, MD, pediatric and adolescent infectious disease specialist at Bronx Care Health System, New York; and staff at the National Institutes of Health, Bethesda, Maryland, and the Centers for Disease Control and Prevention, Washington, D.C., especially Kelly Terry, Customer Service Representative, CDC Non-Surge Generalist Department.

I'd like to acknowledge Walter M. Robinson, a friend of my niece Margo Katz and editor of Eastover Press, an independent press and literary journal. Walter agreed to read a few chapters from my manuscript and responded in the most generous way with two and a half single-spaced pages of important observations and personalized suggestions. These were, he stated, "... intended to improve the manuscript so that it might find a home at a publisher." There is no question that what he wrote did, indeed, make the manuscript better. I am very grateful for his kindness; and Ross Slotten, MD, family medicine specialist with AMITA Health Medical Group, Chicago, Illinois, and author of *Plague Years: A Doctor's Journey Through the AIDS Crisis.* Dr. Slotten gave me excellent guidance about how to get a book published and encouraged me in this process in ways that only another author can do.

You
I was given a curve by life itself.
My heart hardened,
My eyes closed,
And my dreams disappeared.
Before all was forgotten,
A hand reached through my darkened cloud.
There was light.
There was hope.
There was you.

This poem was written in 1991 by Linda Spencer. She and her two sons, Rayshawn, seven, and Floyd, fourteen, attended Birch Family Camp, in Vernon, New Jersey, twice. Linda and Rayshawn were infected with the AIDS virus; Floyd was not. I met the family while producing a fundraising video at the camp. Linda's poem, written while she was at camp, expresses her deep gratitude for the doctors, nurses, and social workers who cared for her and Rayshawn throughout the years of their illness. It also refers to the camp administrators and counselors who saw to it that every day she and her boys spent at camp was filled with unconditional love, unlimited opportunities to experience joy, and the knowledge that, for those few days out of the year, they could all be themselves, with no one judging them.

Rayshawn died at the age of eight in 1992. Linda died less than two years later at age thirty-six.

Introduction

FROM THE MID TO LATE 1980s, articles about acquired immunodeficiency syndrome (AIDS) appeared with increasing frequency in newspapers and magazines and on television. I wanted to learn everything I could about this deadly disease of the immune system, brought about by infection with the human immunodeficiency virus—HIV—although I personally didn't know anyone with the disease. I knew people who *knew people* with AIDS, but it hadn't affected my own life directly.

That changed in 1989.

That was the year I started Heartbeat Productions, a small video production company I ran from my home in Brooklyn Heights, in New York City. My mission was to serve professionals working with special populations. This was my niche for a number of reasons: I held a master's degree in special education from New York University, had been a classroom teacher of students with special needs, and had produced and directed many television shows in the field of special education at WNYE-TV, the New York City Board of Education television station.

One of my clients, Herbert G. Birch Community Services, in Springfield Gardens, New York, a private not-for-profit agency, hired me to create a fundraising video from hours of amateur footage shot at a pilot summer camp project it ran for families of women and children infected with and affected by HIV and AIDS. These families, predominantly African American and Hispanic, came from economically disadvantaged communities in the Bronx. The agency felt it was important for the uninfected siblings to enjoy a summer camp experience, too, as these youngsters were often neglected due to their caregivers' focus on the sick child or children.

The video, *A Week in the Country,* was produced with the hope that viewers would be deeply moved by seeing these heroic families and would donate generously. The project was successful, and I was hired to take my own production crew to camp over the next two summers and produce more fundraising videos.

While at camp, whether I was chatting casually or taping interviews with mothers and other caregivers, I was keenly aware of being in the presence of heroes. Miraculously, these women were able to juggle the elements of their hugely complicated lives. They not only had to manage their own and their children's terminal illnesses but also had to do this while meeting the demands of their healthy children. Most of them were single mothers and did all the housework, shopped and cooked, kept doctor appointments, met with their children's teachers, and so much more in spite of being ill themselves. But, in contrast with other diseases, everything related to this one was cloaked in secrecy.

At this time in the first decade of the AIDS epidemic, people with HIV/AIDS—adults and children alike—experienced unimaginable stigma and discrimination. The most egregious instances of this received widespread news coverage, such as in 1984 when the eight-, nine-, and ten-year-old Ray brothers, who were born with hemophilia and received contaminated blood transfusions, had their home burned down in Florida. In that same year, thirteen-year-old Ryan White from Indiana, also a hemophiliac and infected with AIDS through a contaminated blood transfusion, was not allowed to attend school due to mis-information and widespread fear about AIDS. He was finally admitted, but only after a year-long legal battle. Following his death in 1990, Congress passed the Ryan White CARE Act which, through grant funding, supports a multitude of systems of care and services for people with AIDS.

In the first two decades of the AIDS epidemic there were only a limited number of well-known cases or famous people who were open with their diagnoses. The women attending Birch Family Camp knew it was dangerous to reveal that they had HIV or AIDS. Rarely did their relatives or friends know what their families were going through. None of the recurring illnesses, frequent clinic appointments and hospitalizations, weight loss, and children's absences from school could be explained truthfully. These women were not in denial; they simply could not share what was happening to them because of the stigma and overwhelming fear of AIDS at this time in the history of the epidemic.

Attendance at Birch Family Camp increased from five families that first summer to twenty-four families in the third year. I went from never having known anyone with AIDS to mingling closely with dozens of HIV-positive people. I was humbled that they felt safe enough with me to agree to being videotaped and sharing the intimacies of their lives as they struggled to cope with this horrific virus.

During this time, I was slowly and deeply processing everything I witnessed. It was as if my experience of being with these women and children had altered my DNA. I made a promise to myself that I would try to get a job working with people like the ones I met at camp. I sensed it might possibly be the most meaningful thing I could do in my professional life.

It took five years before I was able to fulfill this promise.

In 1995 my then husband, Rick Flaste, and I moved from Brooklyn to Florida.

Amazingly, within a month, I found the perfect job. I became one of five social workers providing family-centered case management in the Comprehensive Pediatric AIDS Program (CPAP) at Children's Diagnostic & Treatment Center in Fort Lauderdale, Florida.[1]

The center had been founded by Dr. Widmayer in 1983 to promote the optimal health and wellbeing of Broward County children and adolescents with chronic illnesses and disabilities. A broad range of services is offered, including but not limited to early intervention and treatment services for both primary and specialty medical care, developmental evaluations, dental care, family-centered case management, access to research and clinical trials, nutritional support, and emergency assistance.

CPAP was established in 1991 in response to the alarming increase in the number of babies and young children being diagnosed with HIV/AIDS in the county.

The general responsibilities of my new job included coordinating closely with the medical team both at formal weekly meetings and whenever medical issues arose and providing social services for the HIV-positive children in the family, as well as offering social service assistance to anyone living under the client's roof. The families we worked with were predominantly African American and Haitian, living below the poverty threshold. We made frequent home and hospital visits; interacted and advocated with doctors, nurses, and other care

---

1   Despite the fact that neither one of my two degrees was in social work, I was told to use the title of social worker because I would be doing the exact same work that degreed social workers do and that the clients used that title to refer to all of us.

providers; supplied food, clothing, over-the-counter medications, and supplies; advocated with outside agencies for client services; provided psychosocial counseling; attended births and graduations; assisted with funerals; and so much more.

Everything I personally did, witnessed, or planned on doing had to be documented in writing and accounted for in fifteen-minute blocks of time. By painstakingly writing highly detailed notes, I probably made this part of the job more onerous than it had to be, but I learned quickly that, for me, brevity was not useful. When a client called asking for information about something we discussed weeks earlier, I knew I could go to my notes and find all the details of the conversation. An unexpected outcome of having documented so meticulously back then has turned out to be a great bonus now, as I resurrect the details of those long-past years.

Being part of a dedicated team of professionals brought me immense fulfillment and pride. Of course, I had held jobs where people worked closely together, but not at this level of intensity and seriousness of purpose. As a young woman in high school in the early 1960s, there was no Title IX promoting gender equality in athletics. This piece of legislation was not passed until 1972, and so girls my age never got to experience being part of a competitive athletic team, something taken for granted by young men. I never experienced the camaraderie, the bonding, or the satisfaction of working hard together toward the common goal of winning a game. My job, however, was no game.

Over the ten years I worked at Children's Diagnostic, I saw our staff grow from five to seventeen to meet the demands of the exploding numbers of HIV and AIDS cases in Broward County. In 2000, the Comprehensive Pediatric AIDS Program expanded its mission from providing medical care and case management services exclusively to children, to also serving women. The name of our division changed to the Comprehensive Family AIDS Program (CFAP).

It was not uncommon for each of us to handle caseloads of fifty to sixty families, many of which had multiple members infected with the virus. The mental focus required to juggle the complex needs of so many people at the same time was daunting. Each evening when I left my office, I carried my clients and their families home with me in my thoughts. Most nights, uninvited, they moved into my dreams.

My CFAP colleagues and I partnered closely with our clinic's medical team and always consulted on cases together. Before medical protocols became more sophisticated and survival rates improved dramatically, my colleagues and I mourned the deaths of many of our clients. Because we were a small, tightly knit group, any death in the program was felt by everyone. Sadness became a familiar feeling, but it never dampened my enthusiasm for the work or the joy I felt when I was able to help make life better for my families.

The mid 1990s brought a major advancement in AIDS treatment with the introduction of a new class of drugs called protease inhibitors. These powerful agents bind to and block the action of an enzyme necessary for the HIV virus to reproduce in a patient's bloodstream. While not a cure per se, protease inhibitors reduced recipients' chances of developing one or more of the AIDS-related opportunistic infections that ultimately proved fatal for people with the disease.[2]

---

2   Examples of opportunistic infections and diseases include fungal infections, cervical cancer, severe or chronic diarrhea, pneumonia, and much more. People with healthy immune systems would be able to fight off these infectious agents. Immunocompromised patients' bodies are virtually defenseless against these infections and diseases.

At long last, if the new medical regimens were followed, it was possible for men and women who tested positive for the virus to live longer. Prior to the availability of protease inhibitors, life expectancy after an HIV diagnosis was about ten and a half years. With the new medications, that increased to twenty-two and a half years by 2005. In 2023, some people have now lived with AIDS for close to forty years.

However, this improved outcome often came at a high price: namely, severe side effects. Many of our clients refused to take the drugs. The medication regimens they would have to follow were hugely complicated, and the agents could be quite toxic. If they had children to raise and no one to help them, they would not be able to handle those responsibilities while being nauseous and experiencing diarrhea, severe headaches, and other debilitating physical symptoms.

Even when the statistics did begin to reverse and life began winning over death, the poverty our families lived with never seemed to go away. It was always weighing them down even as the certainty of death was being lifted.

My professional job ended in 2005. My latest "job" has been to resurrect the clients' stories as honestly and respectfully as I can. I have tried to be equally honest in examining my own feelings and actions during those years.

By writing this book, I hope to accomplish a number of things. These women and children deserve to be honored for the way they lived their lives in spite of having the deck stacked against them. It's true, sometimes the clients made poor or even disastrous personal choices. Who hasn't? But their bad decisions never altered the way I saw them: people trying their best to survive acute hardship, more often than not with amazing grace and bravery.

Beyond sharing my clients' stories, there were other compelling reasons to write this book. In early 1981 the US Centers for Disease Control and Prevention (CDC) published a report that described unexplained cases of enlarged lymph nodes and other unusual and serious infections in five young gay men in Los Angeles. Later that *same* year, they reported cases of women having been diagnosed with the same symptoms. Unfortunately, the research and investigative studies being conducted in the early and mid 1980s were only in response to the increasing numbers of unexplained deaths of gay men and not focused on why minority and poor women and their babies were getting sick and dying.

The early history of major clinical research studies and an early medication trial show that women were not allowed to participate.

Dr. Susan Widmayer is the founder of Children's Diagnostic and was the executive director from 1983 to 2013. She told me a compelling story that illustrates the frustration and anger medical professionals serving women with AIDS felt about the disparity in treatment care and access to medication in the early years of the epidemic.

"We were desperate to get AZT for women," she recalled. "We had nothing to treat them with, because women were not approved to receive AZT. Some colleagues and I attended a large conference run by the CDC in a hotel in Miami. The last speaker at the podium was a doctor reporting on drugs used to treat AIDS—drugs we knew were available only to men. When he finished speaking and asked for questions, many women lined up at the microphone placed in the front of the auditorium. The first question addressing this lack of treatment options for women was asked in a respectful tone, but when the answer was

'We're working on it. We're doing the best we can,' people in the audience began to stand up and yell. It became chaotic, with the doctors yelling back, trying to defend what the women saw as an indefensible position."

Women had no national advocacy groups, such as Gay Men's Health Crisis (GMHC) and AIDS Coalition to Unleash Power (ACT UP), to take on their cause. Celebrities did not speak out on behalf of women with AIDS as they did for men. The gay and lesbian communities, to their credit, turned out in huge numbers to support ill gay men, but women I served had no organized groups of volunteers to help shop for them or to cook for or feed them when they could no longer do these things for themselves. No one came in to help clean our clients' homes, transport them to appointments, help their kids with homework, or just sit and talk with them.

Throughout the early decades of the AIDS epidemic, all men and women diagnosed with the virus suffered dreadfully on many levels. However, I believe it's fair to say that marginalized minority and poor women suffered more dramatically. They were relegated to the shadows. They never spoke about what was happening to them—often even to family members—for fear of discrimination and abandonment. The truth is that these female lives mattered just as much as the male lives. Too many women died with little public awareness that this was their disease, too. Decades have now passed, but it's never too late to right a wrong.

My last wish for this book is that it will be part of my legacy to my children, Rebecca and Jordan; to my grandchildren, Zachary, Aidan, and Chase; and to my step-grandchildren, Izabella, Elijah, Isaac, and Liam. Hopefully, by reading these stories, they will better understand the serious and determined

xxii	*In Their Presence*

work their mother or grandmother once did and realize how important compassion is to the human spirit.

When I was working in the Comprehensive Family AIDS Program, Rebecca and Jordan were young adults and understandably focused on their own lives and personal and professional aspirations. I hope this book will draw them into a period of my life they didn't know much about and show them details of an unfamiliar side of their mother. For my grandchildren, who were either extremely young or not yet born, I hope my book will encourage them to be brave and step out of their comfort zones to experience the truth of other people's lives— people who, on the surface, may not appear to be like them. As I have learned, doing this can be transformative.

I

What Came Before

1

From the Front of the Classroom
to in Front of a Camera

IMMEDIATELY AFTER RECEIVING MY MASTER of arts degree in special education from New York University in 1981, I took a teaching job at PS 396K, in the Brownsville section of Brooklyn.

In the 1980s, attitudes toward developmentally disabled people were quite different from today. Rarely were they seen out and about. No matter how young or old they were, they were almost an invisible population, not yet fully integrated in schools or even in their own communities.

My mentor Dr. Mark Alter, professor of educational psychology at NYU, had inspired me to specialize in teaching students with profound cognitive and developmental delays. My quick placement was possible because of the great need all over the city for teachers with this specialization.

Even though Brownsville was considered an unsafe neighborhood at the time, I didn't hesitate to accept the job offer presented to me by the principal, Dr. Sidney Miller. In addition to his assurance that the school went to great lengths to ensure the safety of the staff, I liked the placement because it was a reasonable commute from my home in Brooklyn Heights. I could be home when my five-year-old son and nine-year-old daughter returned from school.

PS 396K was made up entirely of special education students. In addition to serious cognitive delays, many of these youngsters had dual diagnoses. The twelve students in my classroom ranged in age from five to twenty-one—something you would never find in a classroom today. Most of them had little to no spoken language, were not toilet trained, and had few independent functioning skills. My students were labeled with the now outdated term "severely and profoundly mentally retarded." At my job interview, I was told they all scored below twenty on their IQ tests. Even I, a brand-new teacher, knew that was an absurd and meaningless figure, revealing nothing helpful about them as young people. Other students in the building were given the equally insensitive labels of "educable" or "trainable." While at NYU, my study of this population filled me with the certainty that the low expectations these students had endured needed to be addressed by good teachers. I was confident I was

Dale in the classroom at PS 396K, Brooklyn, N.Y., 1982.

well prepared to do this kind of work and began the fall term with great hope and enthusiasm. When that first year of teaching ended, I knew that with the help of my three wonderful classroom paraprofessionals—paras, as we called them—we had made measurable impacts on our students' lives.

I returned to the classroom in September 1982. I was delighted to learn that not only had the three paras been reassigned to my room but also that we'd be working with the same twelve children as last year. We picked up right where we had left off. All of us, kids and adults alike, fell into a familiar flow.

One day in the middle of winter, Dr. Miller called me into his office. "Dale, I want you to know you are doing exemplary work. I've chosen your classroom to be part of a series of training videos being made for the benefit of the Committees on the Handicapped."

I had heard the term before but didn't fully understand what their role was. I asked Dr. Miller to explain it.

"The committees are made up of a chairperson, psychologist, teacher, parent representative, and representatives from any of the services the student is going to be offered. That could be speech therapy, physical or occupational therapy, etc. These people create an Individual Educational Plan based on the nature of the child's handicap, what services should be put into place to mitigate the handicap, and where those services will take place. It seems that there has been some confusion on the part of some members of the committees regarding the differences, for example, between autistic students and the kind of students in your classroom with profound cognitive or developmental disabilities. Because of this lack of understanding, some children have mistakenly been placed in wrong classroom settings. The Board of Education wants to remedy this by showing how these children can differ in behaviors and abilities, and what methods of teaching have yielded positive results. The shows will be hosted by the classroom teachers. Does this sound interesting to you, something you'd like to be part of?"

I accepted immediately and thanked him for choosing me.

Dr. Miller explained that a crew from the Board of Education television station, WNYE-TV, would come to the school to start filming toward the end of the following week. I returned to my classroom and told my paras what was going to happen. You've never seen a happier group of women. Over the next week, we cleaned and organized the classroom. We brainstormed about which exercises, activities, and techniques we were going to demonstrate, so that the audience would better understand how children with such significant cognitive delays could be reached. The day the television crew arrived, all of us, students and teaching staff alike, looked like we were about to have an audience with the pope. The parents and group home aides knew their kids would be on TV and dressed them in their Sunday best for their television debuts. My paraprofessionals also took great care choosing their outfits for the shoot. They actually came in looking far too dressed up for a job that entails having to assist with feeding, changing diapers, and teaching toilet training. It was all completely understandable, though. We were ecstatic about this special recognition and wanted to look our best.

The TV crew that arrived was made up of three people. The director, Drew Andreotti, was a gray-haired former advertising director with a big belly, an easy laugh, and a short fuse, even when things went just a little bit awry. Cameraman Stan Niegowski and Steve Roberts, the sound and lighting engineer, moved about the room efficiently, setting things up. They were totally unaffected by Drew's bellicose outbursts of frustration when, for example, a light bulb blew or the honking of cars on the street forced a scene to be reshot. Thanks to having acted in many high school plays, majored in theater in undergraduate school, and studied acting privately, I was comfortable doing this kind of work, and that helped make the crew's job go smoothly. Because we enjoyed working together, all of us regretted when the shooting ended two days later and they had to return to the station.

A few months went by, and the school year was almost over. I received an unexpected call from Drew, the director, asking if I would be able to work with them again, this time on one of a number of shows the station was producing to celebrate the Brooklyn Bridge's one hundredth anniversary. For this particular show in the series, I would be the on-air talent leading the audience on a half hour walking tour of Brooklyn Heights—my neighborhood. I accepted his offer immediately and again had a wonderful time working with Drew, Stan, and Steve.

2

How Many Lives Can Be Changed?

I NEVER THOUGHT MUCH ABOUT THE WNYE people or the station for the remainder of the next school year. Sometime in May 1984, Drew called me at home. While we were catching up, I kept wondering, "Why did he call? Do they need me again?" With two TV shows now under my belt, I was eager to do more. But this time he was calling with a different kind of offer—one that caught me off guard and unprepared to answer.

"The assistant superintendent of special education in the Bronx just got a budget approved for a producer–director to create a monthly magazine-format show on special education. It will be shot in each district in the Bronx, at schools the superintendent chooses. The shows will focus on the great things the principals, teachers, and kids are doing. Are you interested in interviewing for the job?"

At first, I didn't grasp what he was saying, so I asked him to repeat it. This time I stayed better focused.

"But I'll have to leave the classroom to do this, right?" "Yes, you would," he replied. "But you'd still be paid the same and have your summers off. You'd be on the payroll of the Bronx Region Special Education Department."

I knew I should jump at this opportunity, but instead I felt instantly anxious. It meant giving up something I'd worked very hard to get and had expected I'd be doing for a long time.

How could I just walk away from teaching? I'd be letting down the kids. I'd be letting down my principal. I was conflicted about abandoning the relationships I'd formed with the paras and my fellow teachers. I told Drew that I knew this was a great opportunity and that it absolutely intrigued me, but I asked him if I could take a day or two to consider it.

"No problem," he responded. "I'm not recommending anyone else for this position until you tell me you don't want it."

Then, he added a bunch of reasons I'm sure he hoped would seal the deal for me.

"I'm telling you, Dale, you have the perfect credentials, and you'll love it. Did I mention the job is located at WNYE's building on Tillary Street? You could even walk to work when you aren't shooting in the Bronx. On a personal note, even though I won't be working on these shows with you, it'll be great having you around the station. Call me as soon as you make the decision."

I felt I couldn't decide without first talking to Dr. Alter, my former NYU professor. He was a passionate advocate for people with developmental challenges, and I knew he would give me good guidance. Dr. Alter had inspired me to specialize in this field, one that did not appeal to me initially. However, after a couple of courses with him, it became the only area I wanted to work in. I'd be working with a population that in the eyes of many couldn't benefit from an education, but I felt confident I could make a difference in their lives. Of course, I knew there would be frustrations and disappointments when the students couldn't grasp what I was teaching or when they learned a skill one day and forgot it the next, but it was a challenge I felt fully prepared to tackle.

"If what you're trying to do isn't working, find another way," Dr. Alter would say in class. He said it so frequently that it became my personal mantra in my own classroom—as well as in my life. How was I going to tell him I was thinking of giving it all up so quickly? But I steeled myself and made the call. Dr. Alter listened to me without interrupting. When I finished telling him how conflicted I was feeling and bemoaned the position I found myself in, he asked me a question.

"How many students are in your classroom?"

"Twelve."

He paused for a moment. Now it was my turn to listen without interrupting. "So, you're touching the lives of twelve kids now. If you accept this job, you'll have an opportunity to touch the lives of maybe thousands of people over time. You'll be chipping away at the negative images people have of kids with disabilities and replacing those images with the truth about what they *can* do and *can* accomplish. You'll also have a great chance to expose your audience to the wonderful things teachers are doing in special education classrooms. When do special ed teachers get a spotlight shone on them? Not often enough. Television is a powerful tool for change, and you could be helping make those changes one show at a time. I encourage you to take this leap. Don't worry about not doing exactly what you'd prepared for; this is a wonderful opportunity to be an educator of a different sort."

Without using the words he repeated so many times in the classroom, Dr. Alter was telling me I had found "another way" to accomplish something important in my field.

I didn't know my way around the Bronx, so I gave myself plenty of time to get to the interview. I arrived early, which, psychologically, was not the best thing that could have happened. I sat outside the office of the assistant superintendent for special education having nothing to do but worry. Could I pull this off? I had worked on only two WNYE television shows before.

A woman came over and asked if I was here for an interview with Dr. Stephen Benardo. She pointed to a half-open door and told me to go right in. Dr. Benardo quickly came around from behind his desk to introduce himself. He shook my hand very firmly and asked me to sit down. Instead of returning to his chair behind the desk, he hoisted himself onto the front edge of the desk, no more than a foot from me. If I had tried to cross my legs, I would have hit his shoes. Dr. Benardo was a trim, well-dressed man in his mid-thirties, with dark hair and penetrating, dark-brown eyes. There was an intensity about him that justified my earlier anxiety. He leaned toward me, looked directly into my eyes, and fired off some staccato comments and questions. "Let's get right to it. You're the only one the station is recommending at this point. They say you're very good. You've been told what the job is. I have only one question for you. Do you know anything about television?"

Wow. Do I know anything about television? How was I supposed to answer that? Because I hesitated for a moment, he jumped right in and asked, "Do you want to know what I know about television?"

"Sure."

"Well, I know there's a button on the TV, and when you pull it out, you get a picture. And when you push it back in, the picture goes away. Do you know more than that?"

"Yes!" I answered with great confidence, but laughing.

"You've got the job. We start in September," he said, hopping off the edge of the desk. He smiled broadly as he pumped my hand, as though we had just sealed a million-dollar business deal.

3

Learning Some New Ropes
and Hanging from a Few

WNYE-TV WAS NOW MY CLASSROOM, but this time I was the student, not the teacher. I was there to learn how to produce and direct a monthly thirty-minute television show with the super catchy name *Bronx Region Special Education Report*. What I learned immediately was that there would be no formal lessons, no materials to read, no assigned mentors—just jump in the van with the crew and all the equipment and drive up to the Bronx. At the beginning of each month, I'd meet with Dr. Benardo in his office and take notes on which schools and programs he wanted me to include, which principals and teachers I should interview, and which classrooms to film. Beyond that, he stated he had great faith in me and was eager to see the first episode. He had no plans to look over my shoulder or question my creative decisions. That was basically it. Sink or swim.

In the beginning, it was painfully clear to me—and probably to everyone else—that I was doing more sinking than swimming. However, by episode four, whatever insecurities I'd had faded, and I began to truly enjoy the work as well as the companionship of my WNYE colleagues. To my great relief, Dr. Benardo loved every show—genuinely loved them. So did all the teachers, administrators, and students in the special education programs we highlighted.

At first, it took me about two or three weeks to complete preproduction, shoot the video, and laboriously hand-log the tapes so that I was prepared to sit with my editor, who worked on a

Dale at the editing console at WNYE-TV.

state-of-the-art editing console. But I gradually became more skilled and found myself with big blocks of free time.

That's when the station's general manager, Phil Lewis, put me to work in other areas. The crew and I traveled all over the five boroughs taping special features and interviews at famous as well as little-known museums, historic homes, and botanical gardens. I was also recruited to work on both on-air and behind-the-scenes assignments for in-house studio shoots. I produced news programs and interview shows. These shoots were all dramatically different from one another. For me, the only thing they had in common was how they could fill me with angst as I dove into unchartered territory.

By far, the most harrowing assignment was cohosting WNYE's airing of the January 31, 1986, memorial service for the seven astronauts who perished when the NASA space shuttle *Challenger* exploded nine miles above the Earth just seventy-three seconds after lifting off from Cape Canaveral. One member of the seven-member crew was the first private citizen astronaut, Christa McAuliffe, a high school social studies teacher from Concord, New Hampshire. She had been selected by NASA as the primary candidate (out of 11,000 applicants) for their Teacher in Space project. Having been a teacher myself, I was fascinated by her story and in awe of her bravery. While in space, she was to perform various science experiments and teach two lessons to her own students and others around the world live via a special NASA satellite feed. On that tragically doomed day in January, her students and all the students, teachers, and administrators in her school, as well as schoolchildren all over the world, were watching the launch on television. What they saw was horrifying.

Phil Lewis decided we would broadcast the memorial service using ABC-TV's live feed.

The service was held in Houston three days after the tragedy and was presided over by President Ronald Reagan with Vice President George Bush and Mrs. Bush, plus more than four hundred others, in attendance. Each time the network cut to a commercial, WNYE would go live from our studio to fill that commercial block of time. With little advance notice, Phil gave me and my co-anchor, Terence O'Driscoll, the assignment of providing commentary on the memorial service and astronaut- and shuttle-related facts.

Anyone watching the ABC coverage of this deeply moving service would have seen Peter Jennings, a highly skilled journalist and news commentator, deliver a serious narrative of the events; that is, until he became overwhelmed with emotion and couldn't speak for a minute. Anyone watching WNYE would have seen two novices sitting on stools, one doing a relatively good job of pretending to be a newscaster and the other one overcome with emotion, speaking in a shaking voice, and visibly struggling to fight back tears. Guess who that was?

When the first commercial break ended and we went back to airing the ABC news feed, Terence looked at my red nose and watery eyes and took it upon himself to perform an intervention.

"Dale. You're doing a fine job. Try and compose yourself while we're not on the air. Think about something positive or happy."

"Terence, I'm so nervous, and this is just so sad. Even Peter Jennings was emotional," I replied, my voice now sounding high-pitched and constricted. "Believe me, I don't want to cry on live TV!"

Terence tried another approach. In a soothing, nonjudgmental voice, he delivered a pep talk about professionalism.

"I don't know if I can be professional right now!" I snapped. "I keep thinking about all the people watching me fight back tears, and I get panicky."

"Oh. Really? *All* those people?"

Terence had a sarcastic tone in his voice but a smile on his face.

"Let me remind you of two things that might help. Number one, WNYE's signal is so weak, it can't reach into many parts of the five boroughs, so there are lots of people who don't even know we exist. Number two, if you, personally, had a choice of watching the memorial service on WNYE or watching it on ABC, which would you watch? Realistically, there are probably thirty people watching our broadcast right now, and there's got to be something wrong with each one of them.

"You have absolutely no reason to be nervous. If you tear up, virtually no one will know."

I took that in, calmed down, and got through the rest of the production in fine shape.

Another time, New York City mayor Ed Koch was to address his constituents from WNYE's studio. Our makeup artist was absent that day, and I agreed, albeit reluctantly, to stand in for her. Job number one: to keep his honor's bald head from shining under the lights.

Now, as an acting major at Boston University's School of Fine and Applied Arts, I had taken a course in stage makeup. But that was twenty years ago. I did not feel prepared in the least to get Mayor Koch camera ready. Still, duty called.

I adroitly placed a short plastic cape around his shoulders, then dipped a large powder puff into the circular container of powder. So far, so good. But then I forgot the basic Makeup 101 instruction to turn away and tamp off the bulk of the powder clinging to the puff. Instead, I tamped it directly over the mayor's head. A billowing cloud of tan powder rose up and settled on top of Koch's head, face, and the exposed parts of his dark suit pants. I jumped back in horror, apologizing profusely. To my amazement, the irascible mayor didn't yell or make a huge fuss, but it was clear he was very displeased. When the dust, literally, settled, he just looked up at me and said, "Young lady, is this your regular job? If not, I strongly suggest you go back to doing what it is you're supposed to be doing and leave this for someone more experienced."

4

When One Door Closes, Will Another Really Open?

IN LATE SPRING 1987 DR. BENARDO summoned me to his office to deliver some bad news. After three successful seasons of *Bronx Region Special Education Report*, the New York City Board of Education had decided to eliminate the budget for his TV show. The last episode would air in June. We were both deeply disappointed. I couldn't see myself going back to the classroom after three years of being away and working in a dramatically different profession. On my final day at WNYE, I thanked all my colleagues for exhibiting such patience and generosity of spirit while teaching me so many new skills. After saying my goodbyes and leaving the building for the last time, I was very conscious of the possibility that I might never again have a job that offered so much creativity and autonomy. In all, I had produced and directed thirty half-hour episodes and worked on roughly a hundred other shows for the station in a variety of capacities. One of my specials, *If Only We Care Enough*, about the first New York City Very Special Arts Festival—the arts component of the Special Olympics—had been nominated for an Emmy Award. The supportive environment of a small television station had nurtured and "produced" me.

I spent the summer enjoying my children full time and applying for various positions at the New York City Board of Education headquarters on Livingston Street in downtown Brooklyn. My ultimate goal, though, was to find a permanent job in television or video production. When the summer ended,

I was offered and accepted an administrative position at Board headquarters. The job entailed supervising ninety-nine paraprofessionals spread throughout schools in the five boroughs. These men and women worked one-on-one with older, non-toilet-trained students up to age twenty-one who had serious developmental and cognitive delays. All ninety-nine of these students were carriers of hepatitis B. (Yes, you read that correctly.) For the most part, these students had been living in institutions and large group settings where inadequate supervision by some staff members resulted in rampant disease transmission from one resident to another. I taught these paraprofessionals how to use behavior modification techniques to help their charges learn to toilet train.

This was not my dream job, by any means. Whenever someone I'd never met before asked what I did for a living, I dreaded answering because I knew that the conversation would come to a screeching halt. No one really understood what I did, nor did they ask me to elaborate—on anything. After the first few aborted conversations, I realized that further discussion of my work was a bridge too far for most people. The conversations just ended with pained expressions on all our faces.

Although the job held no cachet, I knew that it was an important one for these students and their families. If this method of conditioning was successful, it would add an important level of independence to their lives; however, supervising ninety-nine people, reviewing ninety-nine behavior modification charts every month, and traveling between five different locations was not something I felt I could do or wanted to do for very long.

I lasted one year. I accepted one more unstimulating job at the Board of Education headquarters, this time as an administrative assistant in the Division of Arts Education. The responsibilities of this job were much easier to explain, but it did not give me any more satisfaction.

The time had come for me to resign from the board and focus full time on landing a job in network television or professional video production. Over the course of the next couple of months, I interviewed for a variety of positions with several national TV shows, but my previous experience was never the exact fit they were looking for.

A series of rejections led me to reflect honestly on my prospects.

My master's degree in special education coupled with my television production experience gave me a unique area of expertise that few producers had. I knew a lot about children and adults with developmental disabilities and challenging health conditions. I was comfortable working with them and could relate easily to the caregivers who lived with them. It became clear to me that what I needed to do, and wanted to do, was to start my own video production company. I filed the paperwork for Heartbeat Productions.

II

Being in Their Presence

5

Not Your Average Sleepaway Camp

I'D MET PHYLLIS SUSSER, FOUNDING director of Herbert G. Birch Services, in Springfield Gardens, New York, during my last year at WNYE. She had contracted with the station to produce educational training videos for her staff. At the time, her agency operated two schools for children with autism and developmental disabilities in the borough of Queens as well as group homes for children and adults in that borough and the Bronx. The mission of the agency was to help the students and residents live their lives as fully and independently as possible.

I worked with Phyllis and a few of her top administrators during the time they were shooting in the studio and when they returned to have their tapes edited. They were a decent and compassionate group of people who were all strong advocates for their students and clients. I would have had no way of knowing it at the time, but these encounters would later result in our lives becoming deeply entwined.

In 1990, months after those Birch educational training videotapes were completed, Phyllis called me at home. She had a long story to tell which began with her talking about a few HIV-positive residents who were living in the organization's group homes. She and her good friend Dr. Arye Rubinstein, professor of pediatrics, microbiology, and immunology at Albert Einstein College of Medicine in the Bronx, would often brainstorm about how they might collaborate in response to the AIDS epidemic. This led to the creation of a pilot camping project for five families (twenty campers in total) from Montefiore Hospital's

Comprehensive AIDS Family Care Center. They were all impacted by AIDS, and most of them came from low-income neighborhoods in the Bronx. The camp focused not only on the physical and emotional health of the infected mothers and children but also provided the whole family, including the healthy siblings, with the opportunity to get out of the city and into a rural area where they could shed the unbearable burden of AIDS for a little while.

The stigma AIDS carried with it had placed many obstacles in the way of this project's becoming a reality, but Phyllis had a clear vision and fierce determination to make this camp a reality. The first obstacle, which proved to be the most difficult, was finding a facility that would accept the families. It was Phyllis's job to locate the venue. She and Dr. Rubinstein gave in-person presentations to owners and directors of private sleepaway camps. These presentations included both scientifically documented information and emotional details about the families and the dramatic need for a program like this. Nevertheless, they kept getting turned down. The camp owners and directors, like almost everyone at this time in the early years of the epidemic, were afraid of the disease and could not envision how they could explain to the parents of "regular" campers that women and children with AIDS had been staying on the campgrounds for a week.

After a number of disappointments, Phyllis and Dr. Rubinstein made their presentation to the board of directors at Camp Sussex, in Vernon, New Jersey. Camp Sussex had opened in 1923 and was operated by a nonprofit foundation out of New York City, the Brooklyn Children's Fresh Air Camp Association. Before the actual presentation, Robert Silver, one of the board members and also the president of Camp Sussex, told Phyllis and Dr. Rubinstein that a board member, Elliot Lippin, happened to be an AIDS advocate and frequent donor to AIDS causes. It took Mr. Lippin's impassioned appeal to convince the other members to overcome their initial reservations and agree to host the camp for one week.

Staffing the camp with medical and social service professionals from Montefiore Hospital was Dr. Rubinstein's job. These people not only had to be comfortable leaving behind their duties at the hospital for a week but also had to agree to go beyond their obvious professional roles and become "campers" themselves. His and Phyllis's vision was one of complete immersion with the families, meaning that the staff would eat at the families' tables in the dining hall and, whenever possible, join the children at playtime.

In addition to planning therapeutic group sessions for the caregivers, the social workers, too, were expected to be fully involved in camp activities. This would afford them many opportunities to have private conversations with the caregivers on subjects they weren't comfortable discussing in group settings, such as their sexual relationships or any guilt about leaving their orphaned children to be raised by relatives.

Phyllis told me that a volunteer had videotaped what went on during that week at camp. She wanted to hire me to review and log what he'd shot and then let her know whether there was enough compelling footage to create a fundraising video from it. "If you say you've got enough to work with, I'll hire you to put this together for us." I immediately said I would do it, and Heartbeat Productions had its first client. A few days later, a box containing many VHS half-inch tapes was delivered to my home.

Over the next half hour or so, I popped one tape after another into my videocassette recorder and scanned random sections. There were hours and hours of raw footage. Parts had low or inaudible audio, poorly lit images, bad cuts, and the frequent whining of the camera's motor as it went in and out of close-ups, which is not to say the footage wasn't deeply compelling. It was. However, it would require some magic to turn these into what Phyllis wanted.

After two weeks of transcribing everything said on these tapes, I had filled seven legal pads. Nearing the end of the job, something was becoming very clear to me. In spite of the work being tedious and mind numbing, I didn't want it to stop.

As I counted the minutes and seconds of these women's and children's lives, I found myself pulled into their struggles and awed by their courage. I felt privileged to "be with them" in this strange, voyeuristic way. Watching them push their children on the swings or fishing at the lake, I saw no difference at all between myself and them, and their children and my own children. I was always yanked back to reality, though, when, in a dark moment, a woman would express how depressing it was to live this life of secrecy and how her burdens were so heavy. I could not fathom how they were able to put one foot in front of the other knowing not only that they and their infected children were dying but also that their healthy children were going to be left orphaned. How do you get up every day and face that painful reality?

A particularly moving section on one of the many videotapes was a conversation that took place at the first session of camp. It was a group therapy session held outdoors where the mothers were asked to confront the topic of death.

August 30, 1989

The women walked out of the dining room after lunch and strolled over to wooden benches placed in the shade of a large tree. The hope was the shade would decrease the impact of the midday heat. But little could be done to minimize the discomfort the women would feel once the conversation started. Dr. Anita Septimus, the Director of Psycho-social Services at the Family AIDS Center of the Albert Einstein College of Medicine, was going to bring up a topic they couldn't imagine talking about openly back home in the Bronx. The topic was death: their own and their children's.

"How did you feel when you were told your son's diagnosis? And how have you been dealing with it since then?" Dr. Septimus asked gently. She waited for the first mother to summon the courage to speak.

"When they told me about Peter, I thought I was dreaming," a woman named Isla said, shaking her head in disbelief. "I just wanted to wake up. I couldn't accept it right away. I went through a lot of changes, as did my family. I'm trying to be very positive now, because I know if I let myself go, everybody's going to come down with me. I have to be very strong for my kids. Sometimes I can't help but cry, because I know this is for real. This is actually happening to my son, to me, and my family. It hurts a lot. I'm just going to keep struggling for my life, and my child's."

"Thank you, Isla. What about you, Josie?"

"I found out about a year ago when my son was sick. We didn't know what he had. Two months later, they diagnosed him with having the AIDS. That's how I found out. I was tested after that. My son lasted only two months. He passed away when he was just four and a half months old. It's been hard, but, from the beginning, I never let it pull me down. I just kept going."

"Were you able to tell your family what you were going through?"

"Yes. When it came time to tell my family, I just told them. From then on, they supported me. To this day, they're the reason I'm still going. And my husband, of course; he's my major reason I'm still alive. I have a three-and-a-half-year-old daughter who's negative. My husband is negative. So I just have to deal with myself."

"I haven't told anybody," volunteered Isabel. "My family doesn't know. The only one that knows is my sister and myself— and now you all. Julie's seven. She has an idea. I just tell her that she's sick; that she was born sick. She kinds of accepts it. She kinds of knows. The way she looks at me, I know."

"What does she know?"

"That there's something wrong with her, but she doesn't know what."

"You haven't told her?"

"Oh, no! I don't know how to tell her. How'm I going to tell her?"

"Would you like to tell her?"

"No!" she answered emphatically, shaking her head. "What for? She's a kid. It's nothing for her to deal with, nothing she could do. So why tell her? Let her keep being a kid. Julie asked me, 'Am I gonna die, Mommy?' I tell her we all gonna die. This is my answer to her. What am I gonna tell her? I don't know how to tell her that. I want to be honest, but if I tell her she has AIDS, she'll say, 'What's that?' She won't understand, and she'll play with her little friends and tell them, and then their parents won't let them play with her anymore. That's why I can't tell her. I think she's just too young."

Isla had more to say. "I devote my life and my time to my children. I pray to God that they grow up and don't do bad."

"Does your oldest son know anything about your illness or his brother's?"

"Oh, yes."

"You've told them?"

"I've told Solomon. I've told Matt. Peter, he knows we're both sick, but he does not know why." Isla hesitated, finding it difficult to go on. "The time will come... eventually... when..."

She broke down and sobbed, covering her face with her hands. Dr. Septimus quickly got up and went over to Isla. Sitting down next to her, she put her arm around the woman's shoulder and pulled her close.

Isla apologized for crying, but she couldn't get herself fully under control. In a constricted voice, she said, "I just pray so much. I ask my Lord for guidance. Just keep me strong, the way I feel now. I feel really strong."

As she said this, she pushed up the sleeve of her short-sleeved T-shirt to reveal an unnaturally skinny arm.

"I'm doing it all for them... and for myself."

Isabel's daughter, Julie, died six months after camp ended. She was seven years old. Isabel died a year and a half later. Isla lived to attend camp the following summer, but, sadly, she died two days after the session ended, leaving behind three children, including one son with AIDS.

6

Birch Family Camp

W HEN I FINISHED LOGGING ALL the tapes, I made an appointment to see Phyllis. I was not looking forward to telling her there were many hours of unusable footage that might make it hard to cobble together just what she wanted. Phyllis was not a woman who easily accepted being told something she wanted done couldn't be done. What she said took me by surprise. She said I should just use whatever good footage there was and make a fundraising video out of it. She and Dr. Rubinstein were already totally committed to returning to Camp Sussex in the spring, and they wanted me there to continue telling the story of the lives of these families.

In the spring of 1990, I hired my cameraman, sound engineer, and lighting technician from WNYE-TV to serve as my

Camp Sussex bunk houses (Birch Family Camp).

crew for filming at camp. I drove the one hundred miles from Brooklyn to Vernon, filled with optimism about what might lie ahead over the next couple of days. When I got out of my car and walked onto the camp property, I found myself walking into the exact same scenes I had watched on my TV screen and logged for so many hours. It was a surreal experience. At home, I had to play back those recorded voices over and over again so that I could transcribe the words accurately. Now I would have the opportunity to sit next to and talk with some of those same women. In my mind, they were like celebrities.

Camp Sussex was established in 1923 and was in operation until 2005. It was a picturesque, old-fashioned kind of kids' camp with traditional, rustic-looking wooden buildings and cabins painted white with green trim. For the week the families were there, it was renamed Birch Family Camp.

Its 215 acres featured a good-sized lake stocked with fish and an extensive selection of pedal boats and rowboats. There were a pool, tennis court, gymnasium, seesaws, swings, slides, a sandbox, and lots of open lawns. A cadre of camp counselors had already been signed up for the regular summer season, but the concern was that they might not be comfortable working with these families. There was no need to worry. After the methods of HIV transmission were explained to them and they were reassured they couldn't become infected, they were all eager to make a difference in these children's lives.

The crew and I stayed at camp for only two jam-packed days. Because I was working long hours, I was able to socialize with the women and children only at meals and evening events. The rest of the day, I was scouting locations, setting up shots, making sure the people being interviewed understood what I wanted them to talk about, and doing my best to make everyone feel comfortable about being videotaped.

What I heard and witnessed on that first day overwhelmed me. I had been watching these families on tape for weeks prior to coming to camp, and I felt comfortable being with them— almost as if I knew them. What totally surprised me was how relaxed and unguarded they were with me, a total stranger. I attribute this to the rarefied atmosphere at Birch Family Camp, where there was no judgment or fear of rejection. They knew that the stigma they lived with on a daily basis at home did not follow them onto the campgrounds. Here they could be themselves, safe in the knowledge that no one saw them as threats and everyone valued them. The acceptance I felt from them touched me deeply—so much so that being with these women and children changed my thinking about the direction I wanted my life to go in.

Back in Brooklyn, I began working with a video editor. The two of us stitched together the story of this pioneering project, documenting what could be done to enrich the lives of a hidden and stigmatized population. After *A Week in the Country* was distributed, enough donations flowed in that Phyllis and Dr. Rubinstein could plan yet another week of camp the following season.

By the summer of 1991, the AIDS epidemic was entering its eleventh year. With no vaccine on the horizon, the number of cases was escalating worldwide. There were far more candidates for camp than there had been the first two years. This necessitated finding a new venue with a better equipped infirmary to accommodate the larger number of medically fragile campers. In her search, Phyllis received a commitment from the administrators of legendary actor Paul Newman's brand new, state-of-the-art Hole in the Wall Gang Camp, in Ashford, Connecticut. For those ten days in June, the camp was known as Birch Summer Project.

This amazing facility, constructed in 1988 on three hundred acres of a forest, was intended originally for children with cancer. In time, it grew to include boys and girls affected by many types of chronic and terminal illnesses. For the 1991 session, the Birch Summer Project campers were the first children with HIV or AIDS to attend.

The grounds had been designed to resemble an old-fashioned American frontier village. The families were taken on a tour and shown what they could look forward to: boating and fishing on a pristine forty-four-acre lake, performing onstage in an amazing theater built on a scale for children, playing with animals at a small petting farm, creating arts and crafts projects with materials they likely would never have access to in their schools, swimming in a huge, sparkling-blue pool, horseback riding, and so much more.

In Their Own Words

In the process of writing about the two camps, I found myself discarding draft after draft. It's one thing to videotape short interviews or capture sound bites, but that doesn't communicate much about who the people truly were. I knew I was failing at conveying how much these camps meant to the people who designed them, who worked and volunteered there, and who attended. My struggle ended when I had a double revelation. First, my inability to write about the people I met at the camp was because I hadn't gotten to know them well enough. I had been working for only a few days at each camp, and although my time there had been intense, I wasn't feeling confident enough (more than thirty years later) to write about them in an appropriately comprehensive way.

Second, I realized I had the perfect solution to the frustration I was feeling. I didn't have to write about them because tucked away in a box in my basement were copies of the original camp videos I had made. I mailed off these tapes to be transferred to a digital format. This allowed me to sit in front of my computer and watch all three versions of *A Week in the Country* (1989, 1990, and 1991) back to back. It became instantly clear to me that the words spoken by the people on the videos were more clarifying, more powerful, and far more touching than anything I could write. Their words, put simply, were perfect.

7

Response to an Epidemic

I BEGAN MY VIDEOTAPED INTERVIEW WITH Phyllis by asking how the concept of the camp was developed. She was sitting in an Adirondack chair on the porch of one of the log cabin buildings and was eager to talk about how everything evolved.

"The camp came to be following discussions with Dr. Rubinstein over the last two years about the need for a facility to train potential foster parents of children with AIDS, and biological mothers as well. Dr. Rubinstein feels very strongly

Phyllis Susser at Birch Family Camp (still from VHS tape).

that the primary caregivers of the children are not aware enough of their own power to help the children be healthier and to get fewer opportunistic infections. They needed to learn about infection control, about the nature and progress of the disease, the kinds of things to look for in the children, and then, psychodynamically, to give them an opportunity to be with others who are in the same boat; to learn from one another and to give nurturing and support."

Emergency Call

A real-life drama played out on one of the days I was shooting in the clinic. It demonstrated perfectly how a caregiver's not recognizing her child's physical deterioration can have serious repercussions. Dr. Ziev Harish from Albert Einstein Hospital was examining a child whose foster mother had not mentioned anything to him about the boy showing signs of being sick. He realized at once that the child was, indeed, seriously ill and took immediate action by calling the emergency department at Montefiore Hospital in the Bronx to prepare them for the young patient's arrival.

"I would like to speak with the resident in charge," he said calmly. "I'm in upstate New Jersey. We are running an HIV camp, and one of the kids started having respiratory distress this afternoon with some chest pain. His respiratory rate went up from forty to fifty, and he has some nasal flaring, but he's not in severe distress. He will be in the emergency room in about an hour. We want you to be aware that he is coming."

After the phone call, the boy and his mother climbed into a car while Dr. Harish and the child's social worker, Karen Jackson, looked on. Karen leaned into the car and, in a calming voice, said to the little boy, "Bye, sweetheart. You're going to be fine. I'll say a little prayer for you, and you're going to be fine. Don't worry about anything."

Back in the infirmary, Dr. Rubinstein spoke about the seriousness and necessity for caregivers to recognize events like this.

"I did not expect this child to get sick so soon, although I knew that his system was deteriorating, and at some point something was going to happen. On the other hand, one must say that the foster parent of this child does not realize what's going on, and she would have missed this infection. If the child had been at home, he would have possibly been brought to us after two or three or four days in a catastrophic situation that may not have been reversible. So, by him being here in the camp, we may have saved his life."

The two most common causes for transmission of AIDS in women are sexual transmission from an infected partner who'd contracted the disease through sharing a contaminated needle which had been used to inject drugs such as heroin and that the woman herself is an addict and used a contaminated needle.

Besides understanding how infection occurs, women needed to understand how the virus behaves in the body and how to manage their medications.

In addition to teaching how the disease might progress in the children and how the parents can spot the signs of illness, Dr. Rubinstein also designed a curriculum for the mothers about their own disease and their medications. As he explained to the women in the class, "We can detect those pieces of the virus in the blood, and that tells you something. If there are a lot of these pieces of the virus in the blood, it tells you that the virus is replicating. Take for example AZT. We have many patients who, before they started on AZT, had a lot of this virus in their blood. But when you give them AZT, you can see that the level of this virus is going down, down, down, down, down, and sometimes it disappears."

Marisol, a participant in the class, spoke up. "Sometimes," she admitted, "I forget to take my AZT, and instead of taking my two pills, I'll take four."

"This is not right," Dr. Rubinstein replied patiently. "You should not do that."

"So, if I miss one dose," Marisol asked, "what should I do?"

"Just take what you're supposed to take for the next dose. Don't double up. You see, if you double up, you'll suddenly get a very high peak in your blood. And the higher the peak is in the blood, the more damage you can cause to your blood cells."

The Plan for the Caregivers and Their Children

One of the major goals of the camp, Phyllis Susser explained, was "to give the caregivers the opportunity to get out of the city and be in a place where their medical needs could be taken care of, along with their children's. We wanted to give them an opportunity to literally rest and have someone else take over. There are no stresses of daily life here. The caregivers don't need to wonder what to make for dinner and have to shop for it, and have to cook, and wash and clean, or worry where the children are, worry about getting the child to the doctor if there's a sore throat, or for a medical appointment, or having to go and get medication. We have taken those burdens off their hands and given them an opportunity to enjoy all the things that are enjoyable about life, and, for one week, not have to think about or concentrate on what the difficulties are and what the pains are.

"The primary clients here are children who either have AIDS or are HIV infected and would not be welcomed in other kinds of camps, even in camps for children who are sick. The primary purpose for the children is to get them out of the city and into the same kind of safe environment children who are healthy and well can have in the summer, with all of the recreational experiences that camp offers. That's the major purpose for the kids, that they have fun.

"We also want them to have an opportunity to have relationships with the medical people that are so much a part of their lives back home but in very sterile, clinical settings—the hospital, the doctor's office. The children learned that they could see the doctors and that it didn't always mean they were going to get a needle. Here they're having dinner with them, they're out in the boats together, they're swimming, they're playing together. They began to recognize that you can have a whole host of different relationships with the same person."

Medications

The crew and I had an appointment to videotape Elena Perez, the registered nurse who ran the camp infirmary. At Albert Einstein College of Medicine, she worked with the infected children and their mothers regarding everything related to HIV medications, managing the regimens, how to use the medical supplies and equipment, and how to help the mothers deal with the extremely difficult job of getting their children to take their meds.

In advance of our coming to the infirmary, I had asked Elena to set up a table with the medication regimen for one child at camp. Up until we filmed this sequence, I had been wholly unaware of what a typical routine was and how overwhelming it could be for the mothers and grandmothers to administer it all. When we arrived, Elena had everything set up for us. She had laid out a disturbingly long array of medications and medical equipment on the counter. As the crew set up for the shoot, I told Elena that it seemed almost impossible that one child would have to take all this. She assured me this was not at all unusual.

Elena stood at one end of the counter as the cameraman began to roll tape. Following my directions, she slowly moved along, held up each bottle of medicine and explained what it was and what it was used for.

"Most kids get two to seven or eight medications," she began. "This is David's regimen. Right now he has a bacterial infection that just broke out, so he is getting bacitracin, an over-the-counter topical antibiotic. He has asthma, so he gets two medications for that, Slo-Bid and prednisone. Here is his AZT. It's an antiretroviral medication taken to prevent the replication of the virus in his blood system.

"This medication, Proventil, goes along with another medication, Alupent. They are two types of bronchodilators, and they go inside the nebulizer. The treatment takes twenty to thirty minutes and will open up the airways in his lungs and help him breathe better for the next four to five hours.

"This," Elena continued, "is a can of Ensure, which David must drink at least four to five times a day to supplement his regular food. This is necessary because very often he has no appetite."

Suddenly, without any direction from me, Elena looked up and spoke directly to the camera.

"This is a heavy load for trained medical staff to dispense and oversee. You can only imagine what it must be like for a mom, a grandmother, a foster mom, a caregiver to be able to manage the amount of medication that one child takes."

I was stunned by what I had just seen and heard, and reiterated how hard it must be for David and his mother to have to do this every day. Elena shook her head back and forth, indicating, I thought, that she, too, was still shocked by it. But what she meant was that I had misunderstood.

"Oh, no!" she said. "What you saw is not done once a day for this child. This was just his *morning regimen*. Many of the kids have to take medications and treatments three or four times a day."

These regimens and treatments were typical of what was available for children in 1990. It was quite early in the epidemic, and doctors had a limited number of effective therapies at their disposal. But as far as medications to fight the virus were concerned (antiretrovirals), there was only one, AZT.

Over the next few years, four or five different classes of drugs became available, consisting of two or three different medications, which had to be given three to four times a day. It was very hard to adhere to these medication regimens, and the pills were hard to tolerate because of toxicity.

It is entirely different now. In 2023, pediatric infectious disease specialists have dozens of antiretroviral drugs to choose from. A child or adolescent may have to take only one pill once or twice a day. Inside that pill may be a combination of two or three different medications. An injectable drug given just once a month is even available now for adolescents. Additional good news is that these drugs are all much better tolerated, with fewer side effects.

The Infirmary

Before the children came into the infirmary, the doctor and the nurses had already made the atmosphere as comforting and stress free as possible. Everyone's goal was to keep the young patients calm and distracted from any uncomfortable

Counselor encouraging child to take his medication (still from VHS tape).

procedures or foul-tasting medicine they might have to endure. The counselors stayed by their side, held their hands, or let them sit on their laps to help settle them. There were specially designated clinic toys the children could play with or hold only when they were in the clinic. This gave them something to look forward to at each visit.

8

Why Take Whole Families to Camp?

PHYLLIS SUSSER STRESSED TO ME the importance of having the children's parents and siblings or other caregivers such as grandmothers or aunts join them at camp.

"You know, we could just take the kids. But to bring the family together—the primary caregiver and the healthy siblings of the children—allows the family to spend time together in a way that they don't have an opportunity to do back home. The healthy siblings are able to see sick brothers and sisters in a normal setting, in a very happy environment."

Floyd Spencer, healthy sibling of camper.

The crew and I walked down to the lake and found a tall, lanky teenage boy there. He appeared to be older than most of the children at camp. I introduced myself and the crew, and after explaining what we were doing, I asked him about himself and if he would be comfortable talking on camera about how old he is, why he's at camp, and what he's enjoying the most. He didn't hesitate for a second before saying he would do it. When he sat down for the brief interview, he told us his name was Floyd Spencer, and I learned that he'd accompanied his mother, Linda, and his younger brother, Rayshawn, to camp. Both of them had been diagnosed with AIDS, but thankfully, Floyd had been spared.

"My name is Floyd Spencer. I'm fourteen years old. I'm having a nice time here," he told me, smiling. "I like the gym. I like everything really. I came here for my brother. This is a time that he can enjoy with me, and he feels better that I'm around. He doesn't need to be with me all the time, but as long as he knows I'm around and I'm in the same camp, he can come and see me any time he wants. I think he's having a wonderful time."

The Counselors

A deeply heartwarming dynamic of the camp experience was the relationships that developed between the children and the counselors. When I asked Phyllis Susser to comment on this she said the following:

"The children immediately bonded with the counselors, a couple of whom were themselves HIV-positive, which added yet another dimension to the relationships which would form. They came from all over the country. While these young people come with devotion and dedication and the belief in what they're doing, and wanting to help, and wanting to be involved, seven

days later—by the time they go home—they are emotionally attached to the children and the parents in a way that shocks them."

Waterfront counselor Beth beamed when she recalled the first day of camp. "When the kids got off the bus, and they started running around, I just felt so happy. I think I have smiled more this week than I can ever remember. Even now, just thinking about the kids, I can feel it inside, and it's so warm, and it feels so good. It's the best feeling in the world to see one of the little kids pull a fish out of the water. Their faces just light up."

Another counselor, Troy Morris, admitted that, upon first hearing about the program, "I was a little apprehensive about it because basically it was about my own fears. But after one of the administrators explained to me the program and how you can get AIDS and how you can't get AIDS, I had to do it. I figured that the kids that were coming here really needed this, and I figured if I could give as much of myself as possible, then I would. And I also want them to be able to look back one day and say that they had fun here at Camp Sussex. That would make me very happy, very happy, indeed."

And for Stephanie, in her early twenties, the experience was perhaps especially meaningful. "Last summer, I was at the camp. I have a big love for children, and I'm also HIV-positive," she said. "I don't really know…um…I'm going to get sensitive about it now." The always ebullient young woman choked back tears, then composed herself. "I don't really know if I can have children in the future, so this is my way of kind of, like, giving back to them, and hoping that someday I could have one. I watch how they grow and what they go through. I love their hugs. I love when they notice a miracle for the first time. They're just so full of joy. They're, like, so innocent. Children are so innocent." She added with a laugh, "It makes me want to be a kid again."

A Special Visitor Returns

Throughout her professional life, Ruth Messinger was a tireless and passionate advocate for social change. As borough president of Manhattan from 1989 to 1997, Ms. Messinger was always keenly interested in how best the city could serve families impacted by HIV and AIDS. To help expand her understanding of the dilemmas facing families living in Manhattan and what she could do to make things better for them, she traveled twice to visit with the mothers and caregivers at Birch Family Camp. While I was interviewing her at camp on an early summer day in 1991, she told me the following:

"I come here each year because what matters to me is seeing the ways in which this camp makes a difference for these families," she said. "Frankly, hearing the mothers talk about their life experiences, about how special it is to be in camp, but also about the situations they encounter every day in the hospital, in school, and in the neighborhood, I have to do two things. I have to think about the systems in the city that are not working for individuals and families that are dealing with AIDS, and I have to think about ways to keep this camp alive and to expand its program so that it really has a home and can be operated many months of the summer and on other occasions during the year.

"I think it's very clear when you listen to the women who come here with their children and grandchildren talk that we simply don't have the capacity to create this in the city in the middle of people's lives," she continued. "We can create pieces of it, and we ought to do that, but there is nothing to substitute for the chance to really be away from home in a place where you feel taken care of and entirely respected, and where you get a chance to sort of put your life back together."

Taking Good Care

My first introduction to Dr. Anita Septimus did not occur in person. She was a woman in the videotape footage I was logging for Phyllis Susser. Those videotapes had been shot in 1989 during a group therapy session at the very first season of Birch Family Camp. I was mesmerized as I watched her ever so gently guide mothers with AIDS in a deeply emotional conversation about death. In 1990 I interviewed Dr. Septimus in person at camp, where she spoke passionately about these women and children.

"This camp is a place where families can have a real-life experience with some fun to look back on. It's very important to be able to remember the children happy. These are dying children, and the fact is that these families are going to lose them. Now they can look back and say, 'Well, at least we had some fun, we had some happiness.' If we can counteract some of the pain and suffering, then I think we have done something unusual for these kids and for us also. It's very difficult for staff to care for children knowing they will be dying and having such shortened lives. So, it's also important for us to see these children happy, even though they are going through such a disease.

"Unfortunately," she pointed out, "children with AIDS are massively cared for by single mothers, whether it's natural mothers, foster mothers, adoptive mothers, grandmothers, great-grandmothers, aunts, et cetera. These are extraordinary women. We need to help these women take better care of their children. They are oftentimes isolated, poor, frightened, don't share their life stories with anyone because they are afraid of stigma. It's important to support them, to encourage them to talk, to come out with their stories, and to have the courage to fight for what they deserve."

Amelia, a blond, curly-haired woman who looked like she was in her mid-fifties, became the sole caregiver for her six-year-old granddaughter, Natalie, when Natalie's mother died of AIDS. I asked her how the experience of being at camp was for both of them.

"I've never seen her so happy and enjoying herself. Usually, when we're back in the city, she's always tired or sick. And over here, she's just running around. She hasn't complained. And she's eating a little bit, at least," she said with a smile. "She never eats when we're back home."

I first saw Lauren when she appeared on the videotapes I was logging from the camp's first session in 1989. Lauren was a beautiful dark-eyed child of about three years old, with wavy brown hair and adorable dimples—which didn't come into full view until she walked right up to the camera lens, filled it with her face, and smiled like a Cheshire cat.

There were only five families in attendance that year, which meant that Lauren got a lot of screen time. There was footage of her wriggling into the seat of a kiddie swing, zooming down the slide, sitting on one end of a seesaw while a counselor pumped the other end up and down. But the most touching of her many appearances showed her and her four bunkmates sitting transfixed in the television room while they watched *Cinderella*, the 1950 Disney animated musical film. Lauren had a lollipop in her mouth, and as she watched Cinderella sing the song "A Dream is a Wish Your Heart Makes," she twirled the lollipop around and around, making her rosy lips slick and shiny.

Here are the words:

> *A dream is a wish your heart makes*
> *when you're fast asleep.*
> *In dreams you will lose your heartaches,*
> *whatever you wish for, you keep.*
> *Have faith in your dreams and someday*
> *your rainbow will come smiling through.*
> *No matter how your heart is grieving*
> *If you keep on believing,*
> *The dream that you wish will come true.*

I can clearly remember seeing that movie and listening to that song when I was a little girl in the 1950s. Cinderella's words carried a simple, hopeful message—if I believed hard enough that my dreams would come true, they would. But when I watched the video of those five little children listening to those same words, I was struck with a profound sadness. They were all living with a deadly virus in them and, mercifully, had no awareness that their dreams likely would not come true. The following summer, I met Lauren and her mother, Judith. In one short interview, Judith shared some profoundly personal details that revealed a complicated and compelling story of their lives.

"We adopted Lauren when she was three weeks old. I couldn't carry a child to term. She was ill on and off with severe respiratory distress. At eight months old, she was diagnosed with HIV. The unpredictability of it is still devastating. However, I have great faith and hope in the future and in my daughter specifically—and in my ability, too, to go wherever it must take us.

"Lauren, to me, is a very special child. We've had our horrible times. She has been on doses of corticosteroids that have made her difficult to manage, to say the least. However, now she's developing so wonderfully. She's so much her own person. She's the type of person who dislikes intensely going to sleep and being out of what's happening. I try to give her as much space as possible and to understand that this spirit she has is also what's keeping her alive. This is her struggling to live. I know whatever the future may hold for us, it will always have been wonderful to have been with Lauren and to know her. She's really been a gift—an absolute gift."

Last Day

At dinner on the day before camp ended, I joined a table of mothers who were chatting about what they did during the day. I asked how they were feeling about having to return home to the city. Their answers spoke reams: "Anxious." "Sad to be leaving." The most gut-wrenching response, however, was "I have a sense of dread that I might never attend camp again if my children or I don't survive to the next summer." Every head nodded in agreement.

When I asked what their favorite activities were during the week, their excitement bubbled over. Everyone spoke at once, and I had to ask them to take turns talking. One told me about the trip to a flea market, where they were set loose with some money in their pockets to buy whatever they wanted. Another mother talked about a drive to the top of a mountain to watch the sunset. She said everybody sat in silence on the mountaintop, and she felt a sense of peace just flow through her. I learned about the bowling trip, going to the movies, and getting dessert at Dairy Queen—all simple pleasures, but unforgettable.

There was little likelihood there would ever be another week as enjoyable and unencumbered as this week was for them. Limited finances, the fragile nature of their own and their children's health, plus the crushing responsibilities that would replace all the wonderful things they had experienced here would become their reality again, and they knew it.

On the last day, it was not just the campers, women and children alike, who were deeply emotional. The counselors and staff were visibly heartbroken. They had bonded so quickly and deeply with these children, who they knew they might never see again. These wonderful people had given freely of their attention and affection. They'd made personal investments in the kids' happiness with little or no expectation of ever learning anything about them in the future. The week of camp was intense for everyone, as was the emptiness they felt when the buses drove away with the children they had come to love.

III

A Move South and a New Career

9

Fort Lauderdale to Los Angeles and Back

MY HUSBAND, RICK, WAS APPROACHING his fiftieth birthday and had been working at *The New York Times* for thirty years. On many occasions, Rick had spoken about leaving *The Times* and pursuing freelance writing full time. He felt that if he waited beyond age fifty to make the break, he would be "too old." And so he resigned in 1992 to begin this new phase of his life. For two years, he worked from home in Brooklyn Heights. It was an extremely productive time for him.

For me, however, 1992 marked not the beginning of an exciting new phase of my life but rather the end of one. After three disappointing years of diminishing income from Heartbeat Productions, I sadly filed the legal paperwork to end the business. When I mentioned this in conversation with Phyllis Susser one day, she immediately offered me an administrative position at the Birch executive office in Springfield Gardens, in Queens. I committed to this job fully aware that the bulk of my responsibilities would be middle-level, straight-up administrative work. Only one small facet of the job included producing staff development, fundraising, and public relations videotapes for the agency. Understandably, this was the part I was most interested in, but I knew realistically there would not be that many opportunities for doing this.

Rick and I had talked a number of times about moving out of New York. The flexibility of being a freelancer meant that he could live almost anywhere. If we were to move to another state, his criteria were that it had to be a relatively short flight back to

New York for meetings with his publisher and editor and, ideally, lower taxes. For me, even though I believed fully in Birch's mission and admired and enjoyed my colleagues, over the two years I was employed there, I found the bulk of my administrative work unstimulating. The concept of moving to a new state was appealing.

Rick had grown up in Miami, and we had vacationed there a number of times with the children. It was a familiar place and also met both of Rick's conditions. We decided to fly down to South Florida for a few days to explore our housing options in both Miami and Fort Lauderdale.

Miami lost out to Fort Lauderdale for a variety of reasons, the most serious one being that the two middle-class neighborhoods we had been considering were in the throes of dealing with an unsettling number of robberies and violent incidents. A man seated next to us on the flight to Fort Lauderdale recommended that we speak with his real estate agent in Fort Lauderdale. We took his suggestion and met with Yvonne that afternoon. She listened to us carefully and expressed great confidence that she could find a perfect place for our somewhat atypical taste in houses. She told us how good life could be in Fort Lauderdale, with its many attractive neighborhoods, myriad opportunities for a robust outdoor life, good restaurants, museums, and decent cultural venues. If we wanted to spend time in Miami, it was only about an hour's drive away. As if these attributes weren't enough, she reminded us that everything was bathed in sunshine and surrounded by sparkling water.

Yvonne spun her office chair around to face a large map of Fort Lauderdale hanging on the wall behind her desk. She pointed to a cluster of neighborhoods that we might want to consider: Las Olas Isles, Victoria Park, Colee Hammock, Coral

Ridge, Poinsettia Heights, and the small city of Wilton Manors. Yvonne gave us our own map and encouraged us to drive around and familiarize ourselves with those neighborhoods.

Before we left her office, the agent pointed to the map again. She ran her finger up a long, broad, green line labeled Sistrunk Boulevard. "By the way, while you're driving around, don't go down this road," she warned us, though she didn't say why.

The next day, Yvonne called and told us she had three houses to show us, and we should meet at the first one in Colee Hammock. The neighborhood was certainly charming, but the house didn't appeal to us. The second home, in Wilton Manors, was too large. We followed Yvonne's car to the third house, in Las Olas Isles. She thought it would be ideal for us: perfectly sized for two people and filled with charm. The owners had already purchased their new house and were eager to sell.

Many Fort Lauderdale communities fronted or backed on water, but none of them seemed quite like Las Olas Isles. It was composed of man-made, fingerlike peninsulas interlaced with canals; hence the city's nickname, "The Venice of the Americas." The canals splayed out on either side of Las Olas Boulevard, an elegant, palm tree–lined thoroughfare that led from the picturesque central business district all the way to Fort Lauderdale Beach. Yvonne was right about the house being perfect for us. A two-bedroom, two-bath, 1,400-square-foot cottage had been built in 1948 but renovated recently with Spanish tile floors and unique architectural details. The small plot of land was chockablock with palm trees, bird-of-paradise plants, vivid pink bougainvillea, and a variety of rare specimen plantings. In back of the cottage were three added bonuses: a lovely pool, a dock with electricity, and a canal that flowed into the New River. If we got this house, our new address would be Coconut Isle Drive.

I entertained myself with the thought that life here would be like living in one of the songs on Jimmy Buffett's 1981 album *Coconut Telegraph.*

The next day, we returned with Yvonne to negotiate. While we were talking with the owners, Rick's cell phone rang, and he walked out to the dock to take the call. I watched him as he paced back and forth, alternating between looking very serious and laughing occasionally. It was a long conversation, and I was getting anxious that something might have happened that would prevent us from moving here. I loved the place!

When he came back inside, he told me he had been called by Leslie Abramson, an internationally known Los Angeles criminal defense attorney. She was looking for a coauthor to write her autobiography. In 1989 Ms. Abramson had represented eighteen-year-old Erik Menéndez, one of the infamous Menéndez brothers, who murdered their parents.

Armed with shotguns, Erik and his twenty-one-year-old brother, Lyle, had surprised José and Mary Louise ("Kitty") Menéndez while they were watching television in their Beverly Hills mansion. The entertainment mogul and his wife were shot a total of fifteen times. Ms. Abramson argued that Erik and his brother had endured a lifetime of emotional, physical, and sexual abuse at the hands of their father and feared that he would murder them after they threatened to expose him. In 1996, after three trials, the sensational case came to an end with a verdict of life in prison without the possibility of parole for both the brothers.

Her current assignment, however, was not in a courtroom representing a client but in a courtroom reporting about a murder even more notorious than the Menéndez brothers' case. She was the chief ABC-TV correspondent for the O. J. Simpson murder trial. Ms. Abramson wanted to meet Rick to determine if they "clicked" and if she would feel comfortable working with him on the book. Rick flew to Los Angeles to meet Leslie. They did click, and he got the job. In spite of the fact that we wouldn't be moving into the house on Coconut Isle Drive, we bought it anyway and rented it for the time we'd be gone. We then, in turn, took a year's lease on a house in the Los Angeles suburb of Pacific Palisades.

My Five-Year Promise Fulfilled

Upon our return to Florida in the fall of 1995, we moved into our wonderful new home. Each morning, I would take my breakfast outside and sit by the pool reading the *South Florida Sun-Sentinel* classifieds and look for social service jobs. I knew exactly what I was looking for but wasn't optimistic I would find it. If I saw no listings to pursue, I would get in the car anyway, my résumé on the passenger seat, and drive around hoping to spot possible job opportunities that had not been advertised in the paper.

I was doing just this one day in September when traffic came to a standstill on the Andrews Avenue bridge. It took a few minutes for the raised drawbridge to let the line of waiting tall-masted sailboats, yachts, and large fishing boats pass underneath. While I was stuck there, my curiosity was piqued by a nondescript, gray, two-story building on my right with a sign that read "Children's Diagnostic & Treatment Center." When traffic moved again, I turned into the oversized, mostly empty parking lot, got out, and walked inside. The small lobby was modestly decorated with bare minimum furniture. I asked the receptionist sitting behind a sliding glass window what kind of diagnostic and treatment center this was. She smiled and pointed to a small stack of brochures on a table and suggested I read one rather than having her explain the many programs and services the center provided.

I sat down and began reading. Children's Diagnostic, an affiliate of the North Broward Hospital District,[3] annually served some ten thousand Broward County children and adolescents with disabilities or chronic illnesses, regardless of a family's ability to pay. In addition to medical care, young patients received evaluations, intervention services, and physical and occupational therapy, and the families were offered comprehensive case management and other social service support. What a remarkable place! The center was also a research facility, affording terminally ill children access to the latest drug protocols and state-of-the-art treatments. What sorts of terminal illnesses? I wondered.

The answer came in the fourth paragraph. The building I had accidently discovered featured an outpatient pediatric AIDS clinic. I stopped reading, walked back to the window, and took a deep breath.

"I'd like to apply for a job."

Five minutes later, I was shaking hands with Marie Brown, who introduced herself as a case manager in the Comprehensive Pediatric AIDS Program, known as CPAP. She added that she was being promoted to supervisor. I told her I'd like to be considered for a position—that is, if there were any openings—and handed her my résumé. She stood and read it. I, too, remained standing, deeply aware of the thumping in my chest, as if I'd just completed a four-hundred-meter race.

---

3   Now called Broward Health, a public, nonprofit hospital system governed by the North Broward Hospital District Board of Commissioners.

Marie told me that the center did, in fact, have two openings. I would have to meet with Vickie Tutunick, the current supervisor, who was becoming the program coordinator, and then be interviewed by the executive director, Dr. Susan Widmayer. If they were in agreement that I should be hired, I could actually have my pick of either job.

"One job would be to take over my position as a case manager in CPAP," Marie said. "The other would be as a case manager in the Early Intervention Program, which serves any Broward County child, birth to three, who is born at risk of..."

The rest of Marie's words were being puréed in my brain. I was unable to absorb anything else she was saying. All I wanted was the job she was leaving.

My interviews with Vickie and Dr. Widmayer went very well, and they offered me a position immediately in the Comprehensive Pediatric AIDS Program. It seemed to me that they were as happy to hire me as I was happy to be hired. I felt remarkably lucky that I had so easily fulfilled the five-year-old promise I had made to myself to work with this population.

It took two seemingly endless weeks before the bureaucratic paperwork was completed and I could meet my four new CPAP colleagues. To my delight, they were an enormously welcoming, generous, and diverse group. I would soon know them well enough to add more superlatives to the list: the hardest working, most dedicated, and compassionate people with whom I'd ever worked. Three of my colleagues were degreed social workers, and one had a degree in divinity studies. We all did exactly the same work regardless of our undergraduate majors or advanced degrees. I was told that all the clients called us their social workers and that the agency wanted us to refer to ourselves as that to avoid any confusion about who was doing what work.

Sister Camille Brouillard was in her late forties and fluent in French and Haitian Creole. She worked almost exclusively with the Haitian clients. Sister Camille laughed easily and, much to my amazement, could swear without inhibition when a situation called for it—but always under her breath. Camille was the first Catholic sister I had ever known personally. Of her many contributions to clients and colleagues alike, offering prayers, when requested, was an important one. As a non-praying person, I was surprised one afternoon to see a colleague go up to Sister Camille and ask her to pray for her very ill client—and even more surprised to occasionally see someone take her aside and ask for a personal prayer. In time, I made my own requests for Camille to pray for my clients and, on occasion, even for me. During those short, whispered moments together, Camille would face me, take my hands, close her eyes, and make her appeal for God to bring me strength for the difficult work I had to do. The sincerity and intensity of her words would always leave me feeling uplifted.

Arlene Gurwich, like me, was in her early fifties. Soft-spoken and impossible to rattle, she had gray-flecked, straight, dark-brown hair flowing to the middle of her back. When we met, Arlene was quick to tell me that she worked predominantly with teenagers, her "favorite population." In time, I, too, had a number of teens on my caseload, and truthfully, I found them to be frustratingly challenging. As if their issues of defiance toward authority, teenage angst, raging hormones, and burgeoning sexuality weren't enough, they had, of course, a highly contagious terminal illness thrown into the mix. But Arlene adored her clients and loved guiding them through their myriad problems. Her reward was that they loved her back. She behaved like a mother hen toward her teens. There was no time clock in Arlene's day. No matter the hour of the day or the day of the week, if a client was in crisis and needed to talk, she was always available and ready to help. I considered both Arlene and Sister Camille to be my mentors.

Kim Purinton, in her mid-twenties, was the youngest member of our team. She had a sweet personality, tons of patience, and was the mother of a young baby. In addition to her always upbeat attitude, she had a crystalline soprano voice and, if coaxed, would sing for us, lifting our oftentimes sagging spirits.

David Lord, the only man in CPAP, was in his mid-forties. A married father of two daughters, David was perennially cheerful and somewhat rumpled in appearance. His bachelor's degree was in divinity studies, and he was an ordained minister. He did not have a church or a congregation, but his clients were his "flock," and he looked after them with diligence and warmth.

I brought my own expertise and life experiences into the mix. I had a master's degree in special education and was the parent of two young adults: a nineteen-year-old son in college and a twenty-three-year-old daughter who had graduated college and was living and working in Manhattan. It was understood when I started the job that in addition to being assigned to any client in need of services, I would also be assigned those known to have or suspected of having developmental delays. I also spoke Spanish moderately well and was given the very few Hispanic clients our clinic saw at that time.

The five of us had to squeeze into a relatively small office designed for maybe three people. There were no cubicles, just five mismatched desks and chairs and a couple of filing cabinets. The upside to this imposed physical closeness was that I learned major parts of my job simply by listening to my colleagues' phone conversations and watching them relate to their clients during office visits.

When a client came in to discuss a problem, a chair usually piled high with boxes of donated shoes or stacks of clothes would be cleaned off and pulled up to the side of a desk next to her social worker. Amid ringing phones and the noise of ambient, animated conversations, the social workers and clients would lean in close to each other in order to be heard. In this setting, solutions to the family's health, economic, social, and emotional issues would be discussed.

I revered my new colleagues and learned quickly to model their behaviors. I hoped in time I could be just like them. In addition to my four office mates, Marie, the new supervisor, and Vickie, now the program coordinator, were also generous teachers.

"No Dear, That's Not the Way It's Done"

My new house was about four miles from Children's Diagnostic & Treatment Center. One Garden-of-Eden-like winter morning, before I had any factual understanding of my job, I came up with what I thought was a brilliant idea. I would get some much-needed exercise by biking regularly to work. I had a reliable bike, a wicker basket on the handlebars to hold my pocketbook, and a loud enough bell to alert cars that I was in their vicinity. Off I went, full of anticipation for what the day might hold, and feeling quite proud of myself for doing something good for my health and body.

When I turned into the parking lot, I spotted Dr. Widmayer walking out the front door. I had enjoyed talking with her at my job interview and was now delighted to see her waving at me. I waved back, smiled broadly, and stopped the bike in front of her. Up close, she didn't look quite as delighted to see me as I thought she had looked from a distance. As a matter of fact, she had a quizzical expression on her face.

"Dear, what happened to your car?"

I told Dr. Widmayer I wanted to start a fitness regimen that began with biking to and from work each day. Now a genuine look of dismay crossed her face as she stared at the wicker bicycle basket with my pocketbook filling up every inch of space.

"Dear, how will you do your home visits on a bike?" she asked gently. "If you're on a bike, where are you going to put the bags of food and clothes and children's shoes, and all the other things we routinely deliver to our clients? And, dear, where will the clients sit when they need to be taken places?"

What was I thinking? What was *she* thinking of me? That she'd hired an idiot? I couldn't respond. I felt my face heating up and sensed I was blushing, a very unfamiliar physiological response for me. Nervous laughter came spilling out of me and then careened out of control from embarrassment. Dr. Widmayer smiled at me and started to laugh as well, with a warmth I was only beginning to experience but would come to count on.

10

Death in the Room

DUE TO THE DRAMATICALLY ESCALATING numbers of people becoming infected and needing services, I was told I would soon be getting my own caseload of ten families, per- haps in as little as two weeks. Until then, I would spend time accompanying the social workers on home visits.

I understood that having a caseload meant sooner or later I would be dealing with the death of a client. What I did not know or understand well enough in those first few weeks was the grim fact that death was *always* hovering over our work. Every doctor, nurse, social worker, family resource worker, and administrator accepted this fact and confronted it in their own way. Because no clients had died during the first two weeks of my orientation, I had an incomplete picture of death's impact on my seemingly strong colleagues.

Weekly staff meetings were held in the morning, before cli- ents started dropping by. At my third meeting, we were seated around the conference table waiting for everyone to arrive. People were chatting as they had done before, but in somewhat hushed tones. I expected the agenda would be the same: agency business first, after which staff members would take turns pre- senting their problem cases. Medical Director Dr. Ana Puga, Marie Brown, Vickie Tutunick, and the social workers would comment and offer suggestions for how to approach or improve the situations. It was at the very first of these staff meetings that I observed social workers weighing in on cases that weren't theirs. Although caseloads were large, almost everyone had some level of familiarity with their colleagues' clients. There was an open atmosphere that encouraged others' input and observations. When the last person sat down at the table, a curtain of silence abruptly fell over the room until Sister Camille began to speak. Her hands were clasped in front of her, and her eyes were cast down. Her voice trembled. Suddenly Camille's words came out in sobs as she announced that one of her teenage clients had died over night. Other people also began to cry. Someone jumped up to put her arms around Camille.

I hadn't been denying the probability of this happening to one of my clients, but I had not been thinking too much about it. Surely it wouldn't happen soon. Or would it? I felt awash in fear because I now saw what lay ahead. But in that moment, having witnessed the empathy and tenderness displayed by my colleagues toward Camille, I also understood that I would not have to go through this alone.

Shadowing

Arlene was the first person who took me on a home visit and introduced me to some of the things I would, in time, be seeing and experiencing on a routine basis.

Arlene turned on the air conditioner in her car and began telling me about the family I would be meeting. Her client Antoinette was a single mother in her early twenties with twin toddler sons. Antoinette suffered from a condition known as wasting syndrome, one of the possible complications of advanced AIDS. This had caused her to lose a large amount of weight. She was also battling several opportunistic infections: cryptosporidiosis, caused by a protozoan parasite, produced nausea and unrelenting diarrhea, while her hacking cough signaled pneumonia. As Arlene was explaining Antoinette's symptoms, I thought to myself that I probably had never met anyone as sick as Antoinette in my life. This made me anxious.

During the ride, I learned that Antoinette had been a virgin when she met the father of her boys. He infected her with a virulent strain of HIV, but, amazingly, the boys were not born infected. When the boyfriend learned Antoinette was pregnant, he abandoned her. Because the young woman's physical decline was rapid, her mother realized early on that she would have to move into her daughter's small house to take care of everyone.

An older woman answered the door and welcomed us in. After the front door closed behind us, I had to wait a moment for my eyes to adjust to the darkness. Navy-blue bedsheets serving as drapes covered the large living room window. The only natural light making its way into the room came from two small, distant kitchen windows. Out of the corner of my eye, I saw a small form dash out of the kitchen, raising flecks of dust that danced crazily in the pale rays of sunlight. Flickering light from a small TV on a stand in the corner helped brighten the living room a little.

At the sound of Arlene's hello, Antoinette's two little boys ran in from another room and wrapped themselves around her legs. Antoinette's mother, Jean, who had let us in, peeled the boys off and warmly embraced Arlene herself. Arlene introduced me as her new colleague and asked permission to speak freely in front of me. Jean nodded, took my hand in her two hands, and told me what a blessing Arlene was in their lives. What a beautiful thing to say about someone! I hoped that one day a client of mine might say the same about me.

Jean and Arlene began to chat. I looked around the room at the closed interior doors and wondered why Antoinette hadn't come out to join us. Jean turned on a table lamp, illuminating a small, motionless form curled up on the sofa under blankets, despite the stifling heat. On the floor next to the form stood a galvanized metal bucket.

"Let me introduce you to Antoinette," Arlene said cheerily. We walked over to the sofa, and I saw that the form was, indeed, a woman's. Her head was the size of a small child's, her hair was very sparse, and her cheeks were sunken in, but she flashed a big smile that revealed beautifully straight, bright-white teeth. Arlene introduced me. Antoinette extended a rail-thin arm toward me. I shook her hand and told her how pleased I was to meet her.

"I apologize for my condition," she said in a thin, raspy voice. "I'd like to greet you properly, but I feel too weak to get up right now." I stammered something like, "Please don't worry about it," and hoped she couldn't sense my nervousness.

"I'm sorry for the bucket being here," she added. "I've been throwing up so much lately. I need it right close by."

Antoinette pointed to a chair, indicating I should sit down. She quickly put her arm back under the covers.

"I've got chills that sometimes just shake me to the bone, and awful diarrhea, too. I can't do nothing for my boys anymore, not even play with them."

I don't know if Arlene sensed this might be a lot for me to absorb (it was), but she jumped in and reminded Antoinette that she would be taking her to Broward General Medical Center[4] tomorrow morning to be admitted, and that they would do whatever was necessary to help her feel better. Antoinette admitted she had forgotten. She closed her eyes, and the corners of her mouth turned up into a hint of a smile. Perhaps the thought of

---

4   Now called Broward Health Medical Center.

what would happen tomorrow was giving her a sense of relief. She said nothing more. Arlene promised to bring some books and toys for the boys when she came to pick up Antoinette in the morning. We said our goodbyes, and Jean hugged both of us.

As soon as we got back in the car, I could feel the tension in my body ease. I had questions to ask.

First, I wanted to know why Arlene was personally taking Antoinette to the hospital, when it looked like she was sick enough to have gone by ambulance. And wasn't Arlene anxious about her passenger possibly having a bout of diarrhea in her car? Or throwing up? "Look in the backseat," she said. I turned and saw a neat stack of towels. I didn't need to ask what they were for.

Arlene went on to explain that because very few CFAP clients had cars, the center's policy was to provide free transportation to clinic appointments.[5] Without this service, and with no one to drive them, their medical care would lapse and they'd get sicker. If a client appeared to be seriously ill, injured, or dying, then an ambulance was certainly warranted; but if their condition was more or less routine, and we felt we could take care of it on our own, we should. Bus passes were distributed to those who were well enough to take public transportation and also given to the uninfected caregivers raising infected children or grandchildren.

Arlene obviously felt she was able to handle this level of illness on her own. Would I be able to?

---

5   The practice of transporting clients in our own cars was later discontinued. In its place, CDTC contracted with a local taxi company to bring them to and from the clinic for their appointments.

Next, I asked Arlene why the windows in Jean's home were covered with sheets and why the room was kept so dark.

"As your caseload grows and you start doing your own home visits," Arlene began, "you'll see that many of the clients' homes have dark sheets hung at the windows. It's not only that sheets are cheaper to buy than curtains, but dark materials work better to keep out the heat in the brutally hot months. And there's another important reason dark sheets are preferred. It's because in addition to blocking out the sun, they block out prying eyes. Rumors fly when a neighbor is suspected of having AIDS, and this is one way to protect a person's privacy."

"What will happen tomorrow?" I asked.

"Dr. Puga will call ahead to let Broward General know we are coming, and they will undoubtedly admit Antoinette. I want to be with her to make sure everything goes as smoothly as possible. I also don't want the children to be alarmed by an ambulance taking away their mother, and I don't want the rumor mill to start churning when the neighbors see an ambulance pull up. This should be like any other ride we've taken together—relaxed and pleasant. This might be Antoinette's last ride anywhere. I want it to be with me, not strangers."

Circle of Prayer

Next, it was my turn to shadow David. He told me this was a routine hospital visit at Broward General Medical Center to check in with his client who had been admitted yesterday morning because of dehydration and a urinary tract infection. He came to deliver her bedroom slippers and Bible, which she had forgotten to take from home. David introduced me and, just as Arlene had done, asked his client if she would be comfortable with me staying in the room. She said it would be fine and then sweetly wished me good luck with my new job. I was very touched by her kindness. I asked how she was feeling, and she laughed and answered, "Now? Great! I've had a full day away from my kids, and it's been like a vacation. I hope they don't send me home tomorrow!"

David told her that in all likelihood she would be going home tomorrow, and she made a grumpy face. We all laughed. After David said goodbye and promised to see her when she came into the clinic next, we started walking down the hall toward the elevator. A voice called out his name from one of the rooms, and he poked his head in the doorway. It was Maggie, a client at the center, though she was assigned to another social worker. She'd seen him pass by and invited us in.

David introduced me and, again, asked if she would be comfortable talking to him with me in the room, adding that I could wait outside if she'd prefer. I'd now had a number of opportunities to observe how seriously everyone took the issue of confidentiality. Maggie, sitting in a hospital reclining chair, smiled warmly at me and told me I should stay. The two of them chatted comfortably about nonmedical matters. In spite of the fact that she was not one of David's clients, he knew her well enough to ask how her son was doing on the middle school football team.

When David started to say goodbye, Maggie asked if we could stay for just a few more minutes. She had asked the hospital chaplain to visit and say a prayer for her. She thought he'd be there any minute. As an ordained minister, David understood and was more than happy to wait.

The chaplain arrived, accompanied by one of the nurses assigned to Maggie's care. He asked us to form a semicircle around her chair and said we'd all be holding hands. He stood on Maggie's left side, while the nurse stood on her right, and David and I stood in front of her chair. He and I held each other's hand and reached for the nurse's and the chaplain's hands. The chaplain asked us to wait for a moment before doing that. He reached into his jacket pocket and pulled out several blue latex gloves. He handed a pair to the nurse and gave each of us a pair. He then put on a pair himself. I immediately shot David a glance. He gave a barely perceptible negative shake of his head, indicating I shouldn't say anything.

Now gloved up, we all held hands around Maggie's recliner, and the chaplain began to pray. I was completely unable to focus on his words because I was too upset by his actions—and embarrassed for Maggie.

CFAP had an ironclad commitment to educating our clients, their families, and the community about the modes of transmission if someone has HIV or AIDS. Holding hands was certainly not one of them. The chaplain's actions had to have made Maggie feel as if she were contagious. Even if he was well intentioned and did this to protect patients from any germs that he might be carrying, I wondered why he didn't explain this to Maggie, so that she wouldn't be left thinking that he was afraid to touch her.

I anticipated an awkward silence when the chaplain and the nurse left the room, but David didn't lose a beat. In a matter-of-fact tone, he addressed immediately what had just happened, saying that we all know HIV can't be transmitted through touch. He added that the nurse had to have known this as well but probably put on the gloves out of respect for the clergyman. David expressed disappointment that the chaplain didn't know better, but Maggie brushed it off, noting that it wasn't the first time this had happened.

This encounter occurred at a time in the course of the epidemic when fear and misinformation about how the virus could be spread was rampant. Dealing with the stigma about AIDS, and other people's—even close family members'—fear of it was a constant problem for our clients.

11

A Caseload

MARIE TOOK ME TO MEET Simone, a petite, energetic woman in her late twenties who had been diagnosed in elementary school as developmentally delayed. Given my background in special education, Marie felt that Simone would be a good candidate for my new caseload and, if I agreed, she would become my first client.

Simone lived in a Section 8 (rent-subsidized) three-bedroom cinderblock house, which she shared with her much older boyfriend, Henry. The couple had two daughters, ages one and three. She also had an eight-year-old son from a previous relationship. None of the children were HIV-positive. Simone learned she was infected when she was tested at an early prenatal visit when she was pregnant with her first child with Henry. I learned from Marie that Simone had never shown any interest in her disease, how she contracted it, or what she should do about it. I doubt that the obstetrician who gave her the HIV test results recognized the signs that Simone had developmental delays, and they surely didn't explain things in a simplified way. In the early days of our working together, I noticed how forgetful and easily distracted she was; but as time went on I became aware of her severe lack of understanding about child development, her poor parenting skills, and her inability to make healthy decisions for herself and her children. She was not in the least interested in getting medical care. Her retort was always, "No. I feel fine. There's nothing wrong with me."

Simone was in her neighbor's yard when she saw Marie's car pull up and us get out. She ran barefoot to the car, her year-old baby bouncing up and down on her hip. Marie introduced me as a new social worker and asked if we could talk inside. Simone seemed very excited and ran to her front door with us following behind. The door was locked. As she stood there, presumably trying to remember where the key might be, she scratched vigorously at her arm. I noticed the skin was red, blistery, and raw.

"Oh! The key's next door," she exclaimed and turned to run back to the neighbor's house. Marie stopped her.

"What's going on with your arm?"

Simone told Marie she had bugs under her skin, but it was going to get better because her grandma told her how to cure it.

"What did she say to do?"

"Use Brillo. She told me to just keep rubbing a Brillo pad on my arm, and it'll kill the bugs." Marie looked skyward and exhaled loudly.

"Stop using the Brillo pad immediately!" she said firmly. "It's not going to help, and you're hurting yourself. It could get badly infected."

Marie told Simone that she would pick her up tomorrow and bring her to the clinic, where she'd be seen by a nurse and get real medication. Simone seemed happy enough to do that and promptly ran off to the neighbor's house to fetch the key.

We watched her go inside and waited…and waited. We looked at each other and started walking to the neighbor's, but then Simone came bounding out.

"Sorry!" she shouted. "I got to talking with my friend." Again we stood at Simone's door with no movement on her part to let us in. An awkward few seconds passed. Marie looked at Simone and asked if she was going to open the door or not. The young woman's face fell.

"Oh. I forgot to take the key with me."

She spun around and ran back to the neighbor's. I looked at Marie, nodded affirmatively, and said, "Yup, I'll take her!"

On January 31, 1995, shortly after Simone became my first client, *The New York Times* reported data from the Centers for Disease Control which announced that "AIDS is now the leading killer of Americans from twenty-five to forty-four years old." This was shocking news; it immediately made me worry about what I had just taken on.

Oh-So-Personal Case Management

Vickie assigned Ginny to my caseload. She sat down at my desk to prepare me for my first home visit.

"Ginny is a single mother with three elementary-school-age children, none of whom are infected," she said. "Her children seem happy, and I've never witnessed anything alarming in her relationship with them. Ginny's disease has not yet progressed beyond HIV, and the virus is not impacting her health in any discernable way. She acts and looks robust. In fact, Ginny is actually far too robust. You could say she's grossly overweight. She's also slovenly, and you need to know that her housekeeping and parenting skills are really poor. These are some of the areas I've been working on, and you'll have to continue this work with her."

While driving to the house, Vickie talked about the kinds of help Ginny and the children had needed in the past and what I might find myself doing for them in the future. I understood from that conversation that nothing should be taken for granted with Ginny. Her formal education was limited, her decision-making skills were poor, and she always looked for the easy way out of a situation. If I were to assume she knew how to do something, I might well be surprised to find out otherwise.

"I'll tell you a story that will speak reams about Ginny's personal hygiene skills," Vickie offered. "Ginny often has a strong body odor. She recently came into the clinic with a severe rash under her breasts and her belly. After the nurse examined her, she asked Ginny about her bathing habits and learned she was not washing herself thoroughly. You see, Ginny never realized she had to lift up her breasts and wash underneath them or beneath her sagging belly. Over time, she had a pretty bad buildup of sweat and grime, which turned into a serious rash."

I nodded affirmatively as Vickie spoke, as if this were not the first time I had been told a story like this—but it most definitely was. I asked if the nurse explained to Ginny how she needed to bathe differently.

"Oh, sure. The nurse verbally explained proper bathing techniques, but she also knew Ginny well enough to know that simply talking about why she got this rash and prescribing medication to get rid of it would not be enough. She wanted me to teach Ginny how to wash herself. I was told to do a home visit, and if Ginny were agreeable, we were to go into the bathroom, and I was supposed to ask her to strip to her waist, lift up her breasts, which were very pendulous, and then I was supposed to verbally guide her in how to properly wash under them. I also addressed the other problem area but told her to handle that one on her own the next time she showered."

I was completely mute during this explanation.

"Did she agree to this?" I asked incredulously.

"Yes, she did, with no hesitation. So, I taught her this new skill. It was definitely a first for me!" By discussing the details of this, Vicky taught me an early lesson regarding how very, very intimate and personal social work could be.

American Doll

Individual clients and families were regularly being added to my caseload. My newest addition was the Williams family, consisting of Fitz and Sherisse, their seven-year-old son, Gerard, and their five-year-old daughter, Zoe. They had recently arrived from the Caribbean island of Saint John. Only the mother and daughter were HIV-positive. Back home, their lives had been quite comfortable, and there had never been any thought about emigrating to the United States until Zoe started developing recurrent respiratory infections. It was then that both she and Sherisse were diagnosed with HIV. After that, the decision to move here was made quickly. They sacrificed everything and left behind family and friends in exchange for access to the superior medical care they knew would be available in the States.

My first meeting was only with Mrs. Williams and her daughter. It was brief. I met them in the clinic lobby. They were sitting in a far corner with no one else near them. I sat down next to Sherisse, introduced myself, and explained that we could chat for a bit until Zoe was called in to see the doctor. I reassured her that a home visit would be scheduled very soon, and that would allow us to talk privately and in greater depth about the family. She said she'd enjoy that and promptly told me to take down directions to her house, explaining that some of the streets were dead ends, and she didn't want me to get lost.

Sherisse, twenty-nine, was very attractive, well dressed, and outspoken. She knew exactly what she wanted from the medical staff and told me so, in a lilting Caribbean accent: "The *bes'* possible *everyt'ing* for my child, that's what I want."

I told her she would be very pleased with the medical care in our pediatric clinic, and I then outlined some of the social services the family might qualify for. Sherisse was quick to tell me that they were far from rich but had never received any assistance in the past and weren't looking for any now. Mr. Williams had been employed steadily as a telephone lineman in Saint John and had already signed a contract to work for Florida Power & Light. His new job would start in a couple of weeks. Sherisse had worked as a freelance manicurist and got all her clients by word of mouth. She was "*dahn* good!" she told me proudly but admitted to being anxious about how she would start over in Florida with no friends to recommend her.

Zoe, sitting next to her mother and holding a large, beautiful, brown-skinned doll, was a vision in a black-and-white gingham dress with red bows circling the hem and more red bows around the scoop neckline and the short sleeves. She wore shiny black patent leather shoes and white ankle socks with lace cuffs. The astonishing thing was that Zoe's doll was wearing exactly the same outfit. I was not the only one to notice this. The other little girls in the lobby were staring at Zoe and her doll. One child pointed in Zoe's direction and whispered in her mother's ear. Another one walked right over to Zoe and told her she really liked her doll. Zoe politely thanked her and put the palm of her hand over the doll's head and ran it down her long brown hair. They were then called into the clinic.

When I got back to my desk, a colleague, Irene, told me she had seen me with my new clients in the waiting room and asked if I knew how much the little girl's doll cost. I had no idea. Irene, though, had a daughter and was familiar with those dolls.

"They're called American Girl dolls and can cost about a hundred dollars. They could even cost more, depending on the model and how many outfits you buy," she said with eyebrows raised. Now my eyebrows went up, too. One hundred dollars, plus the cost of the matching outfit!

Sherisse and Zoe returned in a few days to get the test results from Dr. Puga and to discuss Zoe's starting on medication for her respiratory problem. I stayed in the examination room with them. Dr. Puga asked Sherisse whether she would consider starting treatment for herself, but Sherisse refused, saying that she was feeling just fine and would be focused entirely on Zoe's health. This decision was not uncommon among our women, but it was unwise. Dr. Puga told Mrs. Williams that if she delayed taking care of herself too long, all the benefits of early intervention drug therapy might be lost. Sherisse also dismissed any rationale I offered about the importance of her remaining healthy and strong *for* her daughter.

Zoe had brought a different American Girl doll to the appointment, but once again she and the doll wore matching outfits. It was now obvious to me that both dolls' dresses had been handmade by a seamstress. The shoes, this time, were different. Zoe's doll had on white socks and black flats, while Zoe was wearing nylon stockings and small "kitten" heels, as well as glossy pink lipstick.

My first home visit was scheduled to take place in two days, and that's when I planned on going over the family's finances and talking to Sherisse about Zoe's being only six but wearing stockings, heels, and lipstick. Sherisse had requested the visit be my last appointment of the day but wouldn't tell me why. I was happy to accommodate her.

I'd never visited Sherisse's neighborhood before: a middle-class Black community composed of modest one-story single-family homes with well-manicured lawns. When I rang the doorbell, I could hear a child running toward the door and a young boy's voice shouting, "I want to get it! Let me get it!" He opened the door, looked at me, and then ran away. This had to be Zoe's older brother, Gerard.

The moment Gerard opened the front door, a pungent aroma of something exotic cooking filled my nostrils. Sherisse gave me a tour of the house, proudly showing me each piece of art and identifying each relative in the displayed family photographs. She showed me the room the kids shared and the master bedroom. They hadn't been living there long enough to have accumulated too much, but everything they had was brand new. I learned that all their furniture back home had been sold or given to family and friends when they left.

I couldn't contain myself any longer and asked, "What are you cooking? It smells amazing."

"Come in the kitchen. I'll show you."

Sherisse lifted the lid off a large pot simmering on the front burner and told me it was callaloo. My face must have registered that I was hearing this word for the first time.

"It's a *kinda* stew," she explained. "I'm *makin'* it for *dinnuh.* Take a deep sniff."

"It smells wonderful," I told her. "What's in it?"

"*Sahlted* codfish, bacon, onion, scotch bonnet *peppah, gahlic,* chopped tomatoes, and the callaloo, which is *kinda* like collard greens. But you can *trow* a lotta *diffren' t'ings* in it.

I was very touched by her generosity and thanked her. Sherisse led me out the back door, and we sat down at the umbrella table on her small cement patio. She went back into the house and quickly emerged carrying a metal container similar to a suitcase. She sat down and flipped open the lid, revealing trays of brightly colored nail polishes, bottles of liquids, lotions, paint brushes with pointed heads, cotton balls, files, and two gleaming stainless steel cuticle cutters. All these, plus whatever else was hidden in other compartments, were the tools of her manicure business.

Sherisse was an easy conversationalist and very open about her life. She also had a wonderful sense of humor, imitating her grandparents and other family members in an exaggerated thick patois. I had to ask her to stop because I was laughing so hard. I also had to request translations when she was in full patois mode.

"Dale, *lemme* do your nails. Okay?" she asked with an impish smile. So, this was why she wanted me to schedule the home visit at the end of my day. I put up a little fuss but was really quite happy at the thought of Sherisse's wanting to do this for me. I chose a very light, almost translucent pink color called Ballet Slippers. In the time it would take her to do the manicure and the time it would take for my nails to dry, we could talk, and I could cover some social work ground and get a few concerns addressed.

Over the course of the next twenty minutes or so, we discussed the family's finances, their rent, her husband's salary, and her hope that she'd be able to contribute financially once she was known in the area as a skilled manicurist. She repeated what she'd said at our first meeting: that they did not need anything in the way of "handouts," as she called them. We talked about how she felt Zoe's medical care was going, and she reassured me she was very pleased and liked Dr. Puga and Nurse Betty Benivegna. Before I could ask, she reiterated in a firm tone that she was not interested in care for herself. I nodded my head, indicating I understood, but told her I would revisit this topic with her from time to time to make sure she hadn't changed her mind.

"I'd like to ask you a question, Sherisse, and I hope I'm not overstepping my bounds," I said cautiously.

"No, you go ahead. Ask me *anyt'ing*

"The first time I met with you in the clinic, Zoe was wearing a very beautiful dress, and her doll was dressed exactly the same. The second time I saw Zoe, she was holding a similar doll, and they were, again, in matching dresses. I learned from a coworker who has a daughter that those were American Girl dolls and could have cost a hundred dollars each. That's a lot of money to pay for dolls. And the matching outfits had to have been made by a seamstress. I'm sure they, too, were pretty expensive. Now that I know Mr. Williams's salary, what your rent and other expenses are, and the fact that you're not yet able to contribute to the family financially, I'm a bit concerned about your having spent this much on two dolls and handmade clothes.

Sherisse said nothing for what felt like an eternity. At some point, I realized I was holding my breath waiting for her to speak. I made the decision, right or wrong, to fill the void with my other concern.

"One other thing: Sherisse, do you mind telling me why Zoe was dressed in stockings, heels, and wearing lipstick? She's only six but was dressed and made up like a teenager."

I added quickly: "I hope I haven't offended you by asking these questions." Her silence continued for a moment, and then she spoke slowly.

"No, you didn't offend me. I'm *used* to it. This is *somet'ing* I do for my child. For my child who may *nevah* grow up to be a *teen-aguh*, mind you. I want *huh* to have *ev-er-y-t'ing*," she said stretching out the syllables. "All the *bes' t'ings* I can buy or do for *huh*."

Sherisse's voice rose as she continued speaking.

"If I feel like *puttin'* makeup on *huh*, I will *do* it. I may *nevah* see *huh* teenage face, so I look at *huh* this way and *t'ink* it might be what she'd look like when she got older. And, truth be told, she may *nevah* get older, Dale! I have to give it all to *huh* now. I have to see *huh lookin'* like this now because what if I die *fuhst*? I won't get to see *huh* all grown up."

Oh, my God! I felt like my heart had been ripped open. I never imagined she was thinking like this. But of course she was. I started to cry and apologized for being so oblivious, so insensitive. Sherisse got up and walked to my side of the table.

"*Stan'* up, Dale," she said.

I dutifully did what she told me. She then put her arms around me. She was hugging *me*, trying to make *me* feel better! Who was the social worker here?

"Now, you be careful how you hug me with those nails, Dale. Don't you smudge *dem*. I worked hard on *dem*!"

Sherisse had managed to lift the cloak of embarrassment and shame I was feeling and make me laugh. The acknowledgment and sadness of a child's possible early death that hung in the air had been dispelled.

"Now, sit down again and give me your *lef'* hand. Close your eyes." I put my hand in hers and closed my eyes. I could still feel tears burning my eyes. She took my thumb and held it for about three minutes. I sensed the lightest of touches on my nail, like a butterfly kiss you give a toddler when you bat your eyelashes on their cheek. I thought my manicure was already finished. What was she doing?

Sherisse told me to open my eyes and look at my finger. There on my thumbnail was the most exquisite miniature palm tree: golden-brown trunk, green palm fronds, and three minuscule dark-brown coconuts poking out from the fronds.

"Oh, it's gorgeous!" I exclaimed. "I've never seen anything so perfect. Thank you, Sherisse. I'll never forget today."

"Oh, you welcome. And I'll *nevah* forget today either. *Ya* wanna know *somet'ing* funny?" she asked with a grin. "You be the *fuhst* White woman whose nails I *evah* do!"

"Well, if that's the case," I said with a big smile and playfully trying to imitate her accent, "Then I'll be the *fuhst* White woman to give *ya* a really good reference so *ya* can grow *ya* business!"

12

My "Beat"

THE BULK OF MY CLIENTS lived in northwest Fort
Lauderdale. Sistrunk Boulevard, the street I'd been cautioned by my real estate agent not to drive down, is the heavily trafficked corridor that runs squarely through the middle
of the city's African American community. The sidewalks
on Sistrunk were equally teeming with women and children
strolling or shopping and small clusters of out-of-work men
sitting in folding chairs, shooting the breeze. It was a vibrant,
social place.

The vast majority of residents in the community were living
well below the poverty threshold. Most of my clients lived in
government-subsidized Section 8 houses or apartments, many
of which resembled nondescript single-story motel units. These
buildings were poorly maintained both outside and inside.
Front yards were often nothing more than dirt with weeds or
scattered patches of grass poking through. Only the splashes of
red and yellow from the flowering ixora bushes offered a respite
from the drabness.

There were many empty lots on either side of Sistrunk
that, in addition to being choked with weeds, were filled with
mounds of household trash and objects flung from the windows of passing cars. Some freestanding shops and markets had
hand-painted signage on the front or on exposed exterior walls.
A painted advertisement on the exposed side wall of the local
pharmacy listed some of the things that could be purchased
inside. The largest lettering on that wall read "DRUGS"—an

unintended but bold reminder that these were, indeed, plentiful in the community.

For residents, Sistrunk was a typical thoroughfare—a place to shop and catch up with friends and acquaintances. It was also, as our real estate agent had pointedly hinted at, a road mostly avoided by those living in the close-bordering White communities. Over a period of ten years in Florida, I lived in two of those White communities. But, in spite of Yvonne's warning, I actually spent the majority of my professional time on the streets that splayed out from Sistrunk. It became my "beat," and those streets became as familiar and comfortable to me as any street I had lived on in my fifty years up north.

There were definitely moments of uneasiness when I was first learning to navigate my beat. Unemployed men, young and old alike, often hung around outside their apartment units in small groups. They may not have had jobs, but they definitely had responsibilities. I learned they were the "unofficial eyes and ears" for the community. But, as a novice, I couldn't discern if these men were benign or something to be suspicious or even afraid of. I went to my colleagues for guidance.

Arlene reminded me of our ride together in her car to visit Antoinette.

"Did you notice the engraved nameplate on my dashboard?" she asked me. "It said 'Social Worker, Children's Diagnostic & Treatment Center.' Not my name, just my title. I keep it there for a reason.

"In all my years of working in this neighborhood and the Pompano Beach neighborhood, where I have a lot of families, I have never been threatened by anyone. But you want to be sure that everyone knows you're in the neighborhood to do good, to offer assistance to someone. As an unaccompanied White woman, you stand out like a sore thumb. And remember, suspicion goes both ways. Your arrival will automatically raise questions. What's she doing here? Is she from the Department of Children and Family Services? The sign on your dashboard explains everything before you even step out of the car. Everyone in the community knows CDTC and the good work we do. We're very welcome here. Believe me, in an amazingly short time, word will have spread about who you are, where you work, and what your car looks like. You will be fine. The best possible thing you can do is engage with the men right away. 'Hi, how're you doing, guys?' goes a long way. You will probably see the same men each time you come back to that area, and they will remember you. They'll become your buddies once they know you're here to help someone's child or an entire family."

I followed Arlene's advice, and as soon as I got back to the office, I ordered a shiny, silver-toned nameplate. When I had my first opportunity to use it, there was no question that it gave me a feeling of security. I parked in front of my client's housing complex and noticed that the four men sitting in plastic chairs were stretching their necks to see what the sign said. I confidently opened the car door and greeted them.

"Hi, how're you doing, guys?" I asked. (I was a good student.) They all answered my question and, even better, they were all smiling at me. Emboldened, I now improvised from my "script."

"I'll be here for about twenty minutes. Do you mind keeping an eye on my car for me?"

"Sure. Happy to," one answered. The others nodded in agreement. I never had to ask again. With every subsequent visit, they always volunteered to watch my car.

Simone's Boyfriend

In the time since Marie had taken me to meet Simone, my very first client, I'd made a number of routine home visits. Early on, I had read the past documentation and saw that there were serious concerns about Simone's boyfriend, Henry. It stated that he was a lot older than Simone, was sullen, always suspicious, and uncooperative. When I met him for the first time, I immediately saw the obvious difference in their ages. Henry had gray flecks in his hair and deep furrows on either side of his nose. I guessed he was in his mid-fifties.

To be honest, I disliked him from the first day I met him. I was also a bit afraid of him. When Simone told him I was her new social worker, he sneered, let out a nasty laugh, and walked away. During home visits, he would often stand in the living room with his arms crossed and stare at me. He listened to everything I said to Simone, but never said a word. I felt there was a lot of anger bubbling under the surface with this man. I wondered if it was directed at me, someone else, or the world at large. I knew enough not to let my anxiety show, but at each home visit, before getting out of my car, I always said a little prayer: "Please don't let Henry be home."

This was a household in trouble. Because of past concerns about the children's welfare, CDTC was not the only agency working with the family. There was also an open case with the Florida Department of Children and Family Services. I knew very little about how DCF worked, but that was to change quickly.

Mrs. Fields, a DCF social worker, had been assigned to the case. Because Simone's children did not have HIV, they were this woman's clients. Simone was mine, but because CFAP practiced family-centered case management, the needs of everyone in the household had to be taken into consideration. This meant the children and even Henry were, in some ways, "mine," too.

I began developing my relationship with Simone by making weekly home visits. The living room was sparsely furnished with the most basic necessities: a sofa, a stuffed chair, and two end tables with lamps on it them. She also had a glass-fronted breakfront, but there was nothing displayed on the shelves.

I was happy to observe and be able to document that her house always looked clean. It was, however, dramatically different from other clients' homes where children lived. Neither the walls nor the end tables held any framed pictures or school or family photos. The refrigerator had no children's drawings taped to it. There were only a couple of baby toys lying around on the floor. If you didn't happen to see them, you couldn't say for sure that there were children in this household.

I knew there were serious concerns about Simone's ability to provide a safe environment for her kids. She herself never appeared bruised and never complained about Henry mistreating her, but I quickly became troubled by Simone's inability to make good choices for herself and her children or to see the inherent danger in many things.

An early example of this occurred on an unusually hot day. Simone opened the door and told me to come in. She stood next to me as I made a visual sweep of the living room. The baby was sitting on the floor. Next to her was a baby bottle with a slurry of curdled milk caked to its sides and bottom. Before I could get to it, the baby reached down and popped the nipple into her mouth and began to suck. I bolted over and yanked the bottle away from her. My sudden movement and the loss of her bottle made her howl with surprise and anger. I looked to Simone for some sign of recognition that this curdled milk posed a health risk to her daughter. There was none.

I asked Simone to walk me through the steps of what she did with the baby's bottle of milk when she hadn't finished drinking it. Did she put it back in the refrigerator? No. Did she know that heat could spoil the milk? No. Did she use hot water, soap, and a bottlebrush to clean the bottles? No again. I learned that she didn't have a bottlebrush and just swished soapy water around in them. A lesson from me on food spoilage and refrigeration followed, and a note to myself to buy her a bottlebrush.

Over time, I observed that with Simone, Henry was controlling and sullen. With his two little girls, he was distant at best; but with Malcolm, he was verbally abusive. Malcolm was Simone's nine-year-old son from another relationship, which was probably the first of many marks against Malcolm. When I asked Simone whether Henry ever hit Malcolm, her answer was no, but her downcast eyes told another story—one that I couldn't act on because I hadn't seen it for myself.

I did not relish the idea of confronting Henry. However, I knew I had to the day I saw a man's leather belt lying on the sofa. I called his name, and he sauntered out of the bedroom ever so slowly. He was fully dressed, with a belt already on his pants.

"What's this belt on the sofa for?" I asked as if I were just curious.

"I'm still getting dressed."

It was an obvious lie. I summoned the courage from somewhere deep inside me and stated firmly, "You're already wearing a belt. What is this one for?"

I waited, but there was no answer. No verbal answer, that is, but his mouth took on the same sneer I had seen before, and the look on his face said clearly, "Mind your own business, bitch."

Trying hard to keep my voice steady and strong, I warned him that if I were to see that belt out again or learn from Simone that he was using it on the children, I would report it to his DCF worker. His eyes narrowed and met mine, but he said nothing in response. He seemed totally unfazed by my threat, turned his back on me, and slow-walked back into the bedroom.

I had asked Simone a few times to give me a tour of their house, but she always answered nervously, "No. Henry's in the bedroom. You can't go in there. He wouldn't like you going into any of the rooms."

On my ride back to the office, I was thinking about why he appeared to despise me. I believe I figured it out. I was one more of probably a number of unwelcome social service workers in his life, each of whom he saw as having great potential to make trouble for him.

At my next weekly visit, Henry wasn't there. I asked Simone again for a tour and assured her I didn't need to see her and Henry's room. She relaxed right away.

"But I'd like to see the kids' rooms," I said. "Maybe there are a few things I can bring them from our donation room."

We walked into the bedroom shared by her two little girls. I was glad to see that the room was clean, but there was only a crib and a twin bed in it. There were no curtains or blinds on the window, no dresser or shelves for toys or books. When I asked where the girls' clothes were, Simone explained that she put the clothes in the two black trash bags on the floor: one for clean clothes, the other for dirty clothes. If you don't have a dresser, this makes sense; but I wondered why the DCF worker hadn't gotten them one. Two toys lay on the floor, but no books were anywhere to be seen. When I asked her where the rest of the kids' toys were, she replied that the kids always broke them and she would just throw them out.

Malcolm's room was next. She opened the door, and there he was lying on a dirty mattress on the floor. He looked up at us but didn't move. The acrid smell of urine filled my nostrils. Unlike his sisters' mattresses, his had no sheets. But his room, too, had no curtains, no shades, no dresser, and not one toy or book. I was seriously alarmed seeing him lying there.

"Why is Malcolm in here?" I asked.

"He's being punished."

"What did he do?"

"I don't remember."

"How long has he been in here?"

"I don't know. I guess a long time. I forgot he was in there." Suddenly, the stench of urine and the sad face of this little boy in his jail cell of a room made me lightheaded and slightly nauseous. I told Simone to let him go outside and play with his sister. She told him, and he bolted up and ran out of the room. I followed quickly and stood in the doorway to the backyard, deeply breathing in the fresh air.

"Simone, you can't keep Malcolm in his room this long ever again," I cautioned sternly, realizing all the while that it was probably Henry who had banished the boy and apparently had no interest in putting a time limit on his exile. I worried about what other inappropriate and harsh punishments Henry might have doled out to Malcolm.

"And, Simone, when Henry gets home, please ask him to put Malcolm's mattress out on the street for collection. Let him sleep on the sofa tonight or at your sister's house. Tell Henry I'll bring over a new mattress and a box spring tomorrow. Malcolm just can't sleep on that smelly, stained mattress any longer."

Knowing Simone's intellectual limitations, it was imperative that I teach her some simple, useful parenting skills. If Henry was, indeed, the primary disciplinarian, I wanted to demonstrate some easy, less punitive techniques that she could implement when he wasn't around. For example, could she sit down with Malcolm and talk about what he had said or done to get himself in trouble? Could she take away a special privilege instead of confining him in his room? Did he actually *have* any special privileges?

But who was I kidding? Anything I had learned about childhood development in college or as a young mother from Dr. Benjamin Spock's childrearing bible, *Baby and Child Care*, or whatever methods I invented to use with my own kids decades ago, would probably not fly in this household. Nevertheless, I knew I had to try. I decided to teach her about timeout, a concept I thought would be simple enough for her to understand.

"If Malcolm does something that deserves punishment, you can give him what's called a timeout. Make him stay in his room or sit at the table for one minute for every year of his age. He's eight years old now, so his punishment should have been eight minutes. When he's nine, you can increase the time to nine minutes. I'm sorry, Simone, but you just can't make Malcolm stay in his room for hours and hours anymore."

"I didn't do it!" she snapped back, her dark eyes laser focused into my own. "Henry did it. When Henry's not here, I just yell at Malcolm and wait for Henry to come home and punish him."

Worse Than the Belt

I called Mrs. Fields the moment I got back to the office and introduced myself. I knew I had to keep my tone nonconfrontational, but I also had to get some answers as to why Malcolm was sleeping on a urine-soaked mattress on the floor and why none of the kids had dressers or curtains on the windows. She and I were sharing this case and probably would be for a long time, so it was important that I didn't start things off in an accusatory way.

Mrs. Fields didn't answer my questions to my satisfaction. I didn't expect her to admit she knew about this but hadn't done anything (if that were, in fact, the case), but I was hoping to hear more than "I'm working on getting all these things."

Although her caseload had to be much, much bigger than mine, I wondered just how long had she been "working on it." I couldn't let her timeline be my timeline—or Malcolm's.

A colleague had taught me how to get a CDTC voucher for a mattress and directed me to Poverello, a local nonprofit organization with a well-stocked warehouse of household items.

"If you're agreeable, Mrs. Fields, I will get a mattress and box spring for Malcolm tomorrow if you will get the rest of the things for the children's bedrooms." Not surprisingly, she was more than happy to let me do this.

The Poverello warehouse was cavernous and poorly lit. The closer the rows of donated furniture were to the windows and the open double doors in the front and the back, the easier it was to see their condition. The sunlight didn't penetrate too far, so other sections of merchandise were illuminated by fluorescent light fixtures suspended from a very high ceiling. I wandered around until I came to the mattresses. There were a lot of them in different sizes, each one wrapped in gray plastic and leaning against one another like huge slices of bread. As I struggled mightily to push and separate one from the other, my beeper went off. The number was unfamiliar to me. I walked over to the warehouse office and asked to use its phone to return the call. It was Mrs. Fields.

"Dale, something extremely bad has happened. The police have been called to Simone and Henry's house because someone reported hearing a child screaming."

Mrs. Fields's answer to my obvious question of "What happened?" was that Malcolm had done something to anger Henry, and Henry had pulled down Malcolm's pants and burned his buttocks with a cigarette lighter. I was horrified.

By the time I got to the home, the police had already removed all three children and placed them in temporary DCF protective custody. Malcolm had been taken to the hospital, treated, and driven to where his sisters were. Henry was hauled off to jail.

DCF always preferred utilizing family placement rather than putting children in foster care with strangers. Standard procedure was to run background checks on all possible candidates from both sides of the family. Henry had reluctantly given the names of only a few family members, but they were all quickly eliminated because of past criminal records. Next was Simone's family. The young mother was furious with Mrs. Fields for removing her children, and she refused to supply the names of any close relatives. She didn't understand that it was in her and her children's best interests to cooperate fully and give Mrs. Fields all the names she could think of.

Mrs. Fields knew nothing about Simone's family and asked me if I could make recommendations. They needed a suitable relative who could take care of the children until Simone completed the required steps allowing her to regain custody of her kids. The only relative of hers whom I knew seemed highly suitable: Simone's married sister, Caroline, a nurse at Broward General. I told Mrs. Fields I would go straight back to my office and call Caroline and then call her back.

Unfortunately, Simone's sister did not want to care for her nephew and nieces, and her excuses were actually very reasonable. Her house was too small, she had three kids of her own, and she and her husband went to work every day. After some pleading on my part, Caroline promised she would take more time to consider it. On the positive side, she told me she did not want the children living with strangers; plus, the money DCF paid to families caring for children other than their own would certainly help with her bills. I was relieved that she'd think about it and hopeful that she would conclude this was the right thing to do for her sister and the kids.

I knew Simone did not have the capacity to understand the consequences of what Henry had done and how this was going to change her life. In the hopes that we could talk about this, I drove to her house every day after the children had been taken away. Simone never opened the door to me, leaving me baffled and deeply frustrated. We had been getting along very well, and I believed she understood that I wanted to help her, but she wasn't allowing me in—literally and figuratively.

A week passed. Simone and I had an appointment at DCF to learn what would happen next. I was eager to see her. When I got off the elevator, I spotted Simone sitting alone on a bench in the hallway. She looked so forlorn. Her head was down, her shoulders were rounded, and she seemed to have shrunk in size. I walked over and sat down. When she saw me, she immediately sat up straight and moved as far away from me as she could. Before I could finish saying how glad I was that we would finally be able to talk, she jumped up and sprinted down the hall. I jumped up and fast-walked behind her. I saw her turn a corner and was afraid I would lose sight of her. But Simone had run down a dead-end hallway and was standing there, her face pressed against the wall with her hands over her eyes. She would not look at me.

"Simone," I pleaded, "please explain why you're mad at me." She spun around, and her words cut me like razor blades.

"You told DCF Henry was bad! You told them he burned Malcolm! You wanted me to lose my kids!"

I was stunned. Somehow, in trying to understand how this could have happened to her family, Simone forgot about Mrs. Fields's role in it and chose to make me responsible. When she stopped yelling at me, I stated firmly that I had not reported Henry to DCF. I reminded her that I had, indeed, threatened to report Henry if I ever saw him hurting any of the children, but I had not been there to witness him burn Malcolm. I tried to assure her that I did not want her to lose her children and added that now that this had happened, I would work very hard with her to help her get them back. Her response to me was "Blah, blah, blah!"

I had become the enemy.

Simone's Choices

We sat next to each other in a small, windowless conference room. Mrs. Fields introduced her supervisor and asked Simone if she knew why we were all here today. Simone didn't answer. I waited a moment, hoping that she would respond, but when she remained silent, I leaned in close to her and whispered that it would help her case a lot if she would please cooperate. Simone looked away defiantly and said nothing. Mrs. Fields opened a file folder, took out a bunch of papers, and laid them on the table in neat piles in front of her.

She picked up a page and read aloud from some early documentation recounting how the case was originally opened after a neighbor had reported hearing what sounded like a child or children being beaten. An investigation was conducted, and after the parents and the oldest child were interviewed, it was determined that the children were at risk, and the family needed the intervention of the Department of Children and Family Services. DCF, not wanting to remove the children at that time, provided multiple support services to the family to, hopefully, improve the situation.

At that earlier meeting, Simone and Henry had been asked if they understood that the social worker assigned to their case would be making routine home visits and that they would have to attend parenting classes. Additional support services would also be put in place. They were told that physical force or corporal punishment must never again be used against any of their children.

Mrs. Fields showed Simone the piece of paper with her and Henry's signatures indicating that they not only understood and agreed to all the above but also that they understood the children would be removed from the home and placed in DCF custody if the agency received another report of this nature.

She turned the page and read aloud the date of this most recent incident when Henry burned Malcolm on the buttocks. She started to read the details of the call that had been placed but got no further than a dozen or so words before Simone interrupted angrily.

"Who made that call? I *wanna* know who made that call. Why did you take my kids away?" Mrs. Fields looked exasperated.

Rather than continue reading the account of the incident, she spoke directly to Simone.

"Simone, Henry burned Malcolm on the buttocks. That is a fact. You didn't call the police, and by not doing that and not protecting your son, you share responsibility for what happened. We can't leave children in a home where they are not safe."

"Henry never hurt nobody!" was Simone's furious response. There was no response from Mrs. Fields to this outburst. Instead, she presented Simone with two pieces of paper and asked her to read them and sign her name at the bottom of the second page.

"By signing your name, Simone, it will indicate you understand what you have to do in order to be reunified with your children."

Simone looked at me, and I could tell she was confused.

"What's *reunified* mean?" she asked me. I explained the word to her, and she quickly picked up the pen and flipped to the signature page.

"Hold on!" I blurted out. "Don't sign that, Simone. I'm sorry ladies, but Simone is illiterate. I have to read it to her and be satisfied that she knows what she's signing."

Mrs. Fields and her supervisor looked dumbfounded and shot glances at each other. Now they would have to sit there while I slowly read everything out loud and made sure Simone first understood and then agreed to each condition. A few were the same ones that Simone had previously agreed to when DCF first opened the case. She did not comply with them then, and I didn't know if she would comply now, even in light of her children having been taken from her.

There were quite a few conditions, none of them open to negotiation. Simone had to retake parenting classes. She agreed to this with no hesitation. She also had to attend first aid and

CPR classes. Simone didn't know what cardiopulmonary resuscitation was, so I explained it to her. By the look on her face after I finished explaining it, I suspected she still didn't understand, but she stated she would do it. With regard to seeing her children, visitation would initially take place once a week under supervision at the DCF office. I was assigned to carry out the supervision and write my reports for Mrs. Fields. After an unspecified number of these visits over a period of time, as yet to be determined, she could have unsupervised visitation—that is, if all the visits went well.

As I read a few additional conditions relating to these supervised visits, I felt the tension building in me. I was sure Simone was feeling similar tension and, undoubtedly, getting angry. She simply did not have the psychological capacity to deal with the situation. I was emotionally torn knowing what the consequences would be if she resisted or failed to comply with any of them.

I read silently ahead for a moment and felt immediately anxious. What I saw coming up next would be the deal breaker. I took a deep breath and exhaled.

"Simone, if you do everything you're supposed to do, you will be able to get your children back," I said deliberately. Then I paused—not for effect, but to help myself get better control of my shaky voice.

"But—and this is very, very important, Simone—you cannot allow Henry to live in the house with them ever again."

She had been looking down when I was reading, but now her head snapped up. Simone looked straight at me and cocked her head to one side. Her eyes narrowed into slits.

"You *sayin'* he's *gonna* have to move out or I can't get my kids back?" I doubted Simone ever played with her children, and

I knew she was unable to read stories to them, but without them around, her life would be greatly diminished and empty. There was only one correct answer to this, and I was dreading having to say it.

"Yes, that's right."

"*No-o-o-o!* I *won't* kick him out!" she shouted. "*I love him!*" Simone refused to sign the papers. Mrs. Fields's supervisor warned her sternly that this decision was not wise, but the young mother was past the point of listening. She pushed her chair back with great force and charged out of the room. I grabbed my things, apologized quickly to the women, and left the room.

I knew I should run after Simone, but I was immobilized. I had never been in a position like this before—never had the experience of being the bearer of such horrible news. At that moment, I felt neither physically nor emotionally able to rise to the occasion. I was actually afraid of catching up with her. What could I possibly say to calm her down? What words would make her feel less angry about what had just happened?

I stood against the wall and watched her run down the long hall, open the exit door, and dip into the stairwell. Simone disappeared, and the door shut behind her with a heavy clang. I walked to the elevator and waited. When the door opened, and I saw there was no one inside, a wave of relief flooded over me. Misery surely was etched all over my face.

The next day, and twice more, I attempted to visit Simone at home, but, as before, she never came to the door. Unlike the arrangement DCF has with its clients, ours were not mandated to work with us. It was their choice, and it was clear that Simone did not choose to accept my help.

I kept having the same nagging back-and-forth conversation with myself. If I'd been able to talk with Simone before the

DCF meeting, could I have helped her decide to put her children before Henry? But, if that had been possible, was there any reason to believe she was capable of becoming the kind of parent I wanted to help her become? What about Simone's unwillingness to acknowledge her disease and get medical care? How would her early death affect her children? Would they end up living with their Aunt Caroline anyway or, even worse, with Henry? All imponderables and all out of my control.

I consulted with Marie and was told to close the case. Nevertheless, I was able to learn some things about how the family was coping. Mrs. Fields told me the children did go to live with Caroline after all. For a while, Mrs. Fields would call and give me updates. Caroline's mother was regularly helping out while her daughter and son-in-law were at work. Simone's two little girls were doing well, and Malcolm was faring better in school and showing signs that this new stability was helping him become a happier kid. Whenever feelings of my failure with Simone would surface—which was often—I would remind myself of these positive things. Sadly, I never learned anything about how Simone was getting along.

13

The Caregivers

THE RAVAGES OF AIDS OBVIOUSLY included the loss of
patients' lives, but it also resulted in hundreds of thousands
of children in the United States alone being orphaned. Within
the Fort Lauderdale African American community where
I worked, if a child or children were orphaned because of the
death of a parent caregiver and then taken into DCF custody, a
high percentage of those children quickly ended up living with
relatives. These family members would somehow find a way to
care for their orphaned, sick, or dying young relatives regardless of how inconvenient this change of family dynamics and
lifestyle might be.

What commonly occurred after a woman died from
AIDS was that the children's grandmother, aunt, or great-
aunt took in the orphaned youngsters. When elderly relatives
agree to take on childrearing responsibilities, it is often done
at a time in their lives when they are least prepared to be raising young children again. This sacrifice could easily impair
their own health, not just physically but also mentally. If, for
example, a grandmother has a preexisting medical condition such as diabetes, heart disease, or depression, the added
stress of taking care of children—sick or well—can extract
an enormous toll, especially when she puts their health and
wellbeing ahead of her own. And it can't be ignored that she,
too, is grieving the loss of her own child. This generous and
instinctive decision could have devastating consequences,
not the least of which could be the early death of a custodial

grandparent. That would put her young charges through yet another calamitous loss.

Throughout this book, there are examples of families rising to the occasion: a mother putting her life on hold and moving in with her dying daughter and two grandsons; a young boy's great-grandmother and his three great-uncles raising him after his mother's death; a grandmother and an aunt taking custody of and caring for their grandson and nephew whose mother was an HIV-positive drug addict; a great-uncle raising his deceased niece's HIV-positive son and daughter; and a young client's aunt making a deathbed promise to her sister to raise her three children. These are not isolated responses. They were an accepted communitywide response to assume the daunting responsibility of keeping the family together in times of overwhelming sadness and loss.

My First Eulogy

From time to time during my years at Children's Diagnostic, I was asked by a deceased client's family member to speak at the funeral. I would write a eulogy about how I knew the child or woman and, perhaps, how they dealt with the burdens they carried. I wrote about what made them stand out, or made them laugh, or what they did to make others laugh. If what I spoke about brought comfort to a family member, I was pleased. But what I came to realize after giving several eulogies was that it was comforting for me as well, making me feel part of the community of mourners.

When I sat down to compose a eulogy about the short life of eight-year-old Keisha, I decided to write about visiting her in the hospital. Naïvely, I thought my experience might have been unique and thus warranted sharing. What I realized as I read it aloud was that so many people in the church had also been on the receiving end of Keisha's fun-loving and quite demanding personality. A couple of times, my words rocked the sanctuary with laughter, and it felt like Keisha was with us again for a few sweet moments:

"I was Keisha's social worker. Keisha is the first child I lost. Because of that fact alone, I can never forget her. But there are many other, far more important things about her that I prefer to remember.

"She was eight years old and skinny and feisty, and had an attitude that stood out a mile. I'd like to share with you one of my most vivid memories of her.

"The first time I visited Keisha in the hospital, I found her not in her room but sitting in a child-size wheelchair positioned opposite the elevators. Before the doors were fully open, she spotted my face and yelled, 'Dale, you got a *dolla*?'" Upon hearing this, the congregation erupted in raucous laughter; clearly I had not been the only one to receive this kind of welcome.

"'What do you need a dollar for?' I asked naïvely as I stepped out of the elevator.

"'For McDonald's. For french fries.'

"'Sure, I've got a dollar,' I said and handed her a dollar bill from my wallet.

"'Push me down the hall to my room,' she instructed, her index finger pointing the way.

"It was very quickly obvious that she didn't like the way I maneuvered her wheelchair.

"'Faster! Faster!'

"I obeyed. With an empty hallway stretching ahead of us, I put my back into it and zoomed her straight to her room.

"'Put it in my drawer!'

"She barked her orders at me like a drill sergeant. I walked to the night table and opened the drawer. Like one of those trick canisters that explode with coiled snakes the moment the lid is taken off, her drawer exploded with dollar bills collected from family members, nurses, doctors—in short, anyone she could manipulate into parting with a dollar." This elicited more knowing laughter.

"I don't know if she ever bought a single bag of french fries with the money she collected, but she certainly had a great time raking in the loot."

Memorial Service

CFAP used to hold an annual memorial service for the women and children who had died during the past year. It was a highly anticipated event for us, but even more so for the families. Everyone came dressed in their best church outfits. Of course, our own nurses and doctors attended, but so did the Broward General Medical Center staff who'd cared for our clients when they were hospitalized or at the end of their lives. When staff set up chairs for the ceremony, they always placed boxes of tissues at the end of each row. We knew emotions would run high—for the families as well as for us.

Some family funerals had been held a full year ago, and this event gave people not only a second opportunity to remember and talk about their loved ones but also to be together with others who had gone through the same pain and loss as they had.

In anticipation of the approaching service, the social workers would ask the children who had lost family members to tell us a story about their mothers or their siblings who had died. If they were not old enough to write, they could dictate their thoughts and memories to the family social worker. These precious expressions of love were captured on forms designed specifically for the service. At a designated time in the service, the children were invited to come up to the front of the room and read their stories aloud to the guests. If they couldn't read yet or chose not to, we would do it for them.

The year 1996 was heartbreaking for one of my families. Both my young client Keisha and her mother, Diane, died— Diane just months after Keisha. Keisha's younger siblings, April, Louis, and Moses, were eager to share their memories of their sister and mother and happily dictated their stories to me. I had expected that doing this would be a somber experience for them. I was wrong. They actually ended up laughing hilariously when they recalled certain parts of the stories. I saved three of these forms and include them here, twenty-seven years after they were written:

*During our "remembering" we would like to share our
most special, or cherished memories....*

*Please write down a special memory of your loved one for
us to share during the service.*

Our mother would take us just about anywhere we would want. We loved to go to The Red Lobster. She also took us to the movies. Our favorite one was "Tales From The Hood." Moses remembers getting up during The movie to buy popcorn + soda, but with his 25¢ change he went to play a video game. His mama snuck up behind him + bopped him on the side of his head. He didn't laugh but Louis sure did!

Moses and Louis's memories of their mother.

*During our "remembering" we would like to share our
most special, or cherished memories....*

**Please write down a special memory of your loved one for
us to share during the service.**

I remember my mama taking us to The Mizell library to do our homework. She would tell us stories while we were looking out the window – scary stories about the spirits That lived across The street from The library, in one big house. She would read us stories from The books after our homework was done. Afterwards we would sometimes go to Chuckie Cheese and play in The balls while she would sit There eating pizza.

April's memories of her mother.

During our "remembering" we would like to share our most special, or cherished memories....

Please write down a special memory of your loved one for us to share during the service.

We used to always go to ~~Bo~~ Broward General to see Keisha + play with her. She didnt like to sit in The wheelchair. She liked The red wagon. We also had a red wagon at home + we would push her and our little brother in it. One ~~day~~ she was in The front + he was in The back + the back opened up + he fell out. She laughed so hard she couldn't stop. We would even drive her to the store in her red wagon + she would say, "Giddy-up, Giddy-up, Horse!"

April, Louis, and Moses's memories of their sister Keisha.

14

Our New-Old Home

DIRECTLY OPPOSITE THE CHILDREN'S DIAGNOSTIC & Treatment Center's main building, and on the other side of the parking lot, sat a strange-looking one-story building. It used to house a preschool, but when that went out of business, it sat abandoned for a number of years. Located not far from the men's jail and just yards away from a small bail bondsman's office, its proximity to CDTC meant that the pedestrian traffic in the area was somewhat sketchy. To be kind, I'll say this building was no architectural gem and certainly not in the best of shape, but it offered us a lot at a time when we desperately needed to expand our physical space.

Our numbers of both clients and staff had been growing. The serendipity of our need and this building's availability and proximity to the clinic could solve our problem. Dr. Widmayer negotiated with the landlord and rented the property. CFAP could now move out of its cramped quarters and into its own home.

The building provided us with a reception area, a bunch of small offices to be shared, a client laundry area, and a large meeting room that could double as a special events space for family and holiday parties, clothing and school supply giveaways, and educational forums for our teens and parents.

Before moving in, we toured the empty building as a group and decided who would get which office and who would be paired with whom as office mates. This was all done with a great spirit of cooperation. We were giddy with anticipation about what our new space would mean for us and our clients.

On move-in Monday, the staff snaked back and forth across the parking lot, rolling desk chairs and carrying boxes of personal belongings and miscellaneous items. When we fanned out to our chosen offices, we saw that our desks and the few filing cabinets from the main building were already there. To our delight, there were also additional chairs, more filing cabinets, a sofa, and a couple of stuffed armchairs for the clients to relax in. There was a large conference table and, to our great surprise, new computers—not brand new, but certainly newer than what we had been using. Dr. Widmayer told us that everything had been generously donated by the North Broward Hospital District.

Still, there were many missing items we had to supply ourselves. Because there had been overhead lighting in our former shared office, we now needed desk lamps. We also needed a reception desk and wastebaskets. At our first staff meeting in the new space, Marie and Vicki strongly suggested we bring in whatever we could spare from home or, if we could afford it, purchase the smaller items ourselves. We were encouraged to ask friends and relatives for donations and to keep our eyes peeled for things people had thrown out. When I first moved to Fort Lauderdale, I learned that every neighborhood had a once-a-month bulk trash pickup day. You could get very lucky and score great finds by driving around scouring the neighborhoods on those designated days. That's how I found our reception desk, sitting on the sidewalk, while I was driving to work down Sunrise Boulevard one morning.

No one was happier to have an official reception desk than Natalie—an attractive and vivacious nineteen-year-old client who had been volunteering for us and had now been hired to be our receptionist. She was always enthusiastic no matter what assignments she had been given in the past, but now she was ecstatic about being on the payroll and officially part of the team. Having had no desk to sit behind for a number of days, she'd been making the best of it by stationing herself on a chair in the front office and handing out free items and answering questions. Now, with great fervor, she threw herself into designing her new desk space. She placed the center's brochures in a beautiful fanned out design on one corner of the desk. In the middle went a set of matching desk accessories she had purchased in anticipation of one day having a desk. A small white ceramic angel stood next to a potted plant. And the oh-so-important bowl of free condoms went on another corner of the desk so that clients could easily grab some as they entered or exited the building.

All went well that morning—until it didn't.

Natalie complained to Marie and anyone who would listen, "Something smells horrible." She asked people to stand at the threshold to the front office and take a sniff. None of them smelled anything, and they immediately went back to work. Natalie became more and more frustrated. She walked into my office and asked me to give her area the sniff test.

"*Please* come in," she pleaded. "It stinks! Something stinks in that room!" I couldn't detect anything from the doorway, but when I bent down and circled the desk, it hit me: a nauseating stench of urine. I realized immediately that the wooden office desk had probably been sitting on the sidewalk for a few days and had become a convenient fire hydrant for every dog that passed by. Out it went. That piece of trash was no one's treasure.

When the Skies Open Up

When summer arrives in South Florida, weather can become quite predictable. The sky often turns ominously dark in the afternoon, the prelude to a torrential rainstorm. The parking lot between the CFAP building and the clinic-and-administration building had no drainage. When the New River overflowed its seawall, it transformed the parking lot into an ankle-deep lake. A communal pair of donated black rain boots, set in a corner of the clinic vestibule, was always available to employees who had to dash back and forth between the two buildings. If a summer deluge was accompanied by strong winds, there would be actual waves in the water. But add lightning to the mix, and these routine summer weather conditions made the parking lot just plain hazardous to cross.

In addition, our little building leaked badly during downpours. Water would seep in under the doors and around the window frames. We prepared for these days by designing a series of drills. Plan A was to place sandbags at the thresholds and plug rags into the leaking parts of the windows. We did not, however, have a Band-Aid solution to fix the leaking roof. It leaked so badly in places that we were afraid it might even cave in. Buckets would be strategically positioned in the common areas to catch the drips, while we protected our computers with extra-large black trash bags. And if you needed to keep working during a rainstorm, you reverted to plan B: cover yourself and your computer with a makeshift tarp fashioned out of multiple trash bags taped together and type away in the semidarkness. It was like camping in the woods, but in an office.

We truly were a resilient bunch, though, and never let these inconveniences make us resentful or deter us from doing our work. We knew the rain would stop, the sun would return, and eventually the roof would be repaired. Until that happened, we simply made the best of it. In a way, working in that little ramshackle building turned out to have a positive effect. It provided us with firsthand lessons about the hardships our clients faced routinely, humbling us and making us even more empathetic to the people we were serving.

15

Dog Days

THERE WAS NO PLAN B or even a plan A in place when my thirty-one-year marriage to Rick ended in October 1997. He felt stifled and unstimulated in Fort Lauderdale and wanted desperately to return to New York—so much so that he put this relocation in motion before even discussing it with me. Even if I had wanted to go with him, there was no way I could conceive of leaving my new job. I was doing exactly what I wanted to be doing with my life. I had made close attachments to my coworkers and found a wonderful new friend, Eva Axel, a volunteer at CDTC who oversaw our donation room. Eva could always make me laugh after a stressful day. I also enjoyed the bonus of being able to visit with two beloved elderly aunts and an uncle who lived nearby.

The job and these people were hugely important to me. The marriage? Much less so—for Rick as well, obviously. Our relationship had been strained for a long time, even before we headed south. The move, which was never viewed as a way to repair the marriage, actually became the catalyst that brought it to an end.

Having gotten married during my senior year of college, I'd never truly been on my own until the age of fifty-four when Rick left. But within a matter of a few months, I'd adapted completely and felt joyous about being single, with only our sweet, very old Hungarian Vizsla for company. Tessie had been a wonderful member of our family when the kids were growing up, but in the last year or so, she began showing signs of what the vet called canine cognitive dysfunction, or, simply put, dementia. She'd often wake up in the middle of the night and whine pitifully to go outside. We used to walk slowly together down the median, lined with coconut palm trees, to the end of our dead-end block and then turn around and do it again. She would sniff the warm air and smell the ground for wild animals, which, thankfully, never materialized. After a few minutes of this, Tessie would stop abruptly and just stare into space, as if she'd forgotten where she was and why she had wanted to be there. I always joined her for a few minutes of staring at the night sky and enjoying the sound of the rustling palm fronds. By gently tugging on the leash, I could rouse Tessie from her reverie and walk her back inside. But the worst of her symptoms were not as easily handled. They occurred every weekday morning.

My leaving for work was torture for both of us. As I drove away down the block, even with the car windows closed and the air conditioner on, I could hear her howls coming from inside the house. Every day, this shared agony would repeat itself. And, every day it would remind me of the searing pain I used to feel when I had to leave my aged and no longer fully sentient father after visiting him in his nursing home. He wanted so much to go home and be with my mother and sister, but there was no possibility of this ever happening. Dementia, paranoia, and frequent falls ensured that the rest of his life would have to be spent in a congregant setting. His feelings of abject abandonment were always on display when it was time for a visit to end.

As I rolled him in his wheelchair to the elevator and kissed him on the cheek, I could feel the ache of sadness and the tears building up. The elevator doors would close with me on the inside weeping and him positioned just outside the doors, calling desperately, "Take me with you!" over and over, his cries fading as the elevator descended ever so slowly.

Now I was leaving this lovely animal behind, abandoning her. Tessie's helpless howls tortured me and reminded me of the necessary but so painful abandonment of my father in a place that he, too, didn't want to be.

Once I arrived at work, the myriad things demanding my immediate attention served to take my mind off my sad, lonely dog. My stay-at-home neighbors, however, could not escape her incessant, pitiful howling. I would come home at the end of the day to phone messages and the occasional note on my door begging me to do something about the dog.

The only possible solution seemed to be to take her to work with me. It was with great trepidation that I met with Dr. Widmayer to discuss the possibility of doing this. I explained the situation to her and sat tensely awaiting her answer to my unconventional request. She took a moment to think about it.

"Well, dear," she began, "when your husband left, you weren't the only one who experienced the loss of a family member. Tessie has had a loss, too, and she is obviously suffering; plus, she's very old and apparently doesn't respond well to change. Let's give it a try, but there are conditions that must be met in order for this to work. Your office mate must agree to share space with a dog, and Tessie must not cause any commotion or ever be seen by any visitors to the center."

What amazing compassion Dr. Widmayer had for a dog! What insight extended to a dog's emotions! I was ecstatic. The first step was to convince my office mate that life with a canine—a very gassy canine—was going to be fun. I failed. She wanted nothing to do with Tessie's spending the day in our office. So, I went in search of a more amenable coworker who could embrace this unorthodox concept, as well as the accompanying gastrointestinal condition. Amazingly, a good-hearted colleague (who shall remain nameless for obvious reasons) stepped forward.

"I don't mind," she said cheerily. "I've got a lot of gas, too, and I'll bet my office mate would be thrilled to get rid of me. Look, here's my can of room deodorizer. We'll all be just fine together."

After I stopped laughing and told her how relieved and grateful I was for her decision, I began to feel less confident that I could pull this off. Dr. Widmayer's conditions would not be easy to meet. Could I successfully juggle the enormous needs of my job and the needs of this aged dog?

Having satisfied the first condition of finding someone who agreed to share space with Tessie and me, I now had to succeed at keeping the old girl "invisible" and ensure she caused no commotion. This was unbelievably difficult to control. I continually forgot to close the door tightly behind me whenever I walked out of the office, and if Tessie was awake, she would follow me out the door and down the hall. Although she was docile and good natured, when clients came into our building and spotted Tessie, she scared the daylights out of most of them. Dogs in this community were, more often than not, pit bulls, Rottweilers, or a mix of the two breeds. I'd seen many local residents give wide berth to these dogs when they saw them approaching on the street.

Dr. Widmayer's office was across the parking lot and had no windows looking out in the direction of our building. She never heard the full-throated gasps of the adults or witnessed the young children jumping into their mothers' arms, screaming, "It's a dog! It's a dog!" when they saw Tessie.

Tessie didn't always follow me around when she snuck out. She loved to curl up in a sunny spot on the doormat by the tinted-glass front door. We could see out, but no one could see in. It took only a couple of instances of clients opening the door and jumping back in fear to convince me that Tessie could not continue to lounge in this spot. Dr. Widmayer would surely find out, and this noble experiment would fail. I became "doggedly" vigilant about restricting Tessie to my office during regular business hours.

When clinic hours were over and all the clients were gone, I relaxed her curfew. One evening about six o'clock, I was explaining the work we do to some guests in our party room at the rear of the building. My roommate left our office door open when she went home, and Tessie wandered out to find me. To my huge relief, the guests were unfazed by her presence and some even gave her a pat. In spite of their apparent acceptance of a dog in an office setting, or perhaps because of it, they mentioned meeting the dog to Dr. Widmayer when they went back to her office.

I knew this because ten minutes after they left our building, my phone rang. It was Dr. Widmayer. We both now knew that the terms of our agreement had been broken, and I expected the worst. Demonstrating restraint and unfaltering sensitivity to the needs of others, even a dog, she stated simply, with no acrimony or disappointment in her voice, that Tessie had to stay home from now on. I apologized and told her I would definitely see to that.

I set about trying to keep Tessie happy at home with more toys and chewies. I left the TV on and even went to the expense of building a fence around a back portion of the property.

Thankfully, for her remaining days, which were few, her unsettling behavior diminished, along with the neighbors' complaints.

16

Habitat for a Little Piece of Humanity

HOME VISITS WERE MADE FREQUENTLY for clients in crisis, sometimes even daily. When everyone was doing well medically and there were no other pressing problems, home visits did not have to be made as often. I always looked forward to these noncrisis visits because they would give me a chance to see the family interacting like any other family that wasn't dealing with a ticking time bomb.

Two of my families lived on the same block, and I usually tried to visit them on the same day. The first stop was usually to see five-year-old Jeffrey, who lived with his grandmother— known to one and all as Miss Maggie—and his Auntie Alice. These two women loved Jeffrey deeply. Miss Maggie was almost as wide as she was tall, and her condition of morbid obesity was always of great concern to me but not to her. She routinely waved off any discussions I tried broaching about her diet or health. Alice had a face that always seemed to glow with happiness. She was a gentle and soft-spoken person with some developmental challenges. Both of them always made me feel incredibly welcome.

Jeffrey's health was excellent, thanks in large part to Alice's bringing him by bus to the clinic faithfully. They never missed a single appointment. Jeffrey was not on medication yet and therefore not experiencing any disturbing side effects. Although skinny and wiry, he was robust and looked and behaved the same as any five-year-old boy living without a terminal diagnosis.

Jeffrey's mother, Brenda, lived in the area, but it was Miss Maggie and Alice who were raising Jeffrey. Brenda, a drug addict, had lost custody of Jeffrey when he was a baby. To her credit, despite losing custody, she wanted to remain in contact with him and would frequently appear at the house to visit with the family.

Brenda was a force of nature. As soon as she came through the front door, her deep, booming voice seemed to fill up the space, crowding out anyone else's. Flamboyant and boisterous, she often dressed in an inappropriate, seductive fashion. Having her around would usually upset everyone, especially Jeffrey. He once told me, "Brenda gets high and acts crazy." I didn't know if a five-year-old could really understand what getting high meant, but Jeffrey did understand what acting crazy was, and being around his mother when she behaved this way made him uncomfortable.

When I first began working with the family, they lived in a dilapidated wooden one-story shotgun house. Like all shotgun homes, designed originally about a century ago, theirs was narrow (about twelve feet wide) and relatively deep, the four small rooms lined up end to end with no hallway: a sitting room in front; two bedrooms, one behind the other; and a kitchen and small bathroom in the rear. There were doors and windows only at the front and back of the house, allowing breezes to blow straight through. Jeffrey shared a bedroom with Alice. Every time I made a home visit and walked across the treeless, bare yard, I used to look at their house and wonder how it was still standing in spite of so many decades of Florida's often volatile hurricane seasons. But there it was: a testament to history.

At one home visit, Miss Maggie shared some thrilling news.

"Guess what, Miss Dale," she said before I could even sit down. "My church helped me fill out an application to get a new house, and President Jimmy Carter himself chose us! We're getting a new house with three bedrooms and a modern kitchen and one and a half bathrooms! I can even pick the color paint I want."

In the mid 1990s, the sounds of new construction could be heard throughout residential parts of northwest Fort Lauderdale. The highly respected nonprofit organization Habitat for Humanity and the city were working together to demolish various fragile hundred-year-old houses and replace them with homes made with hurricane-proof concrete blocks and wind-resistant windows. Former president Jimmy Carter and his wife, Rosalynn, were not only the faces of the organization, but they also sometimes volunteered to help build the houses. I found it endearing that Miss Maggie believed the president himself had chosen her family.

When I looked into the criteria for applying for a home, I learned that families had to agree to share in doing some kind of physical labor on the house in order to be considered. How could this family made up of a little HIV-positive boy, a morbidly obese grandmother with a strong distaste for moving about, and an auntie with developmental disabilities have contributed in any way with the construction of their new home? I was deeply relieved when Miss Maggie told me the sweat equity condition had been waived in their case.

The new house was being constructed on an empty plot of land across the street and catty-corner from the old house. The day the heavy equipment arrived, Jeffrey's grandmother positioned herself in a chair at the window facing the building lot and began her new "job" of scrutinizing the construction. She did this from early morning until the crew left at the end of the day, six days a week, until move-in day. She told me that watching the house take shape was better than watching her soap operas. When it was nearly finished and time to pick the paint colors, Miss Maggie did not agonize over this decision. She chose her all-time favorite color, blue, for *everything*! Baby blue was her choice for the exterior, and she chose a different shade of blue for every one of the interior rooms.

The construction of the new house was finished in what felt like record time. It stood in all its blue splendor in the middle of the treeless plot of land. Often, when I drove down the block and parked my car near the house, I would see Jeffrey playing in the yard by himself. As soon as he spotted me, he would run toward my car, his head directed backward at the house as he called out to his grandmother at the top of his lungs, "Here go Dale! Here go Dale!"

We'd walk inside holding hands, and I would join Miss Maggie at the dining room table. She was always sitting in the same chair. In all the years I made home visits to the family, I never saw Miss Maggie stand up or walk around. She was usually engrossed in flipping through the pages of wig or hat catalogs. To my delight, my opinion seemed to matter to her. I was routinely invited to give my opinion on which wig was the most beautiful or whether a particular hat was too small for her large frame. It was wonderful to be so included in the day-to-day minutiae of their lives.

Collard Greens

Sierra and Thomas Days, siblings in their early teens, lived with their great-uncle in a house just up the street. Short, stocky Thomas and tall, slender Sierra were soft-spoken, respectful kids and good students. Although their mother had died of the virus, it had not affected them physically in any serious way. They were both on medication that was extremely effective at keeping their viral loads way down. As with many of my young clients, Sierra's and Thomas's excellent health could be attributed to three things: early detection of the virus in their blood when they were very young, the quality health care they received at our pediatric AIDS clinic, and the devoted oversight from their families.

The street was quiet as I walked toward the house. I saw Mr. Days sitting on the porch, but I wasn't sure if he recognized me. He did and shouted out a greeting as he walked down the porch steps to hold the fence gate open for me.

Mr. Days was a trim, personable gentleman, probably in his late sixties, with gray hair, a neat mustache, and a broad smile.

"It's not raining today like it was the last time you were here," he remarked. "I can give you a tour of my garden now, if you'd like."

At my last visit, Mr. Days had told me that farming was in his blood from the time he was a young boy in Georgia. When he and the children moved to Fort Lauderdale and he bought this house with its far smaller piece of land, he just couldn't give up farming. So, he scaled down from a farm to a vegetable garden planted around the perimeter of the property. And what a garden it was: tomatoes, cucumbers, peas, pole beans, Swiss chard, collard greens, and several varieties of peppers and lettuce.

Mr. Days guided me around the yard, describing each grouping of vegetables and advising where they were in their stages of growth. He was justifiably proud of his abundant and gloriously healthy-looking produce. I was amazed by this small rural farm in a semi-urban setting.

After the tour, we went inside the house. The kids wouldn't be home from school for at least an hour, but I didn't need to see them today. We had recently seen each other in the clinic. Today was my day to talk with their great-uncle. Mr. Days served me iced tea and took the opportunity to tell me the story of his niece's illness and death and how he was left to raise her children.

"I want to be clear. Raising these kids was never and will never be a burden for me. It gives my life meaning."

We talked about a number of other things, including Thomas's and Sierra's grades and their social lives, his satisfaction with our clinic, and where he was receiving his own health care. I reminded him about some of the items and referrals we could provide the family.

Leaning close to me, he said emphatically, "I want you to know something: you should never feel you have to bring us anything when you come by. We are very grateful for the bus passes, the back-to-school supplies, and the wonderful Thanksgiving basket and Christmas presents, but we really don't need for much. If there is something, I'll be sure to call you. But, if you'd let me, I'd like to give *you* something to take home."

"What would that be?" I asked.

"Collards."

We went back outside, where Mr. Days dug up four big plants. He soaked their roots under the faucet of an outdoor slop sink and wrapped them in wet newspaper. He then sent me on my way with explicit instructions on how to replant them, care for them, and even how to cook them with some bacon.

At every red light, I couldn't stop myself from glancing down at the collards lying on the floor on the passenger side of the car, their thick gray-green leaves extending out from the wet newspaper cones. I felt as if I were transporting precious cargo. While I drove, I thought about how much I loved all the moments of my job: from the ones some might consider mundane, such as helping Miss Maggie choose a wig or hat from a catalog, to the time spent with Mr. Days, and even to five-alarm hospital visits and every moment in between. Each day, this work gave me opportunity after opportunity to step outside my own life and be welcomed into so many others' lives. I felt exquisitely useful and filled with gratitude.

17

Becoming an Adventurer

I'VE NEVER BEEN PARTICULARLY INTERESTED in making New Year's resolutions; however, in December 1997 I was a newly single woman and felt that I should resolve to do something important on my own in the coming year. But what? I mentally checked off the goals I'd set for myself and achieved, as well as those yet to be reached. At the absolute top of the list of accomplishments was having found my current job. When I accepted the position, I had no clear vision of what it meant to be a witness to an epidemic or to work ten-hour days plus weekend hours when circumstances called for it. It was a hard job, but I never once felt I couldn't face going back to work the next day—although some days I really wished I could have slept in a bit longer.

Naturally, anytime a client died of AIDS, it brought bouts of sadness, but this was juxtaposed with wonderfully warm and relaxed home visits where I was able to simply appreciate my clients and their family members and where I was in my professional life. It was inspiring to be part of such a supportive team of coworkers, and I felt a lot of pride working for such an amazing organization that supported so many thousands of needy families. I loved my job and had the satisfaction of knowing I was good at it.

Although Dr. Widmayer didn't invent this phrase, she often said the following: "If you don't take care of yourselves, how can you care for others?" I decided to embrace this concept and take some time off to care for myself by going on a long-dreamed-of vacation. When I was a teenager, I saw a travelogue about the Amazon River and the rain forest. The wish to explore these two areas went unfulfilled for almost forty years. This would be my 1998 New Year's resolution.

I had no qualms about telling my clients I would be gone for two weeks because I was completely confident my coworkers could and would handle any emergencies that might crop up. We all had a degree of familiarity with one another's clients and they with each of us.

To prepare for this trip, I needed to see a doctor and get an assortment of shots. As I sat on the doctor's examining table, I stared at the silver tray on the counter holding an impressive but wholly intimidating array of needles. These would soon be puncturing my arms for the purpose of keeping me safe from typhoid, yellow fever, hepatitis A, diphtheria, and tetanus. Because there was no vaccine for malaria, the doctor suggested I buy Lariam pills to take prophylactically, in case I got bitten by a mosquito carrying the disease. Perhaps all of this should have been a deterrent, but amazingly, I wasn't in the least bit anxious about contracting any of these awful-sounding illnesses. I refused to entertain any thoughts of becoming sick on this trip. It was too important to me.

Probably to distract me from the pain of the injections, the doctor engaged me in conversation. One of his questions was whether I was planning on going to Machu Picchu while I was in Peru. I told him I had only planned an eight-day boat trip on the Amazon. He was shocked.

"How can you travel all the way to Peru and not see one of the Seven Wonders of the World?" he asked.

Gingerly easing myself off the examining table with already sore arms, I promised him I would look into it. Once I got home,

I did just that and was reminded of and overwhelmed by the pictures I saw of this fifteenth-century Incan citadel eight thousand feet up in the Andes. My trip of a lifetime would now be extended by three additional days exploring Machu Picchu and the surrounding area.

It took eight and a half hours to fly direct from New York to Lima, the capital of Peru. This was the first time in my life I had flown alone; but rather than feeling anxious, I was giddy with anticipation about what I would soon be experiencing. After landing in Lima, I boarded a propeller plane for the two-hour flight to the port city of Iquitos, where the Amazon River excursion was to start.

It was a late-evening flight. As the glow from the airport lights and the city of Lima disappeared, the sky quickly became darker and darker outside my window, until I could see nothing at all. I closed my eyes and managed to doze off for what felt like ten minutes but probably was more. The voice of the pilot woke me up with the announcement that we would be landing shortly. I looked out the window, twisting my neck to spot anything at all in the pitch darkness. Landing? Landing where? Suddenly, I spotted a few distant tiny spots of light set far apart from one another. I had no idea what they were. The pilot's voice came on again to announce that we were flying over the Amazon jungle, where there were no roads, no streetlights, and no house lights. So, what were those specks of light? Again, my question was answered by the pilot. The lights I had seen were fires set in small villages for nighttime illumination.

The driver who took me from the small airport to Iquitos let me off in front of the *Delfin*, a three-tiered, wooden riverboat of a certain age, neatly painted in green and white. This would be my home for eight days. It was tied up at the dock with a

Taxi boat and tourist boat docked at Iquitos, Peru.

jumble of other riverboats. Those, however, were not meant for tourists but were used for commercial purposes or as "taxis" to transport people up and down the river to visit relatives, sell their products, or get to work. Because there were no roads, the Amazon River was their highway.

Colorfully striped cotton hammocks were hung on the decks of those boats for overnight travelers. Some of these hammocks were slowly swinging back and forth with lumpy hidden forms hanging down in the middle. These were passengers relaxing or dozing while they waited for departure time. There were bales of products wrapped in burlap or tarps and stacked high, one upon the other. The boats with no passengers and not scheduled for departure this evening were tied to one another with heavy nautical ropes. They bobbed up and down in place alongside the dock, moving in a merengue-like rhythm on the dark river.

Even though it was twelve thirty at night, Terry Vandeventer was waiting for me there. He introduced himself as the American naturalist guide and a snake wrangler from Mississippi. A snake

Terry Vandeventer holding an Amazon tree boa found hanging over the bow of the Delphin.

wrangler? We didn't have those in Brooklyn, and I was eager to learn more about him and his profession. He told me that a Peruvian naturalist would board the *Delphin* in the morning. We would also pick up freelance guides from local villages whenever we disembarked to hike. They all were specialists in the wildlife and plant life we would see: snakes, turtles, birds, amphibians, fish, pink dolphins, insects, and mammals. Terry guaranteed I would see examples of all these species as we rode to the headwaters of the Amazon, explored its tributaries in a tender, and hiked through the rain forest.

Terry appeared to be in his late forties and sported a neatly trimmed salt-and-pepper Vandyke beard. He had a broad, open face and a pleasing southern lilt to his voice. When Terry reached out and took my bags and asked me to follow him up the wooden gangplank, I noticed he was missing a sizeable chunk of flesh on the palm of one hand by the thumb and wrist. He saw me looking at it.

"Venomous snake," he said matter-of-factly. "I was lucky. I lived." Terry spoke softly, explaining that the ten other passengers had arrived much earlier than me and were already asleep in their rooms on the main deck. That is not where I would be sleeping, however. He led me down a narrow flight of metal stairs to the lower deck. He apologized for my isolation from the other guests, explaining that the rooms on the deck above were all filled. I would be sharing this level with the ship's captain, crew, the two naturalists—and the ship's engine. He told me we'd be departing soon, now that I was on board. Terry gave me specific directions to get to the bathroom.

"Go back up the metal stairway, turn right, and you'll come to the two bathrooms. Men's toilet and shower will be on the left, women's on the right. To use the sinks, you'll need to climb one more set of stairs to the top deck, where you'll see two sinks attached to the stern.

We came to a row of rooms with small screened doors. Terry opened a door and nodded, indicating this was my room and that I should enter. It was all of about eight feet wide by twelve feet long, with a low ceiling. The walls and ceiling were paneled with dark mahogany slats resembling wainscoting. There was a small bunk bed, with the bottom bunk actually resting on the floor. Two folded, thin white towels had been placed on the beds. Two separate shelves were attached to the wall and aligned with the foot of each bed. The one opposite the top bunk, which I had decided to sleep on, had an old-fashioned electric fan on it and just enough room for a few personal items. Terry switched on the fan, and it began to move the heat around the claustrophobic room. There was no closet. On the wall to the left of the screen door were three hooks for my clothes.

When I'd booked my reservation, I had no clear image of what to expect regarding my accommodations. The literature said, "Imagine yourself exploring the upper reaches of the exotic Amazon, one of the world's greatest ecosystems, on a multilevel riverboat with private staterooms." It was, indeed, a multilevel riverboat, and the room was private, but a "stateroom"? That was a huge stretch. But I honestly didn't care and absolutely wasn't disappointed. It was clean and unique. I wasn't looking for luxury.

When Terry left, I lay down on the upper bunk, fully dressed. In a matter of a few minutes, the rattle-pound of the engine filled my ears, and the boat began to pull away from the dock. The mattress was thin, and I could feel wooden slats moving under it whenever I shifted my position. Looking through my screened door from this fully reclined angle, I was able to see the Amazon River flowing by, only about ten feet away from me. The river was almost at the level of the deck. If the Amazon had waves, which it didn't, they would have surely washed over the deck and right into my room.

Now in my bathrobe with my pajamas draped over my left arm, and my showering supplies (which also held a small Spanish–English dictionary) in tow, I tiptoed up the stairs to the main deck and walked in the direction of where I had been told the bathrooms would be. I strolled through an open-air dining room with gleaming dark wood benches and tables already set for breakfast. At the end of the dining room was a short hallway with a door on each side, neither one marked. But I remembered what Terry had said: "Ladies on the right."

The bathroom was the size of a deep, narrow closet, with a high window at the far end. There were no divisions in the room. A toilet (with brown water in the bowl) was under the window. A hook was on the back of the door, and a pipe and showerhead were coming out of the wall. There was a single handle below the showerhead, which I assumed would regulate the flow and temperature of the water. No sink. No mirror. No shower curtain. No amenities. Again, I didn't care. I took off my bathrobe and hung it and my pajamas on the single hook and hoped they wouldn't get wet when the shower turned on.

I stood naked a few feet away from the showerhead and stretched out my arm to turn the handle in the only direction it could go. Cold brown water flowed out. I waited a bit and put my hand in the flow again. It was still cold and still brown. Another couple of minutes passed, and nothing changed. I took a deep breath and stepped into the water, dreading the jolt of its cold temperature on my skin. It was, indeed, uncomfortable, but so what? This would be a week with no hot showers. I knew I could survive.

Walking to the stairwell leading to the third deck, where the sinks would be, I spotted a crew member standing behind the bar folding napkins. I took a chance and spoke to him in my best high school Spanish.

"*¿Por qué no hay agua caliente? ¿Y por qué el agua es el color marrón?*" (Why isn't there hot water? And why is the water brown?)

"*El agua es del río, filtrada de palos y hojas,*" he responded.

I understood the first part. "The water is from the river, and that's why it was brown." I thanked him, took out my little Spanish–English dictionary, and looked up the words *palos* and *hojas*. He was telling me that sticks and leaves were filtered out of the river. I was really glad I had kept my mouth closed during the shower and not swallowed any water. I knew there were piranhas in that river, and who knows what else!

When I climbed up and out of the stairwell, I found myself standing in a place so palpably overwhelming that I gasped. The river was not wide at this point, and as the boat glided smoothly along, the dark silhouettes of trees slid past silently on either shore. I was completely alone in this foreign setting. I stood at the open-air sink, my toothbrush in one hand and a bottle of purified water nestled in the crook of my elbow. I looked up and squinted at the brightness of the full moon. Its intense white light was cascading downward, sparkling crazily off the wake of the brown river water flowing behind the *Delphin*.

"Look at where you are!" I whispered out loud. My eyes filled with tears.

May the Orishas Bless This Building

My time spent on the Amazon River, hiking in the rain forest, and exploring Machu Picchu became for me a trip of a lifetime. Although my head was full of exotic images when I returned home, I had a professional life to attend to and dove right back into it. There were a few times when my private life intersected with my professional life; no example of this was stranger than what happened shortly after CFAP had moved into its new home.

My friend Eva and her boyfriend Joe were extraordinary mambo dancers, and Joe was an obsessed collector of all genres of Latin music spanning many decades. Joe had been living in New York in the mid 1970s when one of his favorite bands, the Grammy Award–winning Cuban Latin jazz band Irakere came there on tour. He and a Cuban friend attended their show. His friend knew one of the two tenor saxophone players, Carlos Averhoff, and when the show ended and the band came offstage to mingle with the audience, Joe was introduced to Carlos.

There was an instant rapport between these two men. Carlos spoke excellent English, albeit with a thick Cuban accent. When he mentioned that he was hoping to buy stereo equipment in New York City to take back to Havana, Joe jumped at the chance to help him. They ended up spending the better part of the next day shopping, eating lunch together, and forming a warm bond of friendship. Many years passed before Carlos returned to New York on tour, but when they reunited, the two men once again spent precious hours together and solidified their friendship. Like so many other relationships between Cubans and American citizens—which benefited family members and friends in both countries—this friendship was sorely tested by both governments' restrictions on travel between the two countries.

The members of famous Cuban bands were considered by their government to be international musical ambassadors and were granted permission to travel out of the country on concert tours. However, this privilege did not come without a price. They were watched vigilantly by Cuban security guards lest someone try to defect. It was at a concert in Miami in the early 1990s that Carlos acted upon his long-considered plan to do just that. He desperately wanted to secure a better life for himself in the United States and to be able to send money home to his family. Sometime between the night of the last concert and the next morning when everyone was to congregate in the hotel lobby for the trip home, he slipped past the guards and disappeared into the well-established Cuban community in Miami. One of the first people he called was his American friend Joe, who was eager to help him get settled in any way he could.

Carlos was now a free man, and I was a newly single woman. Eva and Joe could think of nothing more logical than to fix up their two friends.

I'd never met anyone like Carlos. Along with his Irakere bandmates, he had been a celebrity in Cuba; but here in South Florida, it was a different story. Every day seemed to be a Sisyphean struggle to get the recognition he deserved as a great musician and to make a decent living for himself. He formed a four-piece band and gigged routinely at the Van Dyke Jazz Club on Lincoln Road in Miami Beach, was a guest artist at concerts, taught saxophone privately, and was a professor of music at Florida International University School of Music.

He worked incredibly hard but somehow found the time to have a social life—with me. I was interested in everything he taught me about his life, his music, and Cuban culture. In return, he was fascinated by his gringa girlfriend and everything about my life. He loved meeting my family, going on double dates with Joe and Eva, and hearing about my job. It was on one of the occasions when we were talking about my work that I mentioned we had recently moved into a new building. Carlos became very excited. "It must be blessed—all the rooms, the offices, the desks, the chairs, everything. When can I do it?"

I told him I had absolutely no idea what he was talking about. He then patiently gave me a lesson about *Santería*. Like many native Cubans, Carlos was raised in this Afro-Cuban religion, which combines the beliefs and customs of the African Yoruba people with some elements of Catholicism. Throughout his childhood, he had witnessed both his mother and his grandmother perform rituals for the family as well as for neighbors and friends.

As part of *Santería* custom, Carlos always wore a necklace of colored beads under his shirt. Both inside and outside his apartment in Miami's Little Havana were clusters of white flowers and more hanging beaded necklaces. These symbols reflected his strong belief in the power of the Yoruba deities called orishas.

Now he wanted to bring their beneficence and protection to me and the people I worked with. I was deeply touched by his desire for all of us to be safe from harm and agreed to let him bless the building—even though I had no idea what that would entail.

Carlos drove up from Miami, and we met outside the CFAP building one Sunday morning. I was confident no one would be in either our building or the center's clinic and offices on a Sunday. Knowing he would be performing at a late gig the night before, Carlos had asked me to buy the things he would need for the blessings and bring them with me Sunday morning. It was a shopping list probably no Jewish girl from Long Island had ever had to follow: a cheap cigar, a whole coconut, and a bottle of Florida Water. That last item, a cit-rus-scented eau de cologne, can be used as an aftershave, a body splash, or a scent for sachets. However, shamans who practice *Santería* incorporate it in rituals for purifying, healing, and blessing.

I unlocked the front door. My anxiety began to build the moment we walked in. It was dark inside, so I flipped on the lights.

"Give me the cigar," Carlos said calmly as he took a Bic lighter out of his pocket.

I took it out of the brown paper bag I was clutching tightly and handed it to him. We were only at the very beginning of this caper, but I already felt like a trespasser, an intruder, and not surprisingly, a woman who had lost all common sense.

Carlos lit the cigar and walked into the first office on the right. Quietly, quickly, he said a prayer in Spanish and took a drag on the cigar. He then bent low and walked around the office blowing smoke over the two desks, the chairs, and up and down a tall filing cabinet.

It was the same routine in the next office, and the next, and the conference room, until all the spaces had been blessed. At this point, in addition to my mounting anxiety, I was also beginning to feel nauseated from the pungent odor of cheap cigar smoke hanging in the air in all these tight spaces. Then it dawned on me that the stench from the smoke would probably permeate the whole place and maybe set off the smoke alarm. I was *insane* for agreeing to do this with him. My mind reeled with images of firetrucks pulling up, possibly getting arrested, and worst of all, losing my job. Carlos's voice snapped me out of that nightmarish scenario.

"Please give me the Florida Water."

Carlos retraced all his steps and recited what sounded like a different prayer while liberally sprinkling the Florida Water in each smoke-filled room.

Now it was my turn to pray—to myself. "Please let the stench of the cigar smoke disappear. Please, please make this smell go away before tomorrow morning."

"This part is done," he said smiling happily. "Lock up, and I'll do the last step outside."

"What is the last step?" I asked with dread, knowing that the coconut hadn't played its part yet.

"Let's walk a few steps away from the building and face the door. I'm going to say a prayer to bless the building. I'll raise the coconut over my head and...you know what? I'm not going tell you. You'll see what comes next."

Against my better judgment (of which I had little left), I handed him the coconut. He did, indeed, say a prayer while holding it in both hands. He then raised his arms over his head. I was completely unprepared for what happened next. With great force, Carlos hurled the coconut down onto the ground in front of the door—the glass door! I yelled and jumped back as the coconut broke into dozens of pieces, its milk splashing on the door and running down onto the welcome mat.

"This is wonderful!" he exclaimed. "Sometimes the coconut doesn't break at all, but today? So many pieces! This is wonderful!"

Grinning like he had won the title of World's Most Successful Santero, Carlos walked to the door, stared down in silence for a minute, and then spoke.

"The coconut pieces spell out that the building and everyone who works inside it have been blessed. Everyone will be safe, and all the good work you will be doing for your clients in the future will be successful."

He collected the pieces and put them in the paper bag. I gave Carlos a big hug and thanked him for his kindness in wanting to do this for us. He told me we had to exit in a different direction from which we entered. Now, I don't know the reason why, and I didn't ask, but that last step was easy and caused me no anxiety. It was all over.

Sleep didn't come easily that night. I worried about whether the building could rid itself of the cigar smell overnight and whether the coconut milk splashes on the front door would raise suspicion. Could these conditions possibly be identified by someone as being part of a *Santería* ritual? I knew these concerns were all extremely farfetched and could never be traced back to me, but nevertheless, sleep eluded me.

When I arrived at work the next morning, the glass front door bore no streak marks of coconut milk, the door mat had no specks of the husk or white coconut meat stuck to it, and all the interior spaces, amazingly, smelled just fine. I needn't have worried.

¡Muchísimas gracias, orishas!

18

Give Your Pain to Jesus

MICHAEL WAS SEVEN YEARS OLD when I began working with him and his family. He had full-blown AIDS. He lived with his great-grandmother and her three sons, Michael's great-uncles. None of these men had ever married or had children; and because of this, Michael was treated as their child; they all adored him.

When I made my first home visit to meet the family, I was unprepared for what I would see. The outside of the house resembled any other house on the street. No neighbor or passerby would suspect anything unusual was going on behind that front door. But when I stepped inside, I was shocked to my core. It looked more like a chaotic storage facility than a home. Michael's great-uncle Charles welcomed me in. I could see a small room on the right and a larger room on the left. Both of them had stacks of boxes, newspapers, and magazines piled literally to the ceiling. There was no way to enter or move about in the smaller room, while in the larger room, a narrow passageway had been formed through the stacks. This seemed to be the only means available for someone to get from this room to anywhere else in the house. If, at some point in time, there had been any knickknacks or furniture in either room, they had been swallowed up by the clutter long ago.

Obviously, someone in this household was a compulsive hoarder, psychologically unable to throw things out. I had only minimal familiarity with that term. The popular TV show which took viewers inside the homes of people dealing with this mental disorder would not be in production for about a year.

If I had been told to let myself into the house, I wouldn't have had a clue how to navigate my way through the passageway to find anyone. Mercifully, I didn't have to do this on my own. Very matter-of-factly, with no mention of the condition of the rooms, Charles guided me through to the back of the house, where Miss Moshier was sitting in the small, cluttered kitchen. While dutifully following Charles, I pressed my arms tightly against my sides, fearful that I might brush against one of the piles and cause it to come crashing down. I wasn't so much afraid of getting hurt as I was of being horribly embarrassed that I'd brought attention to the bizarre living conditions in the home.

In a past conversation with Nurse Betty, I'd learned that Miss Moshier had a strong resistance to giving Michael his medications and also did not keep all of his clinic appointments. She was highly religious and believed God would heal her great-grandson, not doctors or medicine. The family's previous CFAP social worker had prepared me for the probability that Miss Moshier would be difficult to work with.

Right from the get-go, I saw for myself that Miss Moshier had little tolerance for outsiders being in her life. She didn't smile or welcome me. This made me a bit nervous, but I introduced myself and made a little friendly chitchat as I opened my notebook and took out a pen to review Michael's case.

"I read Michael's file before coming here today and saw that he has had some hospitalizations. How is he doing now?"

"He's just fine," she stated and said no more.

"I'm very glad to hear that, but he has been quite sick in the recent past. I just want to stress how important it is that he be seen regularly in the clinic and that no appointments are missed. Do you need assistance getting to the clinic?

She fixed me with a blank expression and crossed her arms over her chest. Silence. I was feeling very uncomfortable, but forged on.

"We can send a taxi for you and Michael, if that would help. We'll do whatever it takes to make sure our patients keep their appointments. If a parent waits until a child is in crisis before bringing him to the clinic, it makes it so much harder for our medical staff to help. It's only helping the disease to win, while weakening the child's ability to fight back."

Begrudgingly, Miss Moshier told me they had a car and didn't need the help. She then volunteered some information that I'd already been prepared to hear.

"I don't trust everything I'm told about his health, and I don't trust those pills, either. I don't know what they're doing to him. For all I know, they could be making him worse."

"When I get back to the clinic, I'll find out when Michael's next appointment is," I said, not wanting to take a position regarding what she had just told me. This was, after all, the first time we had met and I wanted to be wholly respectful and not do or say anything to upset her. "They can do a blood test to see if the medication is doing its job. Maybe that will give you some peace of mind."

It was a short visit. Michael was in school and Miss Moshier seemed to have no interest in talking about him anymore or about anything else. Several months later, Dr. Puga called to advise that Michael had been admitted again to Broward General. She added that he was so seriously ill it was unlikely he would survive. She asked me to go to the hospital as soon as possible and speak with Miss Moshier about her refusal to allow the doctors to administer pain medication to him. She hoped I would be able to convince her to change her mind. Dr. Puga added that it was not going to be easy, as no one in our clinic or on the hospital medical staff had been successful. She told me I was, perhaps, Michael's last hope for getting relief. And then she slipped in that she had confidence in my ability to accomplish this. I appreciated her expression of confidence, but my over-riding thought (which I did not share with her) was that I, too, would likely fail in convincing Miss Moshier to do anything she didn't want to do. Dr. Puga knew Michael's great-grandmother far better than I did. What did she imagine I could accomplish with this woman who mistrusted medical science—and me? But I knew that in spite of my feelings of inadequacy, I had to find a way to be successful, for Michael's sake. It was unthink-able that this sweet little boy was suffering. I also couldn't bear the thought that the gaping hole Michael's death would leave in the family would be exacerbated by the knowledge that he'd left this world in pain.

While driving to the hospital, I began hatching a plan to change Miss Moshier's mind about pain medication. When I got off the elevator and walked down the hall to Michael's room, I passed the family waiting area where his three great-uncles were sitting, looking saturated with worry. I waved to them. They all looked up, smiled weakly, and waved back. I sensed that, unlike their mother, they understood perfectly well what was going on. Charles, who often spoke on behalf of them all, had in the past told me about their feelings of helplessness in the face of Miss Moshier's stubbornness.

As I neared Michael's room, I could hear her voice, but I couldn't make out what she was saying. I peeked in the door and saw her sitting at his bedside. Her back was to me; her Bible lay open in her lap. Michael's legs were jerking under the covers, probably from pain and tension. He was moaning and trying to speak, but the words were incomprehensible.

"Give your pain to Jesus," she repeated over and over again.

An immediate sense of helplessness washed over me. Miss Moshier had a lifetime of believing that God would solve all problems. Was there anything I could possibly say that would not challenge her deep faith but would help her accept that God might have another plan to ease her boy's pain?

I tiptoed away back to the family waiting room. From past conversations with Michael's great-uncles in the clinic, I could tell that they were compassionate men and loved the boy dearly. Maybe they could be the allies I needed to help me solve the problem. I sat down on a chair next to them.

"I didn't go inside the room. Your mother is reading the Bible aloud and praying over Michael." They all nodded knowingly. Charles murmured, "That's what she does." All three of them were looking down at the floor. I told them Michael was in a lot of pain and asked if they knew their mother was refusing to allow the doctors to give him any pain medication. They said nothing. Then Charles stated with resignation what I already knew: that their mother was a deeply religious woman and she believed what she believed.

"But," he added with great sadness, "we do not want Michael to suffer."

"Would you feel comfortable telling your mother that God gave scientists the knowledge to develop pain medication?" I asked. "Could you also say that God gave Michael's doctors the skills to use this medication to ease Michael's pain?"

He thought about it for a moment, looked at his brothers, and let out a deep sigh.

"I don't know if it will work, but it's worth a try." Charles stood up and left the room. The three of us sat there in silence, looking through the open door and waiting for his return. Suddenly, there he was, smiling broadly. Without any of us saying a word, we knew what that smile meant. I jumped up and shook his hand with both of mine and ran down the hall to the nurses' station with the news that Miss Moshier had consented to the pain medication. I was so relieved, actually feeling joyous that my efforts had succeeded in allowing Michael to end his short journey through this life free from pain and suffering.

19

Bugs!

IT WOULD BE IMPOSSIBLE FOR social work textbooks to cover every real-life event that students might encounter. Many cannot be imagined or easily explained. Nor can the kind of bravery that's required to deal with certain situations be taught in the classroom. One day I picked up my office phone to hear someone yelling hysterically on the other end.

"Get over here fast! Can you come right now?"

"Who is this? What's happening?" I responded, assuming it was going to be a serious medical problem.

"It's Ginny. Hurry up and get over here! All these bugs are in the house!" I was instantaneously relieved to learn that whatever drama was unfolding in Ginny's house didn't involve a medical emergency. Her audible level of panic, however, did tell me I should stop what I was doing immediately and jump in my car.

I drove the ten minutes to Ginny's home as fast as the law allowed. When I parked in front of her small gray cinderblock house, she was outside with her three kids. All four of them were standing barefoot in the front yard and looking anxious. It was obvious they had quickly evacuated the premises—the same premises I now had to enter. What bugs was she talking about, I wondered.

I walked in tentatively, stood still, and visually examined everything in the living room. It looked like it always did. The beige ceramic tile floor had no bugs running across it. The bedsheet hanging at the big center window had no bugs crawling on it. The same was true of the scratched, black faux-leather sofa and matching armchair, as well as the china cabinet. There was the TV on its small stand and the end table with a lamp and its dented lampshade. Ginny's large upright vacuum cleaner stood in the corner, where it had been abandoned months before in favor of a broom. There were no bugs on or around anything in the living room. So far, so good.

When I came into the house, I purposely left the front door open in anticipation of possibly needing a quick escape. I turned around and called out the door to Ginny. She had her back turned and was talking to a woman, not paying any attention to me.

"Ginny!" I yelled. She didn't turn around.

"Ginny!" I yelled again, louder this time. "What room are the bugs in?"

She turned and yelled back, "They're in the bathroom! Go in the bathroom!"

The bathroom was only a few feet from the living room. It was a small space, and the door was open. I poked my head inside expecting to see small cockroaches, or, more horrifically, perhaps an army of the dreaded large cockroaches called palmetto bugs, Florida's version of New York's water bugs. All types of cockroaches made my skin crawl. Now I could relax a bit having not seen even one of those despised, brown, hard-backed bodies scurrying around at breakneck speed. There were no insects crawling across the floor or on the white sink or toilet. Perhaps they had all left before I got there. The red shower tiles looked okay. No bugs on them, either. Wait! Why were the tiles red? I'd never seen red tiles in the bathrooms of any of these cookie-cutter Section 8 houses.

Sunlight was streaming through the open window centered high on the shower wall. Upon a second, closer look I realized that those tiles were not red. They were white tiles literally covered with thousands of undulating, swarming red ants. I stood perfectly still, terrified. It was like a scene from a horror film. But then I realized I had seen this film before. Up north, there is also seasonal swarming of termites and other species of bugs. Of course, this phenomenon would exist in the humid, even buggier environments of the South.

I backed out of the bathroom and ran outside to Ginny, who was still talking to the woman on the sidewalk.

"Ginny, where is your nearest market or hardware store? I have to buy bug spray immediately." A large majority of our clients did not own cars, and when Ginny began giving me walking directions and sending me down one-way streets the wrong way, I quickly thanked her and jumped in my car. There was bound to be a little market within a few minutes of the house, and I was confident I could find it. In less than ten minutes I was back, bug spray in hand.

Not wanting to fully enter the bathroom, I leaned in as far as I dared. Bzzzt! Bzzzt! Bzzzt! Bzzzt! Bzzzt! The spray hit the shower walls. The chemical fumes filled the air and immediately traveled up my nostrils, while the mist-like droplets of spray settled all over me.

The ants began tumbling off the wall and running for their lives. Those that died right away dropped like small clusters of cherry bombs. The rest slithered off the walls in sheets, hitting the floor and charging crazily in all directions, including toward me. My terrible choice to wear sandals this morning left me wholly vulnerable to the escaping masses. I could feel them climbing over my toes and up my legs. What a sight I must have made: running out of the house and swatting at real and imagined biting red ants running up my lower extremities. I quickly handed off the can of bug spray to Ginny.

"Call the landlord *immediately*," I said. "Tell him to send an exterminator over right away. Ginny, I've done the best I could and simply can't go back in there again. Neither should you or the kids until someone takes care of the situation."

Back in the office and secure in the belief that I was free of the bugs, I began documenting this most atypical home visit. I realized, once again, that a scenario like this would not have been found in a social work textbook. Almost every day, I had to flexibly morph into different personas in order to meet the clients' needs. Whether it called for becoming a vanquisher of swarming bugs or a magician of sorts who could convince someone to let go of lifelong beliefs in favor of modern medical science, every day I was learning that I was truly made for this job.

20

Exclusion, Inclusion, Then Finally... Revelations

THERE IS A LONG, BLEAK history of women being excluded from major AIDS research studies, drug trials, and access to early diagnostic testing and to a potentially life-extending medication for the disease. Dr. Widmayer was witness to this discrimination and shared with me what she saw and experienced in the late 1970s and early 1980s.

At that time, she was working as a researcher in the Department of Pediatrics at the University of Miami School of Medicine. She told me about a medical mystery that was unfolding at nearby Jackson Memorial Hospital. An unexpectedly high percentage of infants born to low-income Haitian, African American, and Hispanic mothers were ending up in the neonatal intensive care unit. The medical staff and researchers knew something was seriously wrong medically to cause those infants to be born so sick, but they didn't know what it was.

In an attempt to figure out why this was happening, and with the mothers' full cooperation, a research nurse was assigned to be with every low-income minority woman throughout labor and delivery. When the baby was born, the placenta and umbilical cord blood samples were placed in dry ice and immediately sent to an outside lab for analysis. However, no practical conclusions could be drawn from these efforts.

After these mothers and newborns were discharged, the researchers followed up with frequent home visits. What they learned was shocking. Not only were those babies not thriving but also they were dying after only a few months. And equally shocking was that the mothers, too, were getting sick and dying.

In early 1981, the CDC published a report that described unexplained cases of enlarged lymph nodes in five previously healthy, young gay men in Los Angeles. They also exhibited other unusual infections, including *Pneumocystis carinii* pneumonia (PCP)—a rare pneumonia—and a rare type of cancer. These diagnoses indicated that the men's immune systems were not functioning properly. Later in 1981, there were reports from the CDC of women being diagnosed with the same rare pneumonia.

The following year, the CDC established the term acquired immunodeficiency syndrome (AIDS) to describe this illness.

Although now there was a name for the condition, no one knew what caused AIDS. It wasn't until 1983 that scientists first identified the culprit: the human immunodeficiency virus. The most advanced stage of HIV is what causes AIDS. This was what was attacking the body's immune system, and because there was no treatment for it at this time, it led to a diagnosis of AIDS and the probability of death.

The early history of major clinical research studies and an early medication trial show that women were not allowed to participate. One example of how women were left out of clinical research studies occurred in 1986, when there was a human trial of a new-old medication called AZT (azidothymidine or zidovudine). The FDA had approved it in 1964 as an anticancer agent, but it proved ineffective. Now it was being assessed in male volunteers as a possible therapeutic against AIDS. Some of the participants were on the actual medication and some were on placebos.[6] The early results of this trial were so promising that the study was halted before the scheduled end date so those men who were receiving the placebo—unbeknownst to them— could be switched to AZT. Although quite toxic (about half of the participants in the study could not tolerate it), it did prove to be somewhat effective in slowing the progression of the virus and in extending some lives—some *men's* lives, that is. Infected women were excluded from participation in this research trial and did not have access to AZT for almost a decade. The language used to describe the criteria for exclusion in the trial used the phrase "No pregnant women and no nonpregnant women" could participate.

The numbers of infected women *appeared* to be extremely low—not because there were so few diagnosed cases but because physicians did not know how to identify symptoms in women. They were using the same criteria they used for the men; however, women's symptoms were dramatically different. For example, physicians did not recognize that recurring yeast infections were early symptoms of HIV disease in women.

It wasn't until 1992—*nine years* after women were first diagnosed with AIDS—that this gender bias in medical research began to change. That was when the Pediatric AIDS Clinical Trials Group 076 study began (ACTG 076 for short). It enrolled HIV-positive pregnant women from across the nation. About nine in ten were either African American (68 percent) or Hispanic (22 percent). Part of the study looked at whether the HIV transmission rate from mother to infant could be reduced by taking AZT during pregnancy and upon the onset of labor.

---

6   A placebo is a substance having no therapeutic effect that is used as a control in testing new drugs.

The name of this medication should sound familiar: it had been part of the medical protocol for men since 1986.

It was another double-blind study, meaning that some of the participants received AZT therapy, while some were administered placebos. None of the enrollees or their physicians knew which drug regimen the participants were on. When the hugely positive results of the ACTG 076 study became available in April 1994, the study was unblinded so all the participants could benefit from taking AZT.

The ACTG 076 study continued post-delivery, with the mothers giving oral AZT to their newborn babies for the first six weeks of their lives. The outcomes of that study were absolutely revelatory: HIV transmission from mother to infant was reduced by more than two thirds, from 22.6 percent to 7.6 percent. The US Public Health Service recommended the administration of AZT to all HIV-infected pregnant women and their newborn infants.

By the early 1990s, Children's Diagnostic & Treatment Center already had an established research department doing behavioral research in HIV/AIDS through the Elizabeth Glaser Pediatric AIDS Research Foundation, the National Institutes of Health (NIH), and other grantors. Over the years, CDTC also collaborated with the CDC, the UCLA Medical Center, the Harvard AIDS Institute, and many other prestigious institutions. CDTC was highly respected around the nation as the only non-university-based clinical research site for HIV/AIDS.

Although our research department had no women enrolled in the ACTG 076 study, we were awarded a grant from the US Health Resources and Services Administration to disseminate its findings. Some of my colleagues and I visited the offices of

Broward County obstetricians and provided doctors and nurses with educational pamphlets about this new standard of care. The goal was to ensure that medical providers and their HIV-positive pregnant patients fully understood the steps that had to be taken to dramatically decrease the odds of having an HIV-positive baby.

One of the largest, if not the largest, research studies Children's Diagnostic participated in at this time was the Ariel Project, named in memory of Elizabeth Glaser and her young daughter, Ariel, both of whom died from AIDS. Elizabeth Glaser was married to actor Paul Michael Glaser, costar of the popular 1970s TV series *Starsky & Hutch*. The celebrity recognition was one of the reasons this case drew so much public attention. Elizabeth Glaser contracted HIV in 1981 through a contaminated emergency blood transfusion when she was giving birth to her daughter. She passed on the virus to Ariel through breastfeeding. Ariel died of AIDS at only eight years of age in 1988. Elizabeth Glaser worked through the grief of losing her child by becoming a passionate activist and a highly visible advocate raising awareness about pediatric AIDS. Before dying herself at the age of forty-seven in 1994, she created the Elizabeth Glaser Pediatric AIDS Foundation to fund research and stop the spread of the deadly disease.

The Ariel Project study, funded by the National Institutes of Health, was conducted at seven clinical sites in the United States. Researchers began enrolling women volunteers in January 1993, and the trial was projected to run until March 1995. This was the first study of its kind with the objective of identifying which factors were or were not associated with the transmission of HIV from mother to child, and which factors increased or decreased those risks. Of those seven participating clinical sites,

Children's Diagnostic & Treatment Center had the distinction of providing the largest number of participants.

The Ariel Project research yielded many results of great significance, one being that HIV-positive women should have only Caesarian deliveries. This birthing method greatly reduced a baby's exposure to a mother's blood and bodily fluids. Later findings concluded that HIV was in breast milk and had the likely potential for infecting the infant.

Thanks to these two groundbreaking women's research studies, hospitals and birthing centers around the world had a new standard of care for HIV-positive pregnant women. Over time, later studies showed that when women received optimum health care, along with the acceptance and application of the new protocols, the transmission rate for maternal–child infection was reduced from 7 percent to 4 percent. As of 2023, with effective HIV treatment and a managed delivery, it can be less than 1 percent.

Protocol for a New Life

The scientific and medical communities had embraced the irrefutable evidence from these two important research studies. The first time I had a pregnant client added to my caseload, I assumed that her obstetrician would be one hundred percent on board; however, that was not the case. I found myself in the unexpected and unenviable position of having to advocate forcefully for my client to ensure her baby could benefit fully from these remarkable scientific findings.

Shonda was in her late twenties and pregnant with her third child when we started working together. She lived in Pompano— about ten miles from Fort Lauderdale—and initially came to Children's Diagnostic only for social service assistance. When she learned she was pregnant, she began her HIV treatment at our clinic. Shonda had a history of drug abuse and, sadly, had already lost custody of her first two children to her mother. I had no experience working with drug addicts and was not completely comfortable about her placement with me. My anxiety eased considerably, however, when I learned that Shonda had taken the first, most important step and signed herself into a hospital detox program.

I met with her immediately after her discharge from detox— and I mean immediately. She walked directly over from the hospital to Children's Diagnostic to meet with me. She was open and honest about her past drug history and other reckless decisions she had made in her life. She also stated with great conviction that she was determined to do whatever was necessary to keep her baby safe from the virus. I wanted so much to believe her. But the worry was there: Would she actually be able to commit to staying clean and sober throughout her pregnancy?

I needn't have worried, for Shonda was a model client and a model patient. In spite of very uncomfortable side effects, she took her antiretroviral medication, AZT, faithfully and never missed appointments for her HIV care or prenatal care with her private obstetrician. She did everything asked of her by our medical staff as well as by her social worker from the Department of Children and Family Services. My monthly reports to her DCF worker always included praise for how compliant Shonda was with everything and how she was remaining drug free. I was very proud of her.

A few weeks before Shonda's due date, she asked me to be her birthing partner. I was both shocked and extremely flattered that, after a relatively short time working together, she felt comfortable enough with me to ask that I share this deeply intimate experience. It was during a home visit that I realized it had little to do with our relationship but was more about how there were no other options. She didn't say this in so many words, but the father of the baby had abandoned her. She continued by saying her mother was both resentful for having to raise Shonda's first two children and angry at her daughter for getting pregnant again.

I had never heard anyone at work discuss being a birthing partner for a client, so I asked around to learn if this was something we were expected to do. The answer was if a client wanted this, and if we felt comfortable doing it, we certainly could. I was not entirely sure that I felt comfortable about doing this, but knowing it was important to Shonda, I promised her I would think about it.

Shonda was hugely impatient and called me every day to see if I had decided. Her insistence indicated to me she really did not want to go through the delivery alone, and so I told her I would stand by her at this important moment in her life.

By 1998, the results of the ACTG 076 research study and the Ariel Project were well known. Shonda understood that a Caesarian delivery would give her baby the best chance of not contracting the virus. It was explained to her that with this type of birth, she would not go into labor, and the baby would not remain in the birth canal for hours being exposed to large amounts of blood and other bodily fluids that harbor the HIV. Although nervous about being cut open, she told me she knew this was the right thing to do.

To prepare for being Shonda's birthing partner, I sat down with Dr. Puga to learn what my role would be. She said that because Shonda would not be going into labor, she would need only one dose of AZT before the surgery began. It was my job to make sure she got it. Other than that, I was to sit by her side and help her stay calm.

After Shonda went for her last prenatal visit, she called to tell me her doctor would be delivering the baby at a Palm Beach County hospital, a facility I had never heard of. It would, indeed, be a Caesarian delivery, and Shonda told me I should be there the day after tomorrow at seven thirty in the morning. After setting my alarm that night for six o'clock, I plugged the hospital's address into Mapquest on my computer and printed out the step-by-step directions. I felt confident I could do the twenty-one miles without a problem.

Upon arriving at the hospital, I was directed to Shonda's room, where I found her covered up to her neck in sheets and looking calm and happy. In contrast, I was definitely *not* but was determined not to show any signs of my mounting nervousness. A nurse was slipping an oversized white shower cap onto Shonda's head when the doctor came in. He glanced at me but neither introduced himself nor asked who I was. In spite of his obvious rudeness, I identified myself to him as Shonda's social worker and birthing partner. His face registered mild displeasure, but he didn't say a word. Not even hello.

"Has Shonda gotten her dose of AZT?" I asked.

To my horror, he stated, "She doesn't need it."

I was completely unprepared for his answer. I knew what my job here entailed and cited a shortened version of the medical protocol about AZT. In a respectful tone of voice, I added that Shonda had been very compliant with her medical regimen and that it would be a shame to risk messing anything up at this late stage.

"She doesn't need it," he said again, this time with genuine annoyance in his voice.

Now *I* was annoyed. I stood my ground and stated emphatically that our clinic director was an infectious disease specialist and had told me how important it was that Shonda get a dose before surgery. I glanced over at Shonda and saw that her eyes were wide open, probably with disbelief that I was talking to her doctor like that. (Actually, I couldn't believe it myself.) But who would fight for her and her baby if I didn't? This was my job. I couldn't help but wonder if I was witnessing blatant racism. Had Shonda been a White woman, would the doctor have dismissed this highly effective protocol as being unnecessary?

I pressed on. "Do you have a single dose available here or *anywhere* in the hospital?" He looked straight at me but didn't answer right away. Had I gone too far? "It's in my office," he stated flatly, with no expression in his voice.

And where was that? At the opposite end of the building, of course. I asked him to please call his nurse and let her know I was coming to get it. To my great relief, he agreed.

From the start, Shonda had done absolutely everything right so she would not pass on the virus to her baby. Now I felt like *I* held that baby's life in my hands. I was not going to drop the ball. I raced through those completely unfamiliar corridors, gasping for breath, and stopping only to ask people for directions. Anger was flooding my brain and pushing me along. I was furious with the obstetrician for his arrogance and indifference to my client's need at this time.

I found his office, got the pill from his nurse, and then raced back; again having to ask for directions all the way back.

Shonda had been moved to a surgical area. A nurse was standing at the window of the swinging door, saw me arriving, and came out. I must have been quite a sight: doubled over from a stabbing pain in my side from running, and panting heavily. I handed off the pill to her and watched as she gave it to Shonda. Mission accomplished!

While I waited outside the door for instructions about what to do next, I looked through the window. I saw Shonda lying on a gurney-like bed. One nurse was setting up a tray with the surgical instruments. Two others were erecting the tent that hid Shonda's belly from her view. It was a team of five. One nurse came out and handed me blue scrubs, a white shower cap like Shonda's, and paper booties to slip over my shoes. I was directed to where I could change and instructed in proper handwashing.

I entered the operating room and sat down on the chair positioned next to Shonda's head. For added moral support, I extended my hand to hold hers. Instead of placing her hand in mine, she put a camera in it.

"I know you weren't expecting this," she said with a sly smile, "but I want you to take pictures." I never expected, nor did I want, to be looking on the other side of the tent. When the doctor told me I should hold off taking pictures until after he had made the major incision, my hostile feelings toward him dissipated somewhat and were replaced by a measure of gratitude. I did not want to end up having to receive some form of resuscitation.

When he gave me the go-ahead, I nervously inched my way to the other side of the tent and stood far out of everyone's way. I was, however, close enough to clearly see him lift Shonda's organs out of her body and place them on her stomach. To my profound amazement, instead of feeling woozy or nauseated by this, I found myself riveted to what was happening. I recalled a decades-old memory of being giddy with delight during the act of dissecting a frog in college biology class and discovering the tiny intestines and stomach inside. Although this was a human

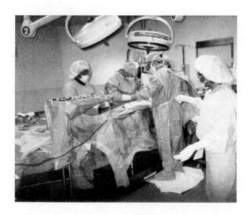

Shonda's Caesarian surgery.

being in front of me and the organs were much bigger, was this so very different? It didn't feel that different. It was thrilling!

There was a long, clear hose running from inside Shonda's body and down into a drainage hole in the floor. The hose was filled with her red blood—blood that, had the baby been exposed to it, might have saddled it with a fate as tragic as its mother's.

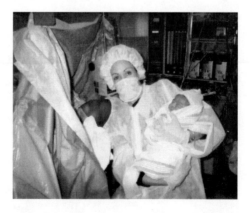

Shonda, Dale, newborn Isaiah.

Miraculously, the baby was lifted out of Shonda's open womb—a perfect little boy. She named him Isaiah. I was snapping pictures like crazy.

Back home, Shonda was just as committed to Isaiah's health as she had been months earlier when she volunteered to enter detox. I called her regularly and made weekly home visits to check on how things were going. She loved to show me any new clothes or toys she had bought the baby or received as gifts. Even though our CFAP clinic medication nurse, Betty Benivegna, also made home visits to check the AZT logbook, Shonda liked to show it to me as well. She faithfully gave Isaiah his antiretroviral medication for the prescribed six weeks. Once again, I was so proud of her. She seemed happy and seriously focused on her new opportunity to be a parent.

Then, one day Shonda walked out of the house and disappeared, leaving Isaiah, her third child, in the care of her mother. She had accomplished her goal of giving her son the best possible chance at a healthy life. Heartbreakingly, to my and many others' deep disappointment, she returned to her addiction, possibly cutting short her own life.

21

The Checked Box

MY NINETEEN-YEAR-OLD CLIENT SERENA HAD schizophrenia, only no one knew it. She seemed normal to me, as well as to Dr. Puga and the clinic nurses. Our only concern about her was that she had refused to start HIV medications, but that was her choice. She had no symptoms of having the disease yet.

Serena's mother, Maggie, was a grocery packer at my local Publix supermarket, and whenever possible, I would go to the checkout counter where she worked so we could chat while she filled my bags. Maggie never reported anything seriously troubling about her daughter other than outbursts between Serena and her younger brothers and other family members, but that was fairly normal behavior for teenagers.

When Serena was offered the opportunity to participate in a national research trial for teenagers with HIV, she agreed. I was surprised because I knew her to be a quiet kid, never one to talk much or join a support group or accept invitations to attend seminars. Many of our teenage clients rejected the chance to be part of this study, but Serena wanted to participate. Maybe it was the small stipend she received for taking part. Or maybe it made her feel important to be part of something as serious as a national research study. Whatever it was that motivated her, Serena showed up faithfully for her appointments. She would take the bus from home to the center, sit at a computer in the research department, and plug in her answers to the study questions.

One day, fairly early into Serena's involvement in the study, Dr. Puga told me to have her come to my office as soon as possible. She wanted me to ask Serena if she was hearing voices.

"Why am I supposed to ask her this?"

"On the research study answer form, Serena checked the box asking if she heard voices," Dr. Puga told me. "We need to know more about this."

I made the call, and Serena came in and sat down. She put her pocketbook on the floor but did not remove her audio headset. For a moment, I considered asking her to take it off so that we could talk without her being distracted by the music, but I thought better of it. I didn't want to possibly trigger a hostile reaction from her. After asking a few perfunctory questions about how she and her family were, I asked the question that was causing my heart to pound.

"Serena, do you ever hear voices in your head?"

"Yes," she answered very matter-of-factly. But she added nothing more. "Can you tell me about them?"

"It's a man and woman."

"When do they talk to you?"

"All the time."

She touched her headset and told me the music sometimes, but not always, blocked out what they were saying. Now I was *so* relieved that I hadn't asked her to remove it. Then Serena completely shocked me by volunteering that she saw the man and the woman today outside the bus window on her way over here.

"You see them? They're not just voices? Tell me about what happened today."

"When the bus stopped to pick up some people, I saw them standing on the sidewalk. They tried to get on the bus, but the driver closed the door fast and drove away."

I asked her what kinds of things the voices tell her to do, and once again, very dryly, with absolutely no emotionality in her voice, she answered, "They want me to hurt people."

Now I was scared, but I knew I had to ask more questions. However, before I could do this, Serena stood up abruptly and walked out of my office. I immediately got up and walked straight to the clinic to report to Dr. Puga that Serena was not only hearing voices but also hallucinating.

The next night, about nine o'clock, I got a call from Serena's mother. Maggie was very upset and asked if I could come over to her mother's house, where Serena had been staying.

"You see, Dale, a couple of weeks ago I told Serena she had to move out. She was constantly fighting with her younger brothers and really frightening them. Serena's grandmother agreed to take her in, but tonight Serena began screaming at my mother. Then she hurled an electric fan at her head. My mother called me and then called the police. They're there now, and they want to talk with you because you're her social worker."

Before asking for the grandmother's address, I asked if Serena had done anything like this before. The answer surprised me.

"Yes, and worse. Much worse. I never told you because I was too embarrassed. She set fire to my house, and she used to sleep with a big knife under her pillow. We're all scared to death of her."

The night was moonless, and the streetlights in Serena's grandmother's neighborhood were dim. In spite of this, I could easily see the outlines of people walking, all in the same direction. There was much more foot traffic than I was used to seeing in this neighborhood during daylight hours. I wondered where they all were going.

As I turned the corner and approached the house, my question was answered. There were two police cars with their lights flashing parked in front of what I assumed was Serena's grandmother's house. The people walking had obviously been drawn out of their homes by the police sirens to see what was going on.

I parked behind the police cars and stepped out of my car. An officer immediately walked over to me, his eyes narrowing with suspicion, and asked what I was doing there. I introduced myself and showed him my CDTC photo ID. He told me Serena had bolted before they arrived and asked if I knew where she might have gone. I assured him I had absolutely no idea. He said that based on the grandmother's statement of what had happened, Serena would be arrested as soon as they found her. It was painful to imagine this young woman being in jail, but I understood that the safety of her family—and maybe the safety of anyone with whom she came in contact—was the important thing now.

At work the next day, I was instructed that if Serena came in to see me, I should take her to the Behavioral Health Department at Imperial Point Hospital, about five miles away, for evaluation. I had absolutely no idea how I would be able to get her to agree to this.

Over the next couple of days, I came up with a few scenarios for how I might handle Serena if she actually did walk into my office. And then she showed up. She was not disheveled, nor did she look like she had gone without sleep. I took a deep breath to calm myself.

"Serena, I'm glad to see you. I want to take you to the hospital to find out if there's something that can be done to stop the voices in your head."

To my utter amazement, she consented to go with me—with conditions.

"I'll go if I don't have to give up my clothes and put on a hospital gown," she stated firmly. "And they can't admit me. I refuse to be admitted!"

It seemed like she had been down this road before. I told her I couldn't promise, but I would do my best to get them to agree to her conditions.

Serena was quiet during the ride to the hospital, and I took my cue from her. No small talk. Besides, I was too scared. I now knew she could be dangerous. What if the man and woman in her head tell her to hurt me? I didn't want to say or do anything that might provoke her—or them.

The silence continued as I parked and as we walked through the door to the behavioral health department. We went down a narrow, surprisingly quiet hall. There was a small, empty waiting room on the right and a nurses' station behind the wall on the left. That wall had a large picture window that looked into the waiting room through the open doorway. It provided only a limited view.

Serena walked into the waiting room and sat down while I signed her in. I quietly apprised the nurses about her hearing voices and her history of aggressive, dangerous behavior; and I then told them that Serena insisted on wearing her own clothes and not having to put on a hospital gown for the assessment. I asked if this would be possible. The nurse said she didn't know but agreed to ask the resident physician when he came in. She let me know that a video camera in the waiting room was connected to a monitor in their office, so that they would be able to see anything going on in there. That gave me some assurance I would be safe while sitting alone with my client.

I walked into the waiting room and sat down opposite Serena. There was a wooden, rectangular coffee table between us with some magazines on it. Serena was looking out the window toward the parking lot.

She turned to me and said again, emphatically, "You can't let them take my clothes. I'm telling you, if they want to take my clothes, I'm gone!"

I assured her that I had advised the nurses of this, which made Serena relax a little and sit back in her chair. A few minutes passed as we sat in silence. A different nurse walked into the waiting room carrying a bundle and handed it to Serena.

"There's a bathroom on your right. Please remove your clothes down to your underwear and put these on," she said tersely. "Here's a questionnaire for you to answer. There are pencils on the lamp table. The resident will be with you shortly." She walked out.

Serena looked at me fiercely and through her clenched teeth growled, "You said I could keep my clothes on! You lied!"

Her eyes darted wildly around the room. She spotted the sharpened pencils on the lamp table, grabbed one in her fist, and lunged at me across the coffee table, her fist stopping just inches from my face.

"I could stab you in the eye with this right now if I wanted to!"

I jerked back in abject terror. Somehow my legs got me up and carried me out of the room and across the hall into the nurses' station. The two nurses were sitting there doing paperwork, heads bowed, and obviously not looking at the video monitor. In a burst of words, I told them what had happened. They jumped up and ran into the waiting room. Of course, Serena was gone.

I ran down the hall and out the door, and scanned the grounds and parking lot. Serena was nowhere to be seen. I had lost my client. She was, again, loose in the world and dangerous. I had survived what was probably the greatest moment of peril in my life. Would the next person she came into contact with be as lucky?

A few days later, Maggie called to tell me her daughter had been found, arrested, and was now in jail. It worried me greatly that she might not get the medical or psychological care she needed while she was incarcerated. I continued to see Maggie regularly at Publix. She always hugged me and thanked me for my work with her daughter. I learned from her that Serena received quite a long sentence. When I asked how the family felt about that, she paused for a second and answered, "Just fine."

I was unprepared for that answer. I thought, "What family is comfortable with their child being in prison?" But then I understood. They had all been traumatized by her, and now they could feel safe.

22

Hard Pills to Swallow

FOR YEARS, THE SCIENTIFIC AND medical communities were intensely focused on how the human immunodeficiency virus was transmitted, how it might be treated, and how, if possible, patients could be cured and the epidemic halted. Progress was definitely made in understanding transmission routes, and by the end of 1995, the FDA had approved the first protease inhibitor, a new class of drugs that offered the hope of extending lives. Over the next three years, these powerful agents proved to reduce the amount of HIV in the blood, sometimes even down to zero. People infected with the virus were developing far fewer opportunistic infections and had a greatly reduced chance of premature death.

However, these results often came at a high price. The medications could be toxic, and patients had great difficulty adhering to their complicated regimens. Many of our clients refused to take them as prescribed or refused to take them at all. Typical daily cocktails of drugs could consist of some pills having to be taken three times a day and others two times a day. Some had to be ingested with meals, others on an empty stomach; some taken every eight hours and others every twelve hours. As if the physical and emotional burdens of living with AIDS weren't challenging enough, these complex regimens overwhelmed the women's lives.

Dr. Ana Puga, by herself or in concert with representatives from the drug manufacturers, would hold frequent educational seminars for clinic and social work staff to learn about the new medications. There were many pros and cons to take into consideration when starting someone on one of these courses of treatment. Yes, lives could be extended; however, if a patient missed doses, the virus could start to multiply in the body, perhaps mutate, and the patient might become immune to that drug. When that happened, any possible life-prolonging or life-saving benefits could disappear quickly.

Making the decision to start on protease inhibitors had to be weighed very carefully, and those who opted to do it would need a lot of support. The medical and social services staffs were always encouraging and sympathetic partners with our clients, but we obviously couldn't be *empathetic*. How could we possibly feel what they felt or experience what they were going through? We couldn't, that is, until the medical staff designed a one-week simulation of what life might be like on an AIDS cocktail. Eighteen of us volunteered to participate in this unique experiment. Small though it was, it yielded quite dramatic results.

The homemade study had two major goals. The first was to help us understand better the enormous commitment and discipline that being compliant entailed—to walk a mile in their shoes—but with some major differences. Obviously, we could not use actual drugs. Instead, our study used placebos such as Tic Tacs, Good & Plenty licorice candies, small mints, and jelly beans. Another big difference was that our "pills" didn't produce any of the toxic side effects of the real HIV pills, such as nausea, vomiting, diarrhea, muscle aches, weakness, rashes, depression, and physical body changes, to name several.

The second goal of the study was to come up with some solutions to make taking all these pills easier for our clients.

At the start of the experiment, we each received an individualized medication regimen. Our pill bottles were labeled with actual HIV medication names and instructions on how the pills were to be taken. Even though our pills were candies, nothing could be chewed; everything had to be swallowed whole. We were instructed to keep a daily journal in which we had to report everything we experienced, did correctly, or did incorrectly. Even our daily thoughts about participating in the study had to be documented. To keep the study results pure, it was essential that we be one hundred percent honest.

All eighteen of us went into this experiment with positive attitudes and the belief that we would be successful. At the end of the week, we handed in our journals to Dr. Puga to review. When she finished reading and recording the findings, we all met again as a group to learn the results.

None of us could have possibly predicted the outcome. The journals showed that sixteen of the eighteen participants failed miserably! Why? We forgot to take our pills with us when we went out. Even when we were home, we forgot to take doses. We took the wrong number of pills. We took them at the wrong times. We forgot to take some pills with food and others without food. Had we actually been HIV-positive, we pretty much would have destroyed our chances of reaping the potential benefits of the new medications.

Dr. Puga and a few clinic nurses participated as well. Surprisingly, they were no more successful than anyone else. At the meeting to review the results, Dr. Puga admitted that she actually felt stigmatized about taking her HIV medications, something she didn't think would be possible in a simulated study. It occurred the day she had a handyman in her kitchen to fix something. He was talking with her when she realized that her pill bottles were right on the counter in full view—and they were clearly labeled with HIV medication names. She told us she felt genuine panic that he would see them and believe she had the virus. When the workman wasn't looking, she sidled over to the bottles and turned their labels around.

One of my colleagues was assigned to take eleven pills a day on a hugely complicated schedule. She told the group, "I wouldn't wish this on anybody. Trying to follow this schedule really messed up my life."

One volunteer was actually a client: an HIV-positive eighteen-year-old woman who was considering starting on meds. Dr. Puga encouraged her to participate in our trial, thinking that if she were disciplined enough to do it with the placebos, she might be a good candidate for the real pills. Her cocktail consisted of nine pills in the morning and nine at night. The first major stumbling block to her success was that she had not told Dr. Puga she'd never had to swallow pills as large as some of these. After choking on them a few times, she began to take only the ones small enough for her to swallow. She admitted to making a lot of mistakes and came to the conclusion that she was not ready to be fully compliant.

The instructions for my own regimen seemed quite complicated, but I was sure I could manage it. I had to take a number of pills three times a day. Some had to be ingested with food, while others had to be swallowed on an empty stomach. I realized quickly how wrong I was. It was a day-to-day, hour-to-hour struggle for me—and an extremely humbling experience.

Here's what we came away with that we hadn't considered before we started the trial: in order for our clients to be successful, we had to be better partners with them. The first few days on our own regimens proved to be a critical time period. To ensure that our clients wouldn't mess up or give up in the early stages, we needed to be more involved and proactive than we had been previously.

We also concluded that more emotional and practical help was needed with managing the medications—more than we alone could provide. To accomplish this, the clients' families had to be brought into the picture and educated about what their loved ones were going through so that they could better support them.

There were also some tangible suggestions made: Clients should be given beepers or receive phone calls to remind them when to take their medications. We needed to set up a twenty-four-hour hotline for providing emotional support or answering their questions. Each patient should receive a pillbox big enough to accommodate the large number of pills these regimens called for.

Initially, we didn't think that the study would enable us to truly empathize with our clients, but, indeed, we had. On a modified and simplified level, we *had* walked in their shoes (although, admittedly, we never had to contend with adverse side effects—a significant obstacle for some patients). At the end of that revelatory week, we had become more compassionate partners and much better able to support our clients in their struggle for survival.

23

A Funeral Conundrum

THERE WERE A NUMBER OF funeral homes in northwest Fort Lauderdale, but only two or three were routinely used by our clients. These companies were family owned and had been in business for decades. I frequently drove past one of them that sat on a fairly large plot of land that was undeveloped on one side. On the undeveloped part of the property, only about seventy-five feet from the front door, sat a discarded child's white vault. It was in full view of anyone driving or walking by. I had no idea how many years it had been sitting there exposed to the elements. It was an inappropriate and baffling landmark. No matter how many times I passed it, I could never avert my eyes. I would try not to look at it, but its sad presence always magnetically drew my gaze away from the road. Why on earth didn't the owners of the funeral home remove it? Had it been there so long they didn't see it anymore? Did the residents in the neighborhood never complain about it? Perhaps in this second decade of AIDS, people had become so inured to the idea of death that they just saw the little vault as nothing more than an unremarkable blip on the landscape.

It was at this same funeral parlor where I would have my first experience of helping a client plan a funeral.

My sister and I had shared the planning of our parents' funerals. Having done that, I didn't see myself as a novice when I went to Roberta's house to discuss preplanning for her sister's funeral. I'd also read a number of exposés about the funeral parlor industry and felt prepared to deal with a possibly pushy funeral director who might try to sell my grieving client over-the-top options and services. I saw shielding Roberta from any manipulative or abusive practices as being part of my job. Naïvely, I thought this was what she would want me to do.

Roberta's sister, Rose, was twenty-seven, had end stage AIDS, and was close to death in the hospital. She would be leaving behind a husband and two young children. During the home visit I had scheduled before going to the funeral home, I told Roberta she shouldn't feel pressured to make any decisions on the spot.

"After we meet with the funeral director tomorrow, you and I can go over the bill together and make sure there aren't any extras on it that you really don't want or need," I explained. "Not everything you'll be offered will be affordable, and I'm sure you don't want to be left paying off a huge bill years after the funeral has taken place."

I was expecting her, at the least, to nod in agreement; however, my comments were met with silence. When I told her that Children's Diagnostic & Treatment Center had a very small fund to help clients with funerals and would contribute $200, Roberta expressed her gratitude. She told me her church would definitely take up a collection for them, and family members and friends would also contribute.

"It'll be fine," she said.

I knew things would likely not be fine. The $200 contribution would make only the smallest dent in a bill that would end up being thousands of dollars. Our CFAP families were deeply affected by the numbers of funerals occurring as well as the high costs involved. Relatives and friends of the deceased, along with local churches and community members, were frequently called on to help with donations. The vast majority of residents in this part of Fort Lauderdale lived below the poverty threshold.

Roberta and I were ushered into the funeral director's office by a serious-looking young man in an ill-fitting black suit. He introduced the funeral director, who came out from behind his desk to shake our hands.

"Please sit down, ladies," he said in a deep, soothing voice. On behalf of myself and my family, I want to express our deepest regret about your sister's illness, Miss Roberta. You are very wise to make these important plans early and not wait until you are in a state of mind that may not be conducive to the best decision-making. We are here to guide you and offer you many options for how you'd like to design your sister's homegoing. I think you'll be very pleased with the array of choices available to you. Are you comfortable with everything I've said so far?"

"Oh, yes," Roberta responded with a smile.

"I imagine you have some ideas about what you'd like, so don't hesitate to speak up and share everything you've thought about. And please ask me any questions as we go along. Let's start with the easiest thing first: the program for the service. We can create it right here on our office computer, and it will be just fine. Or we can send it out to a professional print shop. Whichever style you choose, family and friends will probably save it as a beautiful memento of the day. It's completely your choice which one you prefer. Here are two samples."

Roberta held them in her hands and leaned over to show them to me.

"I like this one better."

Not surprisingly, it was the print shop version. The funeral director told her she'd made an excellent choice.

"Now we're going to walk over to our casket showrooms. Caskets are made from different kinds of wood or metals, they come in different colors, have different hardware on them, and different linings in them. You have a lot of choices, so please don't feel overwhelmed. Take all the time you need. I'm here to help you make a decision you'll be genuinely happy with."

The first room we went into was small and had very simple caskets. He steered her to a plain pine casket and made what I felt was an inappropriate prediction.

"I'm fairly sure you wouldn't want something like this. But, I will say, it is the lowest priced one and very practical if your budget is small."

Roberta told him immediately she didn't want something like that.

"The one to the left of it is also the pine casket, but it's covered in a felt-like fabric. That comes in a variety of color choices." She shook her head no.

The funeral director then led us to a much larger room and gestured toward a handsome mahogany coffin with silver-toned hardware and an interior lined with what looked like puckered white velvet. The price tag made me cringe. I whispered to Roberta, "Look at the price tag." She looked and responded. "It's a man's coffin. I don't want that for my sister."

I mentally heaved a sigh of relief. We moved on down the line to a selection of metal coffins in pale colors with faux silk linings. Roberta made a reasonable choice and picked a mid-priced model in pale pink.

Next, we walked into two viewing/reception rooms where the family and friends would gather for the wake the night before the funeral. After this, we were escorted to the chapel. Roberta's family had not yet decided if they were going to have the funeral in their church or at the funeral home.

We returned to the funeral director's office to hear a number of options: how many staff could be in attendance, embalming, floral arrangements, music, limousines to and from the cemetery, and so on. The funeral director's "script" was frequently dotted with the word *upgrade,* but there was no discussion of what any of them would cost. Roberta never asked, so I did. As her advocate, I saw this as part of my responsibility, but it quickly became clear from her body language that she found my inquiries unsettling. I didn't want to make her uncomfortable and stopped pressing. I knew she didn't want to look cheap or, maybe worse, appear to be poor.

He then spoke directly to me in a patronizingly way.

"Don't worry. There's no pressure to decide anything right now. I'm going to have my secretary work up the figures, and Miss Roberta will take them home with her for consideration."

He assured her that she did not have to take all the options or upgrades *but* made certain to mention that whichever ones she did choose would certainly make the funeral unforgettable for everyone in attendance. A sugarcoated hard sell made in velvet tones.

He never even asked if the family had a budget for the funeral. Our families were often easy targets for an industry that knew how to say all the right things to get people to part with money they didn't have at a time when they were emotionally vulnerable.

The funeral director asked us to wait briefly in the lobby. Five minutes later, he came out and handed Roberta a sealed manila envelope. He told her to open it when she got home and go over it with her family. Clearly, the unspoken message here was "Your social worker needn't be present when you review it."

Walking back to the parking area, I reminded Roberta gently that those wonderful-sounding upgrades would add to a financial burden she'd end up carrying for years to come. As I spoke to her, I heard my own voice mimicking the honeyed tones the funeral director had used, and I was struck by the irony of it. We were both trying to utilize our powers of persuasion, but for totally different ends.

It was getting late, and I asked if I could drop by her house the next day to go over the bill with her. She agreed, but with no enthusiasm in her voice.

The following day, Roberta and I sat at her kitchen table, and she showed me the two-page-long bill filled with a list of all the options and upgrades. On each line, there was a place to check yes or no. To my dismay, she had checked yes to almost all of them. The total amounted to $6,000. I couldn't contain my shock.

"Four limousines?" I exclaimed. "Why four?"

Roberta looked at the kitchen floor as she answered, "Well, one will carry my sister, and the other three limousines will carry the family. We have a big family."

"You could save a lot of money if you had just two—the hearse for your sister and one limousine for the immediate family. Everyone else could take their own cars. I'm sure they wouldn't mind."

"No," she answered curtly. "This is what we want."

I looked over the rest of the bill and didn't say a word about the inflated cost of the flowers and the fee for a three-piece band and a singer, or anything else. I was fighting the impulse to offer another option, which I suspected Roberta would reject: cremation.

"You probably don't know this, but Children's Diagnostic has a relationship with the owners of a local crematorium who offer their services and a very nicely appointed chapel at absolutely no charge. They understand the crisis going on in the community and have genuine compassion for the people impacted by it."

"No. We don't want that," Roberta scolded, this time locking eyes with me. "My people don't do that."

I left regretting deeply that I hadn't used better judgment. When I returned to the CFAP building, I asked my supervisor, if I could meet with her to review the case. I knew I had most likely made some serious mistakes and really wanted to discuss this before I had to deal with the next funeral.

Marie is African American. After hearing how I'd handled things, she told me bluntly that little I'd said to Roberta took into consideration cultural differences. If she had known I was considering presenting cremation as a better financial choice, she would have told me not to bother. Cremation was anathema to our clients. I also learned from Marie that regardless of a family's financial situation, when it came to planning a funeral, frugality was rarely a priority. When planning the last act of love for their deceased relative, the length of time they'd be paying off the bill paled in comparison to knowing they did right by their loved one—and knowing as well that everyone in attendance had been impressed. It had to be a homegoing they could be proud of forever.

I appreciated what Marie had explained to me. This experience had pushed me into unfamiliar waters, and one might assume I drowned. But I chose not to look at it that way. Some genuine positives came out of this. It had been another useful lesson that would go a long way toward making me a better social worker as well as a better human being.

24

My Own Home

ALMOST THREE YEARS HAD PASSED since my husband and I had separated. As part of the separation agreement, Rick had agreed to pay the mortgage on our Las Olas Isles house for three years, and the time had come to sell it and move on to whatever was going to come next. I loved living in that "marital" house with its location on the river, lovely deck and pool, and beautiful specimen plantings, but rather than feeling uncertain about having to leave it, I found myself excited at the prospect. I would use the money from its sale to buy my own home.

I worked again with Yvonne, the realtor who had sold us the Las Olas Isles house. She knew my taste and had actually become a friend. One of the first houses she showed me was in the Fort Lauderdale neighborhood of Poinsettia Heights, a quiet community of pastel, predominantly modest, well-kept one-story houses built in the 1950s. We met in front of 1601 NE 16th Street, and Yvonne told me the home had been on the market for only one day. Its location was ideal: about two miles from my job and three miles from the beach.

I thought it could be a wonderful home, and it was within my price range. It had three bedrooms with handsome original terrazzo floors, and each bedroom had its own *en suite* bathroom. Unlike a lot of 1950s Florida houses, this one featured high ceilings, a solid oak floor in the living and dining rooms, and a brick fireplace, all of which reminded me of the house in Sea Cliff, Long Island, where I grew up. This house had a pool, plus a small pond with a waterfall, and a large variety of tropical plants. The backyard felt like a miniature Garden of Eden. I placed a bid at once, and to my delight it was accepted.

I told my children and friends that I was planning on never moving from this house. Because it was a corner property with a separate side door, ever practical me imagined that the live-in nurse I assumed I would need in my old age would have her own private entrance to her bedroom and bathroom. It was a house for all stages of my life!

Transformative Buoyancy

As the holidays approached, CDTC staff members who worked directly with clients found themselves in the throes of preparing for Christmas. It was definitely the most stressful time of the year for us. On top of the everyday responsibilities that come with large caseloads, we had to take on mountains of extra work to ensure that the neediest children would receive holiday presents. Tidal waves of gifts flowed in from the community and had to be sorted according to gender and age and then wrapped. It would have been impossible to handle the additional workload without the help and organizational skills of our dedicated volunteer auxiliary, the Sunflower Circle of Friends. They transformed the large community room in the main building into a kind of Santa's Workshop, with staff and volunteers taking shifts to sort and wrap thousands of presents.

Each department did its own decorating in the spirit of the holiday. We also had a half-day holiday party for which staff always did a deep creative dive and wrote and produced short plays or holiday songs with traditional or, preferably, original words. The outcome of this extra work was always huge fun, but it did add extra hours to our already full days.

At the end of one of the stressful, preholiday weeks, I decided to give myself a treat and spend a couple of hours on Sunday poking around local yard sales. The classified ad section in the *Sun-Sentinel* listed three yard sales on one street in my own neighborhood. Exiting my car at the first one, I immediately spotted something I had not expected to see but knew I would absolutely buy if the price were right. Awkwardly beached on the front lawn was a used, bright-red Old Town brand kayak with a paddle and life vest. It was love at first sight—and only $75.

When I asked the seller for recommendations of places to kayak, I was amazed to learn that my new house was just four minutes away from a boat ramp on the Middle River in the nearby community of Wilton Manors. I could easily launch the kayak from there and, within minutes, be paddling in an area teeming with wildlife. He also told me which turns to take on the river that would bring me past the backyards of homes no one could see from the road.

Shortly after I had become single, I traded in the family Mazda minivan for a used, low-mileage, sporty, two-door Honda Accord. It was never meant to carry a kayak; yet by folding down the back seats, sliding three quarters of the kayak in, and tying down the trunk over the part that was poking out, I could do it.

Back at work on Monday morning, the hours seemed to drag on endlessly. Since starting this job, I'd never once found work boring, and this day was no exception. However, the mental image of me in my new kayak paddling on the river was a considerable distraction. I made four home visits, met briefly with two clients in the clinic, wrote two essays about clients I hoped would be "adopted" for Christmas presents, caught up with Friday's unfinished documentation, and documented everything I had done today. It was finally time to go home. The red kayak was waiting for me.

I drove the car as close to the boat ramp as I could and lugged the kayak out of the trunk. I positioned it parallel to the river, half in the water and half on the cement ramp so that it wouldn't float away while I parked the car. I stood still for a moment and stared at the river lapping at its sides like liquid fingers beckoning it to get into the water.

Climbing in without assistance required a fine balancing act, but the moment I slid my body into the hull, sat down on the foam-rubber-covered plastic seat, and took my first couple of strokes—I hadn't kayaked in several years—I swear I could feel my blood pressure going down. Finally, I was gliding effortlessly down the river. Any sounds from the street were mostly muffled by the thick mangroves. The loudest sound was my paddle plopping in and out of the water. This was heaven. I felt relaxed and supremely lucky to be here on this calm stretch of the river with no one else around me. There was a light breeze at my back as I rounded a bend and steered myself into a cove densely surrounded by trees and mangroves on all sides.

Amazingly, the movement of my boat did not disturb a flock of white ibis standing on a small patch of sand. There were perhaps twenty of them. Another ten or so were wading in the water up to the knees of their long orange legs. They, too, were oblivious to my presence as they dipped their curved, bright-orange bills into the shallow water, intent on scooping up dinner. After reveling in the serendipity of this exquisite discovery, I let the current slowly carry me away from them. As if this image wasn't enough of a thrill, a lone osprey circled high above me, its shrill screams piercing the silence. I learned that that osprey was well known by local residents and had been named Ozzie. Ozzie would become a familiar sight each time I slipped my kayak into this same cove.

As the seller of my kayak had described, the next phase of my adventure took me past the backyards of homes. I became a floating voyeur. Paddling toward a large, coral-colored stucco home with a huge backyard, my eyes met those of a giant green lizard stretched out on the seawall, basking in the sun. He was at least four feet long, with spikes on his back and a fleshy hanging beard. He was both frightening looking and beautiful at the same time. We stared at each other for a minute. Evidently he was not pleased with what he saw and began a fast, wiggling run along the seawall, his tail swishing from side to side. He dove into the water and disappeared. Although awkward on land, he was a very fast, impressive swimmer.

At the end of the kayak trip, I felt like I had been on an eco-tour to a foreign country. I was relieved of any worry or tension that had built up during the workweek. My thoughts were on the wading ibis, the osprey, the lizard, and the lush mangroves. Paddling alone on the river was free therapy, which I routinely took advantage of for many years.

25

Angels Among Us

YEAR-ROUND, OUR PARTNERSHIPS WITH THE community were absolutely essential. In the mid 1990s, when so many children were seriously ill and dying from AIDS, one local church formed an AIDS ministry and took up collections, ran drives to outfit kids for camp, collected back-to-school supplies, and adopted children for Christmas presents.

In fact, many churches stepped up to help us with these important events, but by far the biggest outpouring of help came at Christmastime. We would create wish lists for the churches by asking our neediest families to give us the following information about their children: first name, gender, age, size, and what presents they would like. Some churches would put each name on a cutout of an angel to be hung on angel trees in the sanctuaries. The parishioners could select names and fulfill those children's special wishes.

But it wasn't only churches that supported us. Private community members, large and small businesses, fraternal and charitable organizations, schools, and our Sunflower Circle of Friends would also "adopt" children. They could do this by writing a check, and our staff would shop for the gifts, or the community members could shop on their own with our clients' wish lists in hand. The latter method was often preferred by families with children. It was seen as an opportunity to teach by example that we all have a responsibility to help others less fortunate.

An additional way to accomplish a part of the overwhelming job of providing so many Christmas presents each year was for the social workers to write short, compelling stories about their neediest clients and submit them to the *Sun-Sentinel* or the Broward edition of the *Miami Herald.* In truth, every one of our CFAP families had a compelling story, and it was not easy to whittle down our entries to only *the* most deserving. If our stories were chosen for publication, we would work hand in hand with the assigned reporters to help link them to the clients and assist with any needed post-publication follow-up.

These stories included personal, sometimes intimate, details about the families to help the papers' readers understand the overwhelming medical, psychological, and financial complexities our children and their parents lived with every day. They also enumerated the items that would genuinely benefit the families' lives. Only a handful of our submissions would appear in the papers, but the readership and exposure were so broad that the outpouring of generosity usually extended far beyond the few highlighted families, as you will see in the stories that follow.

Happy Endings: Three Holiday Stories

A Sofa Tells a Complicated Story

Shortly after Thanksgiving, I made my first home visit to a family recently added to my caseload. The Earlys lived in a low-income housing project known familiarly as the Green Apartments. There were twenty single-story buildings, with four apartments in each building. If viewed aerially, it looked like a large grouping of army barracks. The grounds were mostly devoid of trees and bushes, and the apartments were miserably maintained and infested with roaches. I was familiar with this particular Section 8 complex because a number of my families lived there.

Benita, the mother of nineteen-year-old Kimberly, shook my hand warmly and invited me inside. Kimberly was sitting with her legs tucked under her on a threadbare upholstered wing chair in the corner. She smiled at me but didn't get up. Her black hair was pulled up tightly in a ponytail, a style that accentuated her high cheekbones and dark, almond-shaped eyes. I turned to her and introduced myself as her new social worker. She didn't say anything in response.

Benita began by apologizing for the shabbiness of the cluttered apartment. I assumed the walls had once been painted white, but years of cigarette smoke, as well as neglect on the part of the landlord, had rendered them a dingy yellowish gray. The area rug in front of the sofa was worn thin and stained. Unframed family photos were Scotch-taped to the wall behind the sofa in a haphazard circle near a framed, but askew, photo of Dr. Martin Luther King Jr. giving a speech to a crowd. The end table was cluttered with mail and random small objects. There was one lamp in the room, a pole lamp with only one bulb working. It was doing a poor job of illuminating the room as the sunlight began to fade.

A young boy poked his head into the living room, saw me, and vanished.

"That's Elijah, my son. He's ten. Elijah, come out here and meet Miss Dale."

He walked into the living room and sat on the floor next to Kimberly's chair. Benita sat down on the sofa and indicated that I should, too. As she talked, I opened my notebook and began to document what the physical space was like. The faux leather material on the couch was ripped in a number of places and had been patched with electrical tape. At one point, hoping to avoid the spring that was digging into me but without embarrassing

Benita, I tried to shift my position unobtrusively. In spite of my discrete attempt, she had seen my ever-so-slight shift and apologized again.

"I am so sorry," she said. "It's old, and the springs are shot. My son, Elijah, doesn't have a bed, so he sleeps on the sofa. But he hates it. When he can't fall asleep, he goes into Kimberly's room, lays some blankets on the tile floor, and tries to sleep there."

Benita asked Kimberly and Elijah to go outside so that she could talk to me in private. Neither one of them wanted to go, and they began complaining loudly that there was nothing to do outside. Benita didn't tolerate their arguing with her and repeated herself, this time in a tougher tone of voice. They left, begrudgingly. As soon as the door shut, she began to talk.

"I have stuff I want to tell you about, but alone," she began. "I want you should know some things about me and Kimberly. I'm not ashamed to tell you because, well, it was what it was. DCF took my kids away from me eight years ago and gave them to my brother and his family in North Carolina. Although it tore me apart at the time, I realize it was the right thing to do. I was doing drugs and couldn't be a good mother to them. They lived with him until I got clean, and then I got them back. That was three years ago. But before I got Kimberly back, she was sexually molested, and that's how she got HIV. I believe the whole experience affected her real bad. I've been clean for five years now, and I'm trying to get my life back on a serious track. I'm taking computer courses at Broward Community College, and I work part time."

"You should be very proud of yourself," I told her. "Going to college, taking courses that may lead to a good, steady job, and you're also working part time. That's all wonderful. Would you mind telling me what your salary is and if it's enough to cover all your expenses?"

"I knew you were going to ask me how much money I make. That's okay. I get paid about twelve hundred dollars a month, and Kimberly gets a Social Security check for her disability. There's no way the three of us can live a decent life with this little money. Things that break don't get repaired or replaced—like the broken air conditioner or the refrigerator. You're probably going to say the landlord should pay for those repairs, but he won't. And I don't do any checkups for my car except change the oil. It's eight years old. I'm always afraid it's going to break down and I won't be able to afford to fix it. If that happens, I'm sunk. We have so many bills I don't know if I'll ever get out from under them to give my kids what they deserve."

I asked her to talk some more about Kimberly.

"Kimberly is developmentally challenged. She's like a third grader in a nineteen-year-old woman's body," Benita explained to me. "She's in the special ed program in high school, but even that has challenges for her. And she has big social problems, too. She needs a lot of supervision and support. She gets counseling sessions at CDTC, which is great, but it's not often enough. And she has some bad habits that aren't going to go away easily. When she gets upset or frustrated, which is often, she'll sometimes hurt herself with a sharp object. She also ran away from home a couple of times, which made me crazy with worry. She certainly won't go to college, and maybe never get a job. I'm afraid I'm going to have to take care of her for the rest of my life."

The kids began banging on the front door, demanding to be let inside. Benita sighed and looked at me. Her shoulders slumped. I could tell she had a lot more to say, but it would have to wait. She told me the kids fight a lot, and she didn't want anything to escalate outside where everyone could see and hear it. She got up and let them in.

Benita told Kimberly to show me her bedroom. The teenager led me into her room, and I noticed immediately that there were no curtains or blinds on the window, no dresser, no comforter; and just like in the living room, the walls looked like they hadn't been painted in years. There were two mattresses on her twin bed.

"Why are there two mattresses on your bed?" I asked her. "Well, the first mattress was so old and lumpy that my mother found another mattress and put it on top. Now I've got two mattresses, and they're both of them so lumpy I can't never get comfortable."

Walking back to the living room, I poked my head into the bathroom, and a sour smell hit me. There was mildew on the inside of the shower curtain and on the ceiling. A pile of what appeared to be damp clothes was on the floor. That explained the smell.

Everything I'd seen and heard led me to believe the Earlys would be strong candidates for either the *Sun-Sentinel*'s Santa Holiday Fund drive for needy children or the equivalent holiday drive run by the *Miami Herald*. I explained what they were to Benita and how Children's Diagnostic would also be able to help.

"CDTC's resources are limited, but we can help right away with some of the smaller things you need, like a shower curtain, a hamper, and a new area rug in front of the sofa. If you're agreeable to being interviewed by a reporter from the newspaper and having an article in the paper about your family, possibly with photos, then I will need to write a sensitive story about you all and submit it to the paper. If my story is chosen, then that's the way you'll be able to get the larger items you really need."

"Oh, I'm agreeable, all right! I'll pray every day that we're chosen."

"That's good. If you are chosen, you can expect to get a call from a reporter," I told her. Benita smiled, crossed her fingers on both hands, and gave me a hug.

A week later, a reporter from the *Sun-Sentinel* called me with the wonderful news that Benita's family had been selected. That afternoon, when I knew both kids would be home from school, I drove over to their apartment to tell them. Not surprisingly, they were thrilled. I prepared them for what to expect when the reporter came over.

"Not that I think you'll be shy, but you should be sure to tell the reporter all the important things you need. Just like you did for me, show her around the apartment. Don't forget to also mention some small things that would make a difference for you. Some readers will not be able to donate things like furniture but will want to contribute smaller items. The reporter may come up with some ideas of her own as well."

Elijah jumped up and down and shouted exuberantly, "A new sofa! I want a new sofa!" In mid-December the front page of the local news section carried a lengthy article about the family accompanied by a dramatic photo of the three of them sitting on—what else?—their decrepit old sofa. Benita had obviously taken what I said to heart and went into even greater personal detail about their difficulties than she had done with me. I was surprised she opened up quite so much, but I also understood that she saw a rare opportunity to make things better for her family and didn't want to waste it. Her candidness resulted in the story getting excellent play and an overwhelming response from the public.

The donations included a new sofa *and* loveseat, a kitchen table with four chairs, three floor lamps, a dresser and desk for Kimberly, bed pillows for all of them, china service for four, pots and pans, and some new clothing for everyone. Benita got a new full-size bed, and the kids got bunk beds. In addition, there was an unexpected surprise donation from Broward Community College and local radio station Y100: an all-expense-paid trip to Disney World, plus $200 in spending money.

Besides the Earlys getting everything they'd hoped for, there was a totally unexpected outcome to this story: the public donated such an overwhelming number of beds and mattresses that CDTC was able to provide many other struggling families with much-needed bedroom furniture. It was wonderful to realize that my one short story about the family moved so many people to donate so generously. In this case, a little effort went a *very* long way.

LESS THAN SIX DEGREES OF SEPARATION

When Christmas season rolled around the following year, I profiled five of the families I worked with and again submitted them to the *Sun-Sentinel* and the *Miami Herald* in the hopes that one or two would get adopted for Christmas presents by the papers' readers. On the first Saturday in December, I was working on the submissions while having my hair done. My hairdresser George asked what I was doing, and when I told him, he was intrigued.

George had no family members living in South Florida, so every Christmas he would fly to Puerto Rico to spend time with his nieces and nephews. He told me that this year he was unable to travel and was looking for something special to do in the holiday spirit. "Tell me about the families you're hoping will get adopted," he said. "I might want to pick one and buy presents for those kids."

I read the first two stories out loud to George and was in the middle of reading the third one when he said, "Stop!" That's the family I want."

Like George, Marisol was Puerto Rican, but he was drawn to this woman and her children because of far more meaningful reasons than a shared nationality.

After Marisol's biological children had grown and moved out of the house, she became a foster mother to dozens of special needs children over many years. She also adopted four of them: three young African American girls with AIDS, and the fourth with attention deficit hyperactivity disorder, or ADHD. One of the children with AIDS had died five years ago. What made the story even more touching was that Marisol herself had been diagnosed seven months earlier with biliary liver disease—a chronic disease in which the bile ducts in the liver are slowly destroyed. It can eventually lead to liver failure. She was desperately in need of a liver transplant.

George's enthusiasm for helping this family was off the charts. Marisol's three surviving adopted daughters, ages seven, five, and four, had made wish lists full of Barbie dolls, games they'd seen advertised on TV, and lots of new clothes. George began shopping as soon as the matchup was approved. He delivered his gifts on Christmas morning and called me the next day.

"When I was driving there, much to my surprise, I felt myself getting anxious," he said. "I was a total stranger coming into their home. I almost decided to just introduce myself, drop off the presents, and leave."

Thankfully, George's desire to meet this remarkable woman and her little girls trumped his feelings of anxiety. He told me the whole story, in great detail.

"Marisol was very warm and gracious. The little girls immediately began chattering and trying to guess what was inside their presents. Marisol got up to make coffee, and I followed her into the kitchen. She asked me where I was from in Puerto Rico, and we were both amazed to learn that we had grown up in the same small town.

"As she was making the coffee, I looked at the jumble of photographs on her refrigerator door. My eyes fell on a photo of a couple, dressed for a special occasion. It looked like it had been taken a long time ago. There was something familiar about those faces, so I moved closer to see them better. I couldn't believe my eyes. They were *my mother and father*! I asked Marisol how she knew these people, and she told me that the woman in the picture, my mother, was her mother's best friend throughout her school years in Puerto Rico. The photograph had been taken at Marisol's mother's wedding."

George then told Marisol that those people were his parents. Marisol screamed in surprise and threw her arms around him. Her parents had attended George's parents' wedding, too.

"I felt like I was in *The Twilight Zone*," he said laughing.

It got even stranger. As they talked about the relationships, George learned that his aunt was married to Marisol's uncle, meaning that he and Marisol were actually cousins by marriage.

Because of Marisol's failing health, George didn't waste any time setting up a grand reunion between his mother and Marisol. The two friends had not seen each other in twenty-four years. He arranged to fly his mother from Puerto Rico to Fort Lauderdale. Before this amazing, serendipitous event, George had had no relatives living in Florida. Now, because of it, he'd gained a wonderful extended family.

Do You See What I See?

Because I had lived up north for more than five decades, winter in Fort Lauderdale took a bit of getting used to. The arrival of December brought with it strange and incompatible feelings. How could it be eighty degrees outside, no forecast of snow—some days, not even a chill in the air—and yet the Department of Parks and Recreation employees were stringing up holiday lights all over town? Las Olas Boulevard, the famed main street filled with colorful downtown shops, restaurants, and galleries, was transformed into a dazzling wonderland with sparkling lights winding around bushes and palm tree trunks. The stores glowed with vibrant colors emanating from the outside as well as the inside. For local children, artificial snow was delivered and dumped on a side street for them to experience, perhaps for the first time in their lives.

But my clients' neighborhood didn't reflect much of this in any discernable way. Most families lived well below poverty level and couldn't consider using their limited funds to purchase holiday lights. Even the stores did little to acknowledge the holiday season with outdoor decorations. Whereas our families knew they could count on Children's Diagnostic and other nonprofits and local organizations to provide basic presents such as clothing, shoes, and toys, none of them, to my knowledge, gave Christmas lights as gifts.

My client Robert was eight years old and lived with his mother and older sister in a Section 8 apartment complex made up of four units. He was small for his age, thin, and not much of a talker. Because his diagnosis of AIDS had progressed, Robert had been hospitalized twice in the last year, and his prognosis was not good. Robert's mother had told me that he used to be boisterous and often got into trouble. Failing health had transformed him into a calmer, quieter child, one with low energy and no sparkle in his formerly lively brown eyes. Now his eyelids hung low, giving him the appearance of needing a good night's sleep. At this point in the progression of his illness, I knew that neither our medical staff nor I could make that sparkle return permanently, but I wanted to try to bring it back, if only for an hour or so.

At the end of my day, I drove over to Robert's apartment and asked his mother whether he had ever seen the Christmas lights on Las Olas Boulevard.

"No, he hasn't seen them. Nobody in my family has. I don't think I even know exactly where Las Olas Boulevard is," she answered.

I asked her for permission to drive him over there to see the lights.

"Of course. Come back any time after dinner, and he'll be ready to go," she said. "I know he'll love it."

While driving home, I made a decision to extend our ride together this evening by cruising by some other places Robert may never have seen. I plotted a circuitous route that would end at the holiday lights but include a few things along the way that a little boy might enjoy.

Robert answered the door when I rang the bell. I noticed he had changed his clothes, and I complimented him on how handsome he looked. He told me his mother said this was a special occasion and he should wear his church pants and shirt. I was very touched by how important his mother thought this little outing was going to be for him. I so hoped he wouldn't be disappointed.

When we got to my car, I told Robert he could sit up in the front with me, where he'd be able to see better, and I helped him fasten his seat belt. He sat there without speaking. Timewise, the drive from Robert's house to Las Olas Boulevard should take about ten minutes. Sociologically, in those few minutes, he would be journeying to what might as well be another country. He, like a lot of children in our program whose parents didn't own a car, rarely traveled outside his own neighborhood.

It was already dark when we drove out of his neighborhood and onto Federal Highway. I drove slowly so that he could look into the car dealerships on both sides of the street. Being holiday time, all the showrooms were lit up inside with gleaming cars vying for best-looking model. One in particular caught his eye: a sporty, two-door, shiny red Toyota Solara with an enormous white satin ribbon on its roof. Suddenly, my previously quiet passenger was bubbling up with chatter.

"Look at that one with the ribbon!" he shouted. "I think that car is going to be a really big Christmas present for someone. How will they get it under the tree?" He laughed with gusto, something I had *never* heard him do. I couldn't help but join in.

"What's that store up ahead?" he called out.

"You tell me what the sign says."

"It says toy store. Can we go in there?"

"We can't go in, Robert, but as we pass it, look inside and tell me what they're selling." Robert sat up tall in his seat as we slowly drove by.

"Cars, more cars. But why is it called a toy store?"

"They sell very expensive cars that really rich people buy," I answered. "Do you think it's possible those people might think of their cars as their toys?"

"Oh, maybe," he replied. "I would never think of a car as a toy—unless it's a Matchbox car!" He laughed again uproariously. "Get it? A Matchbox car!"

"I do get it," I said, laughing along. "You are quite the jokester today, kiddo."

Seeing Robert animated and enjoying himself like this was amazing. It filled me with happiness. The next turn I made sandwiched us in between downtown Fort Lauderdale's canyons of steel and marble office buildings. Robert tilted his head back as far as he could trying to look up into the multitude of lighted windows.

"Who lives in there?" he asked. "I don't see any people in any of the windows." I explained to him that these buildings were where people worked, not lived, and they had all gone home for the night. The lit-up windows were the offices being cleaned for the arrival of the workers the next morning.

I made a U-turn to head us back in the direction of Las Olas Boulevard. Suddenly we heard the clanging of bells. I knew what this meant, but I wasn't sure that Robert did. I couldn't believe our good fortune. We were going to be stopped by the lowering of the crossing gates for the freight trains that crept across Andrews Avenue once or twice a day on their way north to unload their goods. The clanging would always fill me with the dread of being made late for wherever I was going, but not now. What a serendipitous opportunity to delight a little boy.

I put my car in park, rolled down the front windows, and asked Robert if he knew what was going to happen. He did not. I explained it to him.

"Look to your left and see if you can spot the first train. You'll see a small white headlight coming slowly down the tracks toward us. As it gets closer and closer, it will get larger and larger, and then the parade of freight cars will start. There will be many, many cars, I promise you. We'll be here for a while as the trains s-l-o-w-l-y chug their way through the crossing."

Robert tucked his legs under him and sat up tall in his seat again watching for the first train. He yelled with excitement as the single bright headlight appeared in the distance.

"I see it! It's moving really slowly, but I see it!"

"Do you want to count the cars with me?" I asked.

"Sure I do!" he exclaimed as they began to rumble through. "One...two...three...four...sixteen...twenty-seven...twenty-eight... forty-five... forty-six... fifty-four... sixty-one... sixty-two... sixty-three...."

On and on and on it went until we had counted seventy-eight freight cars. His body and mind seemed to be locked in concentration while he was counting, but as soon as the last car disappeared from sight, his shoulders relaxed, he slumped back in the seat, and exhaled loudly.

"Whew! That was crazy. It was so long!"

A few minutes later, we were approaching Las Olas Boulevard, and Robert spotted the strings of white lights wrapped around the trunks of the coconut palms that lined the boulevard. The street was dripping with white and multicolored lights. The sound of Christmas carols wafted out the open store doors and into our open car windows.

"This is beautiful," he said softly. "I wish my mom and sister could see this."

Robert grew quiet again and stayed that way as I drove to the end of the shops and made a U-turn so he could see everything again. All the things Robert saw that evening delighted him, as it did me. It may be clichéd, but it's still meaningful to say how remarkable it is to be able to see the world through a child's eyes. I saw everything differently, with a certain wonder that hadn't been there for a long while. It wasn't only the holiday lights on Las Olas Boulevard; it was the skyscrapers, the car dealership windows ablaze with light, and the endless freight trains. I'd seen all these things a multitude of times, but in my haste to get somewhere, I had stopped noticing them. This evening, the mundane had become magical because of Robert.

Even though Robert's life was short, I know these images remained vivid in his mind. He told me so every time I saw him.

26

Little White Lie

A FEW WEEKS AFTER MY JOYOUS ride with Robert to see the holiday lights, my job took an undeniably different turn. In adjoining rooms at Broward General Medical Center, two of my clients lay in medically induced comas. Both six-year-old Janae and eighteen-month-old Sarita had come to the end of their short lives. It was unthinkable that I had two young children in beds not thirty feet from each other dying at the same time. Every day, I'd visit the hospital and go back and forth between their two rooms, trying to be useful and comforting to both families, knowing full well that no one could change the outcomes of these little girls' lives.

I would always find Janae's mother, Dawn, sitting there alone. Was her solitary state the result of her resistance to sharing her own or Janae's diagnosis with anyone? For family and friends, had she made up a different terminal diagnosis for Janae, one much less fraught with stigma?

Janae was Dawn's beloved only child. Dawn, a businesswoman, was assertive, strong willed, and a devoted single mother. She was, as the expression goes, in denial—but not about her daughter's AIDS diagnosis; that she acknowledged but couldn't share. At this point, her denial was about Janae's being at the end of her life.

Dawn's mindset about her own diagnosis was formed because she did not yet have any ill effects from HIV, and she told me quite adamantly that there was no reason to do anything about it—or even discuss it. When talking with a new client for the first time, I would always ask about her health and if she was receiving treatment or wanted to come to our clinic for care. I tried to have this conversation with Dawn, but she shut me down immediately. She said brusquely that her focus was her daughter and asked me not to bring this up again. I told her I would never push the issue with her but would always be available should she have any questions about medications, side effects, or anything related to our women's clinic or our medical staff.

Not wanting to leave Janae's bedside, Dawn had taken a leave of absence from her job. She stayed in the hospital room all day and slept in a reclining chair all night. Dawn's expectation was that Janae would wake up and be well or, at least, be well enough to go home. Every day, I would sit with Dawn in the hospital room, and we would chat, but never about Janae's impending death.

"It's National Bicycle Safety Day!" Dawn informed me one morning in a rush of words as I walked into the room. "The hospital is selling children's bike helmets for five dollars, and I just got her a new bike, but I haven't bought a helmet yet. Will you sit and watch Janae so I can go down to the lobby and buy one? She'll be so excited when she wakes up and I show it to her."

I couldn't bring myself to tell her that Janae would never wake up. I knew she had been told this before, as well as other upsetting things about her daughter's downhill slide and prognosis. Her response was always to flare up in anger at the medical staff. What purpose would it serve at this time for me to be yet another discouraging voice? Soon enough Dawn would be facing the unendurable truth.

So, I agreed to sit and watch Janae. But I suggested to Dawn that instead of buying her a bike helmet, which she might not be able to use for a while, that she buy Janae a bunch of balloons.

I lied and said, "You can attach them to the end of her bed, and when Janae wakes up, the balloons will be the first thing she'll see. They'll make the room more cheerful and make her really happy. What do you think?"

Dawn loved the idea, got up immediately, and went downstairs to the gift shop. When she returned, she was smiling broadly and carrying two large bunches of multicolored, bouncing balloons.

"I got a little carried away," she said, laughing. I had actually never seen her laugh. I made some silly joke about how that might have literally happened if the balloons were filled with helium. She laughed again. It was lovely to see her having a couple of moments of levity in a time of such seriousness. We busied ourselves tying the two balloon bunches to the ends of the bed.

Janae died a couple of days later. I never regretted telling Dawn that lie. It did, after all, give her a few days more of peace and hope. What could be wrong with that?

27

Rosie

IN THE ADJOINING HOSPITAL ROOM was eighteen-month-old Sarita, called Rosie by her family because of the reddish tint to her brown skin. Rosie's nineteen-year-old mother, S'marra, in stark contrast to Janae's mother, was always surrounded by family. Most days, there were three generations of women in the room. They sat and watched this tiny motionless baby who had tubes going down her throat and nose and projecting out from both sides of her chest, draining the fluid in her lungs.

S'marra's mother and grandmother did not sit in silence. When I walked in the room, I always found them chatting about relatives, friends, church, or meals they were going to cook. As soon as they saw me, their casual chatting stopped, and I knew they would start asking me to explain what the nurse or doctor had said to them. They told me they felt it wasn't their place to question a doctor or ask for something to be explained in simpler terms. They knew I would be there every day and looked to me for that. The women were very religious and believed the baby would go straight to heaven; however, they really wanted to understand what was happening to her before that took place. Anticipating this responsibility and fearing that I might not be able to rise to the occasion, I always stopped at the nurses' station and asked for a review of how the baby passed the night and early morning.

S'marra rarely asked me any questions and was always extremely quiet when I was there. I had witnessed the same behavior when she would bring Rosie into clinic. Months earlier, Dr. Puga told me that she'd had to chastise S'marra for often waiting until Rosie was quite sick before bringing her in to be seen, and mentioned that she rarely spoke while she was in clinic. In the hospital room, she always seemed to be listening carefully when we talked about Rosie's condition or treatment, but she never joined the conversation. I wondered if the thought that this might be her own fate may have been preying on her mind. I felt great tenderness for S'marra. No one teaches you how to act while watching your child die.

My phone rang one night about midnight. It was S'marra, and she was sobbing. "Can you come to the hospital? Rosie just passed. I don't know what to do."

Forty minutes later, I was at her side. Even though this outcome was expected, the three women looked shell-shocked. They were standing around Rosie's hospital bed, wiping away tears and not speaking. A nurse entered the room just seconds after I arrived. She asked S'marra if she would like all of Rosie's tubes removed so she could hold her, something she hadn't been able to do for nearly two weeks. I looked to them for a response, but there was none.

"Yes. Please do this," I said on their behalf. "We'll step outside." A second nurse entered the room, and the four of us exited and stood in the corridor. No one spoke. Because of the late hour, it was very quiet except for the hushed voices at the nurses' station and the beeping of the telemetry machines.

When we reentered the room, it was the first time any of us had seen Rosie without a blanket covering her and without tubes coming out of her. The nurse had dressed her in a sweet, pink floral nightgown. Now untethered from all the tubes, she looked like any sleeping baby as she lay there, so small and delicate.

Wordlessly, S'marra walked over to the night table and opened the top drawer. She took out a jar, unscrewed the lid, and dipped her middle finger into it. Tenderly, she put small dabs of cream on Rosie's face and smoothed it into her forehead, cheeks, and chin. Rosie's face would shine as she made her way to heaven. S'marra then leaned over her baby and began to cornrow Rosie's remaining thin wisps of hair. Because of the placement of the tubes, she had never been able to lift Rosie's head off the pillow. You could tell S'marra was on a mission. She would make her baby look just the way she used to look before this horrible virus changed everything.

When she finished grooming Rosie, S'marra turned to me and asked, "What do I do now?"

"Would you like to sit in the rocking chair with Rosie? You haven't been able to hold her for weeks. Now you can."

It was a heartbreaking image, this young mother rocking and caressing her dead baby. When S'marra finished, she stood up and wordlessly handed the baby to her mother. Her mother sat down in the rocking chair and glided back and forth with her motionless little granddaughter pressed against her breast. She, in turn, placed Rosie in her mother's arms to rock. I stood against the wall, my fist pressed against my mouth, holding back the sobs that wanted so much to escape. I watched in silence, overwhelmed both by the sad choreography of the women's movements and by a feeling of deep gratitude that the family had asked me to be with them at this time.

S'marra's grandmother stood up and placed Rosie back in S'marra's arms. S'marra walked the few steps to the bed and laid her down ever so gently. She ran her hands over the pink nightgown, smoothing out imaginary wrinkles. She leaned over the bed and tenderly kissed her baby's forehead, allowing her lips to linger there. S'marra's tears ran down her own face and onto Rosie's.

When she turned her head and looked up at me, she said, sobbing, "What do I do now?"

"Now we'll all go home," I answered.

Channeling Rosie's Poem

Janae's funeral was for family only. Being able to attend Rosie's funeral helped me, in part, to get over the sadness of going through both those little girls' consecutive deaths. Even now, if I recount this story to someone, when I talk about Rosie lying in the hospital bed after the tubes had been removed from her tiny body, even now, my throat tightens with emotion.

A week after Rosie's funeral, I was home sitting at my computer when I was unexpectedly gripped by those hospital room images. I had never in my life experienced anything like watching those three women caress and care for that little deceased baby. I began writing a poem, the words pouring out of me. I had the unexplainable sensation that standing at my shoulder, guiding me, were the women I had come to know who were stumbling through the terrifying experience of watching their children become sick and die.

In 1994, President Bill Clinton issued a proclamation recognizing December 1 as World AIDS Day and encouraged "every American to participate in appropriate commemorative programs and ceremonies . . . to reach out to protect and educate our children and to help and comfort all people who are living with HIV and AIDS."

A few months after Rosie's passing, I was asked to read "Last Acts" at Fort Lauderdale's World AIDS Day event on

December 1, 1998. I was honored but not comfortable reading it myself. Instead, I asked one of my African American colleagues to read it in my place. I didn't feel my voice could do justice to the words.

I invited S'marra to join me at the event. There was a huge crowd. To my delight, she showed up and stood next to me, clutching a framed photograph of Rosie in one hand and a framed copy of the poem I had given her in the other.

"They're next to each other on my mother's wall," she said. "They'll always be together there."

My eyes filled with tears. I gave S'marra a long hug and let her know how much this meant to me. Social workers don't get financial bonuses or tangible rewards, but the nature of the work we do can afford us invaluable moments like this when we know how important our work is and how much we are able to touch people's lives.

Many years later, in 2017, I got a phone call from my son, Jordan. He was on vacation in Fort Lauderdale with his husband, Nicholas, and they were attending the World AIDS Day event. He told me the most amazing thing. They had been part of a candle-lit march to a spot where people from various local AIDS organizations were addressing the assembled crowd. A woman from Children's Diagnostic & Treatment Center came up to the podium and announced that she would read a poem called "Last Acts," written by me during the mid 1990s when so many women and children were dying from AIDS. Jordan's shock at hearing his mother's name and listening to the words of the poem he had never heard before so overwhelmed him that he called me in tears and told me how proud of me he was.

That day, I learned that Rosie's life and the life of her mother have been spoken of and memorialized for decades. What a wonderful thing for them and a treasure for me. The life of a tiny African American baby was neither forgotten nor ignored but held up as a symbol of so many thousands of other children who were deeply loved but perished because of AIDS.

Last Acts

Let me plait your hair
my sweetheart, my Rosie.
Weeks have passed
with your head resting on the pillow,
hair napping up,
braids untwisting.
Let me comb out your knots.
I'll be careful not to pull too hard.
I know it can't hurt you now
but even so, I'll still be gentle.
I'll make the rows so neat.
My fingers will make the familiar journey
up and down your head
for the last time.
They'll never weave these paths again.
Let me grease your face
and make you shine for eternity, Rosie.
I want your skin to glow
as you make your way to God.
Let me rock you now in the hard wooden chair.
We'll glide back and forth
as if on the swells of an ocean you've never seen.
And then…
and then…
I'll go home too.

28

Tina

TINA WAS SIXTEEN YEARS OLD when she was placed on my caseload. She was a petite, thin young woman with high cheekbones and intense dark eyes that never seemed to meet mine. I don't recall ever seeing her in any shoes other than flip-flops or bedroom slippers. I also don't recall her ever smiling. Her mother, Janelle, and her two-year-old sister, Carina, had already been working with another social worker when Tina decided to come into care. All of them were infected.

Over the four years I worked with Tina, I always found her to be frustratingly reticent, except when she wanted something tangible such as a bus pass, or when she would show up unannounced expecting to see a doctor right away for what she had determined was a medical emergency. Tina's suspicions were rarely wrong on these occasions. Why? She routinely did not appear for her regularly scheduled clinic appointments. If she was feeling well, she didn't see the sense in coming. But when a condition worsened, she became demanding and expected to be seen immediately.

We got along well because I accepted the reality that the only way I was going to be successful at helping her become healthier was by doing what she asked—if I could. She needed to feel assured that, if the request was reasonable, I would go out of my way for her. When she wanted to be seen by the doctor immediately, I would gently prepare her for the probability that it wouldn't happen, walk with her down the hall to the clinic, and advocate for her to be seen. In spite of my best efforts, if they were not able to see her that day, her temper would flare up at the clinic staff. She had a short fuse and no veneer of "niceness." If stressed, she immediately became confrontational.

Tina was a nomad. Arranging a home visit was almost as difficult as setting up a face-to-face meeting with the president of the United States. She moved around a lot and never wanted to commit to a day or time for me to come by. Sometimes she lived with her mother, but more often than not, she stayed with a relative or a friend.

Over the course of less than two years, I remember Tina having three medical emergencies. Two of them were the unpleasant consequences of having had unprotected sex, and all of them required the attention of specialists. It was while sitting together in the gynecologist's and the surgeon's waiting rooms that I tried to get to know her better. It was a struggle. She answered my questions but offered little or no additional information. I told her about the teen-specific services we could offer and tried to interest her in participating in a weekly group session run by our CFAP psychologist. She would have none of it. I offered to show her the little house we had set up two blocks away from the clinic as a drop-in center for teens. Tina told me she preferred hanging out with older people.

When I asked why she wasn't in school, she answered very matter-of-factly that she had dropped out when she was fourteen because it was a waste of time. It wasn't until I broached the subject of drug use that she turned around and looked me squarely in the eyes. With no hesitation, she admitted that she "came up" around drugs and started smoking pot with her friends when she was thirteen. I asked if she had ever used anything stronger, and her demeanor shifted. She leaned closer to me.

"No! I haven't, and I never will! I *know* what addictions do to people." She said nothing more. I thanked her for telling me this and made a mental note to speak with her mother's social worker about any addiction in the family. Perhaps this was why she rarely stayed at Janelle's.

Each of the three times Tina was called into the examination rooms for what would be three physically uncomfortable procedures, she asked me to come in with her. She told me to stand by her side and asked if I would hold her hand. The first time she asked me to do this I became flooded with feelings of tenderness toward her to the point where I had to hold back tears. Infrequent as these expressions of her vulnerability were, they revealed chinks in her seemingly impenetrable façade and were powerful reminders to me of how young and in need of kindness and nurturing she truly was.

Unable to learn much about the teenager's life from Tina, I asked her if she would be comfortable letting me talk to her mother. She said she didn't mind, and I invited Janelle to meet with me in my office. I learned far more from her than I could have possibly imagined.

Unlike her daughter, Janelle had a gregarious personality and was a loquacious talker. She exhibited no inhibitions when it came to sharing aspects of her own and her daughter's lives, no matter how dark and disturbing many of them were. She made no excuses for herself—neither for her behavior nor for the poor choices she had made in her life. She accepted responsibility, at least in part, for some of the things she had done in the past that had negatively affected Tina's life. This willingness to reflect honestly and own up to the hurt she had caused others is an essential part of the Narcotics Anonymous healing process for recovering addicts. Janelle didn't just accept this but embraced it.

She was not surprised when I told her Tina wouldn't open up much to me. She said she wanted her daughter to get some help, and in order for me to help her, Janelle felt I needed to understand how Tina had become so suspicious of others and walled herself off to avoid getting hurt.

Janelle was only seventeen when her daughter was born. For many years of Tina's life, their relationship was fraught with problems; however, when describing her as a little child, Janelle insisted that Tina grew up feeling loved. Her father spoiled her and took her everywhere he went. She was smart and pretty, and she loved to color, sing, and dance. That description could have applied to tens of millions of little girls; unfortunately, Tina's happy life began to crumble before she turned three years old, dramatically separating her life from that of most other little girls.

Janelle had not used drugs when she was pregnant, but sometime after Tina was born, she relapsed and went back to using crack. Tina's father, Johnny, was also a crack addict. Janelle admitted that their lifestyle made it impossible for them to provide their daughter with a healthy home environment.

Her recounting of the next series of events felt, at first, like listening to an audio book. Although she was telling me this particular story eight years after it occurred, she demonstrated an almost photographic memory for events. Not only was the information told in vivid detail but her words were delivered rapid-fire, with fierce emotional intensity.

A deeply consequential turning point came when Tina was eight years old. Johnny learned that an acquaintance of his had a lot of money in his house and decided to rob him. Janelle argued with him unsuccessfully, warning him not to do this. He went into the man's house anyway, carrying a pellet gun in his pocket. Janelle stood across the street, anxiously waiting. The robbery failed, and no shots were fired, but the victim called the police. Despite Janelle's not having taken part in the robbery, both she and Johnny were arrested and jailed for three months. Tina went to live with Johnny's sister LaDon in West Palm Beach.

When Janelle was released from jail, the first thing she did was take a bus to LaDon's to pick up Tina. But LaDon refused to give her back. After a heated argument, Janelle left, realizing she probably would not be able to get Tina back on her own. Because of her three-month incarceration, Janelle had lost her apartment and had to move in with her sister, Laura, in Fort Lauderdale.

While she was living there, a relative in Palm Beach County called to tell her that Johnny had been released from prison and had taken Tina back from his sister to live with him. This relative added some enormously disturbing news: Johnny was using Tina to steal crack for him. The dealers would often hide their packages of crack on the ground under fallen palm tree fronds. Tina and her father would watch them from a distance and wait for the dealers to leave. At her father's direction, Tina would then run to the trees, grab the drugs, and run back to Johnny with them.

Upon hearing this, Janelle became deeply alarmed for Tina's safety and knew she had to get her away from Johnny immediately. But because Tina had become a valuable asset to her father, Janelle realized any attempt on her part to take Tina away from him could turn quite dangerous. She hatched a plan to rescue her daughter by having Laura, her brother, a male cousin, and a male friend come with her.

They all drove to Johnny's house in a van. Janelle and her sister walked up to the house and knocked on the door while the others watched from inside the vehicle.

Johnny opened the door, saw them, and knew immediately they weren't there for a friendly visit. From inside, Tina spotted her mother through the open door and was so happy to see her that she charged right past her father and jumped into Janelle's arms. With Tina clinging to her, Janelle turned and ran toward the van. Johnny raced after them and yanked Tina out of Janelle's arms. Father and daughter fell to the ground with him on top of her. Tina squirmed and screamed and resisted so much that Johnny wrapped his legs around her to hold her still. Janelle said she and Laura were also screaming and described the whole event as an awful scene.

By now, the three men in the van had poured out and began punching Johnny while Janelle and her sister pried Johnny's legs off Tina. Janelle grabbed Tina by the hand and ran with her to the van. In short order, Johnny had been subdued and was lying prostrate on the ground. Having successfully rescued Tina, everyone climbed into the van and headed back to Fort Lauderdale.

For addicts, incarceration is often a kind of involuntary rehab. Janelle went into jail addicted. Three months later, she came out clean but without any support systems in place. Not surprisingly, she immediately returned to using crack. In spite of this, Janelle was determined to restore some semblance of normalcy to Tina's life. The first thing she had noticed when Tina ran through the open door and into her arms was that

Tina's hair was unwashed, uncombed, and totally nappy. This problem was easy to see and easy to solve, but the next one was a hidden problem Tina did not tell her mother about right away. She was suffering from an advanced case of pinworms. It was so serious that when she had a bowel movement, the worms were clearly visible all over the surface of the stool. Janelle, horrified, took her immediately to a clinic. The condition was quickly treated with medication.

The next "condition" she learned about could not be cured quickly or treated with medication. Tina told her mother about a twenty-year-old man who used to routinely come over to her auntie's house and "mess with her." Although being quite sure what "mess with" meant, I asked Janelle to define it for me. In a low voice, with her eyes cast down, she said, "Have sex with her." *Tina was eight years old.*

When I asked whether charges were ever brought against this man, I learned that a case manager had helped Janelle do this. On the day Tina was scheduled to go before the judge and relate what had happened to her, there were family members waiting in the courthouse hallway. Some of these people had a long history of not getting along with one another. Janelle then recounted a convoluted story about how a huge fight broke out among the relatives, with punches being thrown wildly. Three family members were put in a holding cell and Tina's court date was postponed. Janelle didn't know what happened to Tina's abuser, and most unexpectedly, she told me they never went back to court again.

Despite Janelle's addiction to crack, most aspects of her life began to improve around this time. She got a good job with benefits in the bakery department at a Publix supermarket. She rented a studio apartment and fashioned a private little room in it for Tina. The most hopeful change was that Janelle made a new friend who became a mentor to her and took her to weekly Narcotics Anonymous meetings. Soon after meeting him, she stopped smoking crack and began attending court-mandated counseling.

When Tina was nine years old and in the fourth grade, her teacher reported that she was doing well both academically and socially. At home, however, she was an entirely different child. She refused to go anywhere or do anything with Janelle. She would either rage at her or not speak to her at all. Janelle had little patience for this behavior. She felt she had done so much personal work to make things better for Tina and for their lives, yet in spite of her best efforts, her daughter didn't seem to care. She was always angry.

Janelle complained to her counselor about Tina's nasty attitude, and the counselor suggested Tina come in to talk with her. At first, Tina refused to go but ultimately gave in to her mother's pleadings.

At one unforgettable session, the counselor was trying to give Tina an opportunity to talk about the abuse she had endured. She asked Tina what she would do if she had a chance to get back at the man who hurt her so much. Tina didn't answer. The counselor handed Tina a stuffed male doll and asked her to pretend the doll was that man. With not a moment's hesitation, Tina threw it against the wall, stomped on it, and twisted its neck. She did everything she could to "torture" the doll.

Witnessing the depth of her daughter's fury made it clear to Janelle how much trauma Tina had experienced. She felt both hopeless and helpless to change anything and resorted to doing what many addicts do in the face of overwhelming pain or guilt:

she returned to using drugs. She told me dejectedly, "I did all I did for nothing."

Over the next five years, Janelle and Tina's relationship grew worse. They argued about everything. A particularly bad moment for Janelle came when she learned that fourteen-year-old Tina and a friend had been robbing school kids and taking their book bags and cell phones. While watching local news on TV one night, Janelle saw her own daughter being chased by the police and outrunning them. As Janelle talked and I listened, the revelations became exponentially more alarming and difficult to listen to.

Janelle had started a new relationship with a man named Phillip and had become pregnant by him. In her third month of pregnancy, Janelle was tested for HIV and learned she was positive. She had been tested before, and the results had always been negative. Phillip had never shared his diagnosis with her, and upon learning of her HIV status, she was both enraged and shattered. Something even more shattering would soon come on the heels of this.

One afternoon Janelle returned home after visiting her mother. She was walking toward the bathroom and passed her and Phillip's bedroom. The door was open, and she looked in and saw Phillip and Tina both standing in the room looking "strange." The bedsheets, as well as Tina's clothes, were messed up. Automatically suspicious, she asked Tina why her clothes looked like that. She received an answer no parent ever wants to hear.

"Phillip raped me, Ma! He raped me!"

Phillip denied it forcefully but was unable to make eye contact with Janelle.

"You ruined *my* life and maybe my unborn baby's life!" Janelle screamed at him. "And now you did it to *her*?"

The police were called, and Phillip was arrested and jailed. Tina and Janelle were driven by a DCF social worker to a doctor's office, where Tina was examined by a rape specialist and given an HIV test.

Janelle did not sit idly by. She retained a Legal Aid Society attorney and took Phillip to court for raping a minor. He was found guilty and sentenced to eight years in prison—an incredibly lenient sentence for raping a young girl and infecting her with a terminal illness.

No case was brought against Phillip for infecting Janelle, which, sadly, resulted in the transmission of the virus to Janelle's unborn daughter. Carina was born in 1994 and would die of AIDS at the tender age of four and a half. All this pain was caused by the actions of one thoroughly irresponsible and depraved man.

Tina loved her little sister, as did everyone who met her. Carina was an animated, loving, adorable little girl. The emotion Tina exhibited while talking about Carina's early death was not just sadness but also anger that her baby sister had been mortally hurt by this same person who had so grievously harmed her and her mother.

Without Janelle's openness and willingness to share so much of Tina's deeply troubled childhood, I would not have understood anything about the root causes of her challenging teenage personality. Tina had been exposed to a dangerous world at a young age and had learned to survive against terrible odds. When she was old enough to navigate her own life, she always tried to do it on her terms. Once I understood the traumas she had experienced, these behaviors were no longer mysterious or off-putting, and I was better able to accept Tina where she was.

29

Sex and Stigma

WHEN MIRIAM MARRIED HER SECOND husband, he brought with him his two-year-old son and an infant daughter. Having raised four children of her own who were already adults, Miriam knew a lot about childrearing, yet she couldn't understand why this baby was sick so often. The family took her from one doctor to another, yet none would render a definitive diagnosis. Finally, Miriam found a physician who was savvy enough to order a blood test for HIV. Carla tested positive. Although this information was shocking and deeply sad, it answered the question about the child's health that Miriam had been struggling with for so long.

Knowing Carla was positive did not deter her from loving her stepdaughter as her own or from staying focused on her mission to keep the girl as healthy as possible for as long as possible. Even after Miriam's husband walked out, she continued to raise his two children; however, over time it became harder and harder.

Carla became my client when she was fourteen. She was naïve, too trusting, and incredibly headstrong. Like teenagers everywhere, she didn't want to listen to reason and didn't want to be told what to do. But there were two big differences between Carla and most other kids her age: she not only had HIV but also was severely delayed developmentally. Her stubbornness and poor decision-making often led to disastrous results.

Miriam didn't have a car, so to help Carla get around and hopefully to facilitate her trip from school to clinic appointments,

I arranged for her to have her own bus pass. Sometimes she did come by herself directly from school. Other times, Miriam accompanied her on the bus, or they came together by taxi. Quite often, she was a no-show.

Carla refused to take her medications regularly, something she and her mother argued about all the time. She refused to believe Miriam, me, or the clinic staff when we all told her that this would negate her medication's effectiveness and allow the virus to multiply, making her sicker. It didn't matter what anyone said. If Carla felt well, which, thankfully, she did most of the time, she did not want to think about having an incurable disease or what her future might hold.

A major concern for Miriam and everyone involved with her case was that we all knew Carla was having sex. When asked, she didn't hesitate to admit it. None of us could stop her, so we had to do the only proactive things we could: keep her well supplied with condoms, routinely reiterate how HIV was passed from one person to another, raise the issue of her responsibility to a sexual partner, and remind her of the guilt she would feel if she learned she had infected another student.

Was I confident that she would insist her partners wear the condoms? No. Even our adult clients found this to be a near-impossible position to take in their relationships. Did she seem to understand what it meant to put her classmates at risk? Again, no. Carla wanted desperately to be popular and attract the attention of boys. Unfortunately, she was incapable of differentiating between good and bad attention.

Whether or not we knew our clients were sexually active, all of us who worked with adolescents had to address this issue. We also had to help them deal with the stigma they would face if they should share their diagnoses. Not many of our young clients were the slightest bit interested in doing this, but Carla, for some reason, was.

The teen attended a special education program in a large public high school. No matter how many times she was warned about the social risks of telling people she had HIV, she did so anyway. The desire to unburden herself must have been overwhelming. She made the decision that it would be okay if she told only one person: her best girlfriend. One day between classes—hardly a perfect time—Carla shared her secret and made her girlfriend promise not to tell anyone. Her girlfriend kept Carla's secret only until the buzzer signaled the changing of the next class.

Earlier that morning, Carla had gotten off the school bus an ordinary girl with friends she trusted. By the afternoon, unbeknownst to her, she had become a social pariah, as news that the girl was HIV-positive passed rapidly from student to student. She was taunted, humiliated, and whispered about not only by kids known to her, but by kids she had never met.

Later that day, Miriam phoned me to say that Carla had come home in tears and told her the catastrophic results of having confessed her HIV status to her friend. Miriam tried to protect her daughter from further hurt by telling her she didn't have to go to school the next day. Carla agreed to this temporary "solution" and walked into her room looking dejected and depressed. She didn't come out until dinner. When she did emerge, she had done an about-face. Carla told her mother that she actually *wanted* to go to school because she wasn't going to "let them win."

In her adolescent way of dealing with what happened, she summed it all up with a kind of bravado by saying, "They're just stupid. They can't hurt me."

I talked to Carla about this at her next clinic appointment.

"When it happened, I felt more angry than hurt," she said thoughtfully, showing a surprising level of maturity in identifying her emotions. "I was angry at my friend for breaking her promise to me and angry at the other kids in the school for gossiping about me."

I asked gently if she might also be angry about having been born with a disease that had caused her so much unhappiness. She thought about my question for a moment and shrugged her shoulders.

"I don't really understand how I got it from the woman who gave birth to me. She gave birth to me and just disappeared. I don't remember her."

Since she had no memory of her birth mother and had never even seen a picture of her, it was difficult for her to focus her anger there. However, with genuine insight, Carla stated she knew it was impossible for her to be the only infected person in her entire large school.

"I know kids who are absent a lot. I even know of one who died. Maybe they had it, too. I once had a conversation with a girl who said her uncle had 'that shit.'"

What Carla didn't realize, nor I at the time, was that by revealing her diagnosis and having that news spread throughout the school, she had done what none of us could: she abruptly ended her high school sex life and all our concerns about it as well.

Keeping Confidentiality

It was Carla's choice to share her HIV status. She was under no legal constraint to keep her own diagnosis confidential. All the employees at Children's Diagnostic, however, were absolutely prohibited from revealing anyone's medical information. We had to follow the guidelines of the Health Insurance Portability and Accountability Act (HIPAA) which states, among other things, that as healthcare providers and employees of a healthcare business, we are prohibited from disclosing protected information to anyone other than a patient and the patient's authorized representatives without their consent. However, unlike doctors or attorneys, who have to take an oath to uphold certain standards, including patient or client confidentiality, we did not have to take a formal oath. We were taught and reminded regularly that we had the professional obligation to never reveal the medical diagnoses or treatment regimens of the patients and clients the agency served. I can say with confidence that we all knew this in the depths of our souls. We strove to take this responsibility as seriously as do priests who hear secrets in confession.

On its face, this seems like an easy thing to do: you just never tell anyone your client's diagnosis unless that person has a genuine need to know. Who would have such a need to know? Examples might be consulting doctors, dentists, or emergency medical technicians. However, these people were trained to assume that everyone they treated might have HIV, and they knew to take the necessary precautions. Teachers do not have a need to know their students' medical conditions. Attorneys do not need to know their clients' medical conditions—unless, of course, their case revolves around a client's diagnosis or medical condition. A landlord does not need to know a prospective tenant's diagnosis.

One might assume that no landlord would ever ask such a question. Yet one of my clients was turned away by a landlord at the door of an apartment she was considering renting. She was furious and certain that she had been turned away because she was Black. I told her that in all likelihood she was right. She was furious at him and asked me to talk to the man and try to find out why he wouldn't even let her in the door. Even though I suspected my advocacy would be futile, I did call him. I introduced myself, told him I was from Children's Diagnostic, and that I was calling about a client of mine whom he recently met and wouldn't show her an apartment.

"Oh. I know about you," he stated in an unpleasant tone of voice. "You take care of sick children, but you also take care of people with AIDS. Does she have AIDS? If she does, well, I don't rent to people with AIDS."

I snapped right back at him and told him she did not have AIDS (which was actually true; she had HIV) and informed him that it was illegal for him to discriminate against any prospective tenant based on his suspicion that the person might have AIDS. He hung up on me.

My client was certainly right. From the landlord's behavior and words, I was confident he initially discriminated against her because of her color. He then double discriminated against her because of a disease he only suspected she had.

Not only were employees of Children's Diagnostic not allowed to disclose anyone's medical condition or diagnosis, we also had to be extremely cautious about revealing something unintentionally through nonverbal behavior. As an example, attendance at certain events can place us in a kind of confidentiality minefield. At clients' funerals, I always had to be mindful that there might be people at the service whom I knew to be HIV-positive. I could not acknowledge any of them with a greeting, a smile, or even something as minimally suggestive as nodding my head. In the highly segregated African American neighborhoods where I worked, White people attending the funeral of a Black HIV-positive person would likely be medical or social services staff who had worked with the deceased. Any demonstrable recognition of someone in the pews could raise suspicion that the one being greeted was also receiving HIV services.

There were, however, other venues or events where this issue was not front and center in my mind. One Sunday afternoon my friend Eva and I were walking across the Sunrise Boulevard drawbridge on our way to a special event taking place on Las Olas Beach. There were streams of people coming and going across the bridge. I spotted one of my teenage clients walking toward us with a small group of friends. She saw me, too. I opened my mouth ever so slightly to smile at her and say hello. The moment I did that, my client's eyes grew huge with abject fear, communicating "Please don't acknowledge me!" I extinguished my smile and looked away.

Saying hi or simply smiling had seemed innocent enough until I saw the terror on her face. My smile could have wreaked havoc on her life. Undoubtedly, one of her friends would have asked, "How do you know that White lady?" If my client were a nimble thinker, she might have come up with a quick response that her friends would have accepted. But if she couldn't think quickly enough on her feet, I might have put her in a terribly awkward position. That encounter lasted only a matter of seconds, but it has stayed in my memory all these years.

Another brush with the challenges of not breaching confidentiality lasted not seconds but weeks. My friends Barbara and Gerald owned a spacious home with a small apartment attached to it in the nearby city of Hollywood. Barbara told me in a phone call that they had recently offered it to an adorable couple with a three-year-old daughter. They had met this family at a local street fair and spent part of the afternoon together chatting and watching the little girl run from one ride and game to another. The wife was from Switzerland, the husband Cuban, and they were currently living in Miami, where they shared a cramped apartment with friends. Neither they nor their friends were happy about this situation; however, the couple was unable to move out until the husband got a steady job and was able to save enough money for a deposit on an apartment.

Barbara and Gerald were so taken with this little family, so touched by their plight and charmed by their little girl that they offered to let them stay in their apartment rent free until the husband could find work. I was surprised by how easily they had invited these strangers into their lives without first checking references or getting a credit report. All of them were happy about the outcome, so I chose not to mention my concerns. End of story—or so I thought.

Shortly after my conversation with Barbara, a new family was added to my caseload: an HIV-positive Swiss woman in her early thirties named Mireille; her Cuban husband, Raúl, in his late twenties and not HIV-positive; and Sarah, their three-year-old daughter, who was HIV-positive. Both parents were unemployed and lived in Hollywood. It was immediately obvious to me that these people were Barbara and Gerald's new tenants. This was an amazing coincidence and one I hoped would not end up putting me in an awkward position.

Before I officially met Mireille, Sarah, and Raúl, they were seen in the clinic. Raúl, of course, was not being seen medically but accompanied his wife and daughter to their appointments. Mireille was a slender, attractive woman, about five foot five, with light brown hair and blue eyes. Her Swiss accent was strong, but her English was excellent, and she was engaging and open. She volunteered that she had already started on HIV medications when they were living in Miami but hated taking them. In answer to my question about whether she was experiencing side effects, Mireille assured me she was not, at least not yet, but it was a struggle to remember when and how to take which pills. Having been part of our own CFAP placebo medication experiment, I understood quite well what she was talking about and told her of my own and my colleagues' experiences. She was amazed that we had done that.

Raúl, slim at about five foot ten, with dark hair and dark-brown eyes, had received an engineering degree from a Cuban university. He had a strong accent and his English was not terribly good. He defected to the States, hoping to make a better life for himself here, but as an undocumented immigrant with mediocre English skills, he found it impossible to find work as an engineer, so he had been applying for jobs as a handyman. He expressed frustration at having so much trouble finding work. I told him how to enroll in a free English as a second language (ESL) course, gave him my copy of the *Sun-Sentinel*, and told him to look through the classified ads. I also encouraged him to pick up a copy of the Hollywood *Pennysaver* and look for jobs there.

Sarah was quieter than most three-year-olds. She sat contentedly on her mother's lap the whole time her parents and I talked. The little girl resembled her mother much more than her father. She was thin, perhaps too thin. Mireille reported that the doctor recommended Sarah drink as much Ensure as she could tolerate every day, because it contained vital nutrients and also might help her put on some weight. Sarah caught colds very easily and had a history of mild respiratory infections. She was not on any medications.

When a first visit with a client wasn't a home visit, naturally, there had to be a conversation about where the clients live. This was the part I knew might make me a little uneasy because I already knew where they lived. I had come to the conclusion that the best way for me to handle this was just to listen, take notes, and make generic comments when appropriate. Mireille described exactly the same scenario that Barbara had: they'd all met at a street fair. Both Mireille and Raúl gushed with gratitude when talking about Barbara and Gerald and the apartment they felt so lucky to have. I agreed with them and expressed amazement at their good fortune.

I set them up with monthly bus passes, a referral to the Poverello Food Bank, and a voucher from a thrift shop where they could get some furniture for their new place. When we were finished talking, I gave Sarah a pair of shorts and a T-shirt with Cookie Monster on it that I had previously selected for her from our donation room. They left with all this, plus the requisite bag of condoms.

About a week after meeting the three of them, I came home to find water flowing out of my laundry room and onto my kitchen floor. The water heater had ruptured. I mopped up the mess and drove to Sears Roebuck to buy a new water heater. It would be delivered on Saturday, and I knew exactly who could install it for me.

On Saturday morning Raúl took the bus from Hollywood to CDTC, where I picked him up and drove him to my house. He had a satchel of tools and worked quietly and with intensity installing the new water heater. We didn't talk while he was working, but once it was hooked up and running perfectly, I invited him into the kitchen and offered him a soda. He wanted to talk about how generous their landlords were and how they would sometimes drive them places. They had even provided them with sheets, towels, dishes, and pots and pans. Once again, I listened and restated how very lucky they were to meet these people.

It was getting late, so I paid Raúl and drove him to the bus stop. This had worked out perfectly. Raúl made some money, and I got my water heater fixed. Those two results were just as important to me as was the fact that the issue of confidentiality never came up.

Barbara and I saw each other only once in the next month, but we talked on the phone more frequently. She always gave me updates on her tenants and never went without mentioning how much she had come to love the little girl. During one conversation, she told me that Sarah had been sick, and Mireille took her by bus to a clinic in Fort Lauderdale.

"Could it possibly have been your clinic?" she asked me. I lied. I said I really didn't know and remarked that there were other clinics in town, plus we had a number of different clinics at CDTC. I mentioned that even if Sarah were going to one of our clinics, I might never know that. Barbara seemed satisfied with my answer. However, she brought the subject up again in a later conversation.

"Mireille had to take Sarah to this clinic again," she said. "It *is* Children's Diagnostic & Treatment Center—where you work! Are you sure you don't know them?"

I knew I couldn't admit to knowing them, but I felt uncomfortable lying to my friend. My pause provoked another question from Barbara.

"Do Sarah and Mireille have HIV?"

"Barbara…" I said, and just stopped talking. Mercifully, I didn't have to say another word because Barbara instantaneously jumped in.

"It's okay if they do. We don't care. We love them. So let's not talk about it ever again." Just like that day when I crossed paths with my teenage client and my decision not to smile at her or say a word saved her day, this time my silence—and my friend's sensitivity—saved my day.

Keeping Secrets

I was attending the funeral of a child who was not on my caseload but whom I knew fairly well. As I sat quietly next to her social worker before the service began, I let my eyes wander over the people already seated in the pews and those filing down the aisle. I recognized a colleague's client who was there with her husband. I spotted one of my own clients sitting next to her boyfriend. I knew that all four of these people were HIV-positive, and I also knew that none of them had shared their diagnosis with their partners. I did not make eye contact or acknowledge any of them.

A few months earlier, a member of our clinic team had asked me to go to Broward General to meet with a twenty-two-year-old woman who was coming there to get the result of her HIV test. Her name was Dionna and she had tested positive. The hospital counted on social workers from CFAP to be with the women when they received this deeply upsetting news. My colleagues and I had been trained in how to deliver positive HIV test results to women who had had their tests done in our clinic, but I had not yet been called on to do this. I felt quite lucky about that because I honestly didn't know if I'd be up to the task.

Dionna and I were seated in a small windowless room while we waited for the nurse to come in. Because I already knew the results, I was dreading the impending moment of truth. Understandably, Dionna appeared exceedingly tense. She kept crossing and uncrossing her legs, looking up at the ceiling, and quietly exhaling. The wait was short. When the nurse reported that the test result was positive, Dionna's shoulders slumped, her mouth fell open, and she made one sharp gasp like someone had punched her in the belly. She lowered her head and wept into her hands. I put my arm around Dionna's shoulders hoping it would help her feel less alone; but the moment carried such weight and sadness that I, too, was swept away by it and had to force myself not to cry.

Between sobs, Dionna told us she had been a virgin when she met her boyfriend. Before they had sex for the first time, she asked him about his HIV status and he assured her he was negative. She said she had believed him, but now she knew he had lied to her. And, at that moment, she most certainly realized that her expectations for a long and healthy life had been shattered.

The nurse asked Dionna if she would reveal her diagnosis to her boyfriend. Her answer was that in spite of this betrayal, she would not under any circumstances tell him. I was not surprised by her response, as my colleagues and I had discussed how this question had been answered similarly in the past by clients in the same predicament.

The answer seems irrational if you're not able to imagine yourself in these women's shoes. They were deeply fearful that if their boyfriends or husbands learned they had gotten a positive test result, they would become angry (or feign anger) and abandon them. Unbelievably, this could be their partner's response even if he knew he was the one who had transmitted HIV to his partner.

The first couple of times I heard a client refuse to tell her partner her new HIV status, I have to admit I was baffled. Why didn't she confront him? My reaction was no different from that of someone who can't fathom why a woman would stay in an abusive relationship. There are dozens of reasons why someone doesn't leave, but until someone tells or reminds you about the abuser's issues of control and the imbalance of power in some relationships, it's easy to prejudge a situation. The circumstances of marginalized women's lives can be so stressful and financially dependent on their partners—especially if there are shared children—that the women can see no alternative but to accept what others may view as intolerable. I did not judge my clients for their choice to remain silent. No one wants to face being abandoned with no resources, and no one wants to become ill and die alone.

30

Letting Go

UNDER OUR SERVICE MODEL OF family-centered case
management, the HIV-positive women and children were
our primary clients; however, if there were other family members residing in the home who were in need of help—whether
infected with the virus or not—we assessed their needs and
responded in whatever ways we could. For the purposes of data
keeping and documentation, if my caseload was fifty actual clients, that might translate into seventy-five to a hundred people.
It was deeply satisfying to know I was helping to make so many
lives better, but the work could become overwhelming.

Like the families, I was deeply disappointed and saddened
by the fact that despite our best efforts, a senseless, untimely
death was all too often the outcome. An unanticipated form of
emotional relief came from attending my clients' funerals. It
was a way I could allow myself the freedom to let go. I didn't
have to be the professional. I could mourn with everyone else
who had been tossed around in the same turbulence stirred up
by AIDS.

I never wanted to miss a single funeral. Some were very simple and others quite elaborate, but none of that mattered to me. I
always left the services feeling uplifted and inspired.

What was not uplifting, but anxiety filled, was the difficulty
I had trying to find the churches where these funerals were
being held. Within the first few months of my employment, I
had learned how to get to everyone's homes, the five hospitals
that made up the North Broward Hospital District, and even

some of the children's schools. I knew how to get to the courthouse, the women's detention center in Pompano, and the local funeral homes. But I did not know where all the churches were. The maze-like geography of Fort Lauderdale could thwart my ability to get to the services on time.

Like much of South Florida, Fort Lauderdale is laid out on a grid. The roads are designated N, E, S, W, as well as NW, NE, SW, and SE. They are then divided into streets, avenues, roads, drives, terraces, circles, boulevards, lanes, and courts. There was no GPS, no Google Maps, and no Siri to help me easily navigate from point A to point B. When I knew I would have to open a street map, I would often start to hyperventilate. And if I got lost on my way to a funeral held at an unfamiliar church tucked away on an unfamiliar street I had never been down, I could almost feel my blood pressure rise and a mild form of panic set in. I *had* to get there! I couldn't miss a minute of the chance to shed my professional side and finally grieve with others. Only when I was finally seated in the pew could I relax.

Because of the number of African American funerals I attended, I developed a level of familiarity with the structure and rituals. I loved the certainty of knowing what would be coming next in the service. Only once was I surprised by a regal presentation like nothing I had ever seen in my life. The organ music began, and the doors in the back of the church opened. All heads turned to see the procession. The organ music reached a crescendo, and four employees of the funeral home entered, dressed not in the expected black business suits but in formal black coattails. Like advancing honor guards, they moved dramatically down the aisle in a slow, choreographed, precision-perfect, high-stepping style. They were followed by pallbearers carrying the casket. It was stunning, and in my experience, an infrequent option chosen by the families.

For most of the funerals I attended, the casket was already up front, flanked by floral arrangements, or the pallbearers entered from the back of the church and walked with the casket up to the front.

Once the casket was delivered to the front of the church, the tempo of the organ music slowed, and the volume decreased. The pastor entered, and the service began. He welcomed us and then talked about the child or young woman we were honoring at this homegoing. Relatives and friends came up to read poems or passages from the Bible. A vocal solo was usually performed. Next, the deceased was remembered with eulogies that were filled with praise for the way the young adult or child had led their life. Sometimes, there were flashes of laughter. But always, whether it was spoken of or went unspoken, there was the understanding that this person was cruelly cheated out of a future that would never be realized.

My favorite part of the service was joining in the singing of gospel hymns. I'd been familiar with gospel music from a fairly young age. When I was fifteen, two of my girlfriends conned my mother into agreeing to let me go with them to a five-day sleepaway summer camp run by their gospel church. My mother voiced her objections, stating, "This would not be a suitable place for a Jewish girl." But Leslie and Marilyn stepped up their sales pitch and swore that the camp had absolutely no religious mission; it was just a place to have fun. Against her better judgment, my mother gave in, and off I went with my friends to gospel camp—just to have fun.

Within the first hour of arriving, I realized that "no religious mission" was a bald-faced lie. True, we had an hour and a half in the morning and afternoon to swim, play volleyball, go on scavenger hunts, and water ski on Long Island Sound, but the rest of the day and evening were devoted to Bible studies, memorizing and reciting psalms and Bible passages, watching movies of the Reverend Billy Graham proselytizing around the world, and round robin prayer held in small groups before going to bed.

There was, however, an unexpected upside to this experience. I heard and sang gospel music every day. I loved its energy, the rhythms, and the emotionality of songs praising God's love and forgiveness, and the promise of a glorious reward in heaven. I came home from camp hooked on this type of music. *Hallelujah!*

My clients' funerals always featured gospel music. Whether I knew the words or not, I always joined in as soon as I picked up the tune and could hum along. When the singing stopped and the pastor began his sermon, his voice started low and then gradually crescendoed almost to a roar. People rocked and stood up, raised their arms in the air, praised Jesus. People called out "Amen!" in agreement with the preacher's words. Women dressed in white filed down the aisles offering tissues to anyone swept up by the emotions of the moment. I saw the attendees' unrestrained participation as wholly befitting the magnitude of the tragic loss of life that had occurred.

At the end of every sermon, the church fell silent for a moment. With no visible cue, the organist started playing again, and the funeral home staff walked solemnly to the casket and removed any floral arrangements from the top. The lid was raised, and they positioned themselves on each side of the casket with their hands folded in front of them. This was the signal for the family members seated in the front row to rise and walk up to the now open casket. Physically strong male relatives stood at the ready to support and, if need be, catch the emotional mothers, grandmothers, and aunties as they gazed down at the child or young woman in the casket. It was not unusual for some to collapse in grief, their sobbing, pleading voices rising upward, hanging in the warm, breezeless air.

After the last family member was seated back in the pews, everyone else in the church stood up. In orderly row-by-row fashion, we moved to the front of the sanctuary and filed past the casket to say our last goodbyes. I created an exercise for myself for this moment. When I looked down at a young client's face, I tried to remember sharing a particular happy moment or event. I didn't want their disease or their death to define how I remembered them or what they had meant to me.

31

Love Birds

WHEN I BECAME LEILA'S SOCIAL worker, she and Shawn were newlyweds. They had been married by Shawn's father, the pastor of a small Baptist church in the community. Shawn was studying with his father to be ordained as the church's assistant pastor. When I first met Leila, she told me that she was HIV-positive but Shawn was negative. I suspected strongly that he might not have told her the truth because he refused to get tested, saying he knew already that he was "fine."

The young couple was inseparable. They would come by bus to attend all of Leila's clinic and social service appointments. I often saw these tall, skinny twenty-year-olds holding hands at various bus stops along Broward and Sunrise Boulevards. They were the perfect picture of young love. All this changed, however, when Leila decided to get her general equivalency diploma.

"I want to do something special with my life. I didn't finish high school, and I want to do better than work at McDonald's or Popeye's, so I signed up to get my GED. We had a fight about it because Shawn is dead set against me going back to school," she said bitterly. "I don't think he wants me to be able to get a good job. He thinks he should be the only important thing in my life."

Leila had attended only two GED classes when she told me that Shawn began showing up at her school. He would stand outside the classroom door and stare at her through the glass panel. The third time he went, he opened the door, walked in, and whispered something in the teacher's ear. Then he walked over to Leila's chair, took ahold of her arm, and guided her out the door without a word. But as soon as they were out of the building, he lit into her, saying he had been watching how a particular male student kept looking at her, and he didn't like it one bit. He accused her of being attracted to that man and forbade her from attending any more classes. No amount of Leila's tears or denials about Shawn's suspicions could convince him otherwise. Leila was devastated, and I was very worried about her safety because it was apparent to me that Shawn was a textbook domestic abuser.

Shortly after this happened, Leila learned she was pregnant. Shawn thought being pregnant would make her so happy that she would now definitely want to stay home. She told me his belief was that since she was going to be a mother, why would she need a GED to do that? However, knowing she was pregnant made Leila even more desperate to finish school. She knew that once the baby was born, there would be no opportunity to get her GED.

"This is what I do, Miss Dale," Leila confided to me in the clinic on a rare day when Shawn did not accompany her. "When Shawn leaves the house in the morning to go to the church, if I know he won't be back for a few hours, I sneak out and take the bus to school. I do my homework on the bus ride back, and I hide the books as soon as I get home."

I knew this was extremely risky and told her so. I warned her that his behavior was unreasonable, frighteningly controlling, and if he caught her doing it again, there might be terrible consequences. I understood she was desperate to better herself in the little time she had left before the baby's birth, so I didn't try to dissuade her any more strongly than that warning. What a terrible mistake.

Shortly after she had explained to me how she secretly attended class, Leila called to tell me that Shawn had found out about her continuing to go to school. She was crying so hard it was hard to understand her. Without giving her a reason, Shawn told her to sit still in the living room and not get up. He then went into the bedroom and came out carrying her schoolbooks, which she'd hidden in the back of the closet under a pile of her clothes. He hurled them on the floor and raged at Leila. He slapped her, yanked her off the sofa, and shoved her against the wall. The formerly adoring young man had transformed into someone unrecognizable.

"You have to call the police immediately, Leila," I cautioned. "This is domestic violence."

"You don't understand!" she wailed. "You don't know how important my father-in-law is in the community. And Shawn's his assistant pastor now. I can't call the police! Shawn's just starting out as a pastor. I don't want to damage his reputation or his career."

I could hear her pacing back and forth on the ceramic tile floor as we spoke. I certainly understood why Leila was scared, but it was difficult for me to accept her concern over Shawn's reputation being damaged. My primary concerns were that his physical violence toward her could seriously injure her or the baby and that it might become the new dynamic between them whenever she behaved in a way he viewed as being willful.

She pleaded with me not to call the police, saying that she wanted to give Shawn a chance to calm down and maybe even apologize. Leila did, however, agree to my insistence that she sleep at her parents' house that night. Her mother and father were extremely upset when she told them what Shawn had done, and they convinced her to tell him to move out.

The next morning, accompanied by her parents, Leila returned to her apartment and confronted Shawn. He ranted a bit, but stopped himself from saying or doing anything inappropriate, undoubtedly because Leila's folks were there. Although quite visibly upset, he put a few things in a bag and left. Leila's father installed a new lock on the front door of their ground-floor apartment, and she told me naïvely that she now felt safe enough to move back in.

Shawn had no intention of staying away and returned to the apartment the next day. It was sheer luck that Leila was not at home. When he tried his key in the lock and realized it had been changed, he evidently went wild.

My phone rang.

"Shawn broke into the apartment!" Leila was sobbing. "He trashed everything! Can you please come over right now and see what he did. I'm scared!"

"I'll be right there, but now you *have* to call the police." She promised she would. I met Leila at her apartment, and she walked me through the rooms, pointing out the damage Shawn had done. Their framed wedding pictures, which had hung on the living room wall, had been smashed on the floor. Glass was everywhere. Lamps were broken. He had set fire to articles of Leila's clothing he had piled up in the center of the floor and taken a scissors to what was left of her clothes hanging in the bedroom closet. The kitchen floor was littered with broken plates and cups.

The police arrived and took pictures and made notes. After they left, I drove Leila to the police station to give her statement.

Leila moved in with her parents, and we were all confident that Shawn would be held accountable for his actions. He was indeed arrested and jailed; however, he was held only until his father bailed him out just a few hours later.

The district attorney assigned Leila's case to a pro bono prosecutor—an attorney in private practice functioning as an assistant district attorney for no pay. I met with him once when he called me into his office to give a deposition. It was a short visit. I was asked to identify myself and my relationship to the victim. He asked for a few facts about Leila and Shawn's relationship. I stated how they were newlyweds with no apparent problems until Leila expressed her wish to better her life by getting a GED. I told him Shawn had forbidden her to take the classes, stalked her, and then physically abused her when he found out she had defied his "orders." The prosecutor took a few notes and didn't ask any follow-up questions. I started to give him my accounting of what I saw in Leila's apartment the day of the break-in. He told me it wasn't necessary because he had the police report. When we were done, he told me I would not be called on to testify at the hearing. I was shocked and massively disappointed when I heard this. I was absolutely sure my testimony could help Leila's case.

Throughout our brief meeting, the prosecutor seemed both distracted and disinterested. He wanted to talk more about how overworked he was than to discuss the case. I immediately began to worry he was not capable of mounting a strong case against Shawn.

I spent a restless night worrying that I had done a terrible job at the deposition. In the face of the attorney's minimal level of interest, why hadn't I pushed him to pay more attention to what I was saying? I replayed over and over again what I had said and what he hadn't said or asked. Why hadn't I gone into more depth about Shawn's jealous and controlling behavior? I should have told him Shawn was exhibiting textbook behaviors of a domestic abuser. Maybe he would have used that expression in court—that is, if I had said it. But I didn't. My restless brain went back and forth over my failings at the meeting. As the night wore on, I realized I was driving myself nuts and decided to try letting it go. It was the first time I had ever given a deposition, and I did the best I could under those circumstances. Now it was necessary to accept the reality that I couldn't play a meaningful role here. Leila was wholly dependent on the district attorney to advocate for her properly and paint as negative a picture of Shawn as he could. I believed that wouldn't be too hard.

On the day of the hearing, the sun was shining brightly, and the sky was cornflower blue, with only a few clouds. The beautiful weather stood in sharp contrast to the ugliness of what was about to happen inside the courtroom.

Leila walked in with her parents and sat down in the first row of the gallery, behind the prosecutor. She looked so pretty and so young. Her ankle-length, floral-print sundress hung softly over her now rounded belly. Was that hope or fear I saw in her eyes? My question was answered when Shawn entered the courtroom wearing a black suit and a preacher's white collar. He sat down in the first row on the opposite side of the aisle. Shawn was flanked by his father, also wearing a black suit and preacher's collar, and the attorney his father had paid for. One private attorney, two men of God, and one frightened and victimized young woman. There was no doubt that inequality of power was on display here, and it answered my question: that was fear I saw in Leila's eyes.

The prosecutor always goes first in a criminal trial, and he stood up and gave what I recognized as a horribly inadequate and incomplete explanation of what had occurred. With his first few words, my stomach was in knots. His affect was flat. His was a very controlled, unemotional retelling of the facts—and not even all of the facts. He expressed no outrage at what this young woman had to endure.

It was time for the defense attorney to speak. Shawn was entitled to the presumption of innocence, and his attorney did a grand job of describing his innocence. He began his opening statement by introducing his client as a newly married young man deeply in love with his wife. He went on to say that Shawn had a wonderful future ahead of him as the assistant pastor of his father's church and was well on his way to becoming a respected figure in the community.

He then posed the question "Why would he risk all of this by doing such a reckless, senseless act? It makes no sense."

He moved on to introduce Leila by way of attacking her. The absurd scenario he created was that it might have been Leila herself who orchestrated the break-in, cut up and burned her own clothes, smashed the framed wedding photographs, and trashed the kitchen. According to him, she was setting Shawn up to be a dangerous person whom she could not possibly be married to any longer.

"But why would she do this?" he asked, shrugging his shoulders and raising his palms in the air. He paused for effect. His voice rose.

"Your Honor, what we have here is a fickle young woman who had met another man in her GED class and decided she didn't want to be married to Shawn any longer. So, she brazenly fabricated this elaborate break-in to frame him!"

Up to that point, the absolute worst thing about this attack on my client was not that Shawn's attorney was presenting this ridiculous scenario, but that there were *no* objections from the prosecutor

I was sitting in the second row, behind and to the left of him throughout this barrage of lies. I kept stretching forward and twisting my head toward him in the hopes of catching his eye. I wanted to glare at him and will him to say something in her defense. It was hopeless. He was staring at paperwork in front of him and jotting down notes. For all I knew, he may have been working on his next case and not reviewing Leila's notes at all. I wanted to scream at him, "Speak up! Defend her!" But I was impotent.

The entire false retelling of events suddenly took a turn more awful than I could have possibly imagined. Shawn's attorney, in open court, disclosed Leila's HIV-positive status. This was an enormous breach of confidentiality and had absolutely no bearing on the case. It should have been objected to by the prosecutor or stricken from the record by the judge. However, neither person said anything.

It seemed to me that introducing Leila's HIV status into the record was done so that the defense attorney could make it germane to Shawn's defense. His attorney posited that Leila kept this information from Shawn when they married, and that this trickery was indicative of her dishonest character. My own suspicion, from the time I first got the case, was that Shawn's refusal to get tested for HIV pointed to the probability that *he* was the one who had infected her.

The judge was swayed by the defense attorney's tactic of turning Leila into the perpetrator of the crime and dismissed the case against Shawn. Leila's sobs pierced my heart like daggers.

As the involved parties and the observers were shuffling out, I overheard Shawn's attorney advising him of a possible legal option open to him. He told Shawn he could file a case against Leila. I couldn't clearly hear what kind of case he was talking about, but I did hear that if Shawn won and she went to jail, and the baby was born while she was incarcerated, the child would be placed in his custody. I never mentioned this to Leila because I was one hundred percent certain that Shawn would never pursue a case against Leila. As he knew he was guilty, why would he want to open himself up to further investigation?

I drove home in a state of mind bordering on fury. I was sure that my anger, disbelief, and disappointment were surpassed by Leila's feelings; plus, she'd experienced the injustice and humiliation of having her HIV-positive status revealed in court. The legal system failed my client miserably that day.

32

Camp Hope

For a little more than a week in the summers of 1998 and 1999, I accompanied young clients from our program to sleepaway camp. Selected CFAP social work staff, Dr. Puga, medication nurse Betty Benivegna, and a large contingent of our pediatric AIDS patients were invited to attend the newly opened Camp for All, in Burton, Texas. This impressive facility was the shared vision of a group of doctors from Texas Children's Hospital, together with several Houston corporations and private business owners, as well as community members. It took five years for their vision to become a reality.

Each week during the summer, Camp for All served a different population of children with special needs, serious illnesses, or life-threatening diseases. During the week that we attended, it was exclusively for HIV-positive children from the Houston area and us. We were deeply honored to be the first out-of-state group invited to participate. All year long, our kids looked forward to the life-affirming experience of attending camp. The promise of going for the first time as well as the anticipation of returning to camp was an unbelievably powerful incentive for the kids to attend their clinic appointments, take their medications, and sit through their treatment therapies. Time and time again, we witnessed the miracle of seeing seriously ill children will themselves to live long enough to return to camp one last time. We gave Camp for All a different, unique name while we were there for our week. For our children, it was Camp Hope.

Well before the departure date for Camp Hope, two important things had to happen. CFAP, with help from the CDTC's volunteer auxiliary, the Sunflower Circle of Friends, and other community AIDS organizations, would begin fundraising to pay for the campers' clothing and supplies. Community members could either donate $150, and the CFAP staff would shop for a child for a week of camp, or they could "adopt" a camper and do the shopping for this child themselves. Similar to what always happened at Christmastime, some families chose to take their children shopping with them and used the experience as an opportunity to teach their kids about those less fortunate than themselves, as well as how to shop on a budget.

After the children who would attend camp were selected, CFAP staff held informational meetings for those youngsters and their parents. These meetings were designed to teach them what to expect and how to prepare for camp. The topics included, but certainly were not limited to, sharing a cabin with other children, communal dining, and the all-important role the camp infirmary would play. Parents were asked to either cornrow their children's hair or tightly braid it. The hope was that these styles would last the whole week. This request was made because we knew the majority of camp counselors would be White and wouldn't know how to plait an African American or Haitian child's hair.

Being homesick was an important topic of the pre-camp discussion. Most children had never been separated from their families, and the possibility of becoming homesick was a genuine concern. Everyone did their best to anticipate and allay the children's anxieties before the day of departure. We knew this week would be like nothing they'd ever experienced before or could even imagine having. We took our responsibility of carefully preparing them very, very seriously.

Our first-time campers, not unlike most of their family members, had never flown before. They had to be instructed in appropriate airport and airplane demeanor. They were told that from the moment they walked through the revolving doors into Fort Lauderdale–Hollywood Airport, throughout the whole week at camp, and until the moment they walked out of the airport doors and into their families' arms, they were to think of themselves as ambassadors of Children's Diagnostic & Treatment Center. They never let us down.

First You Have to Find Them

Collecting the children on the morning of our flight always began before sunrise. Staff would pair up in cars and cruise slowly through the dark neighborhoods, squinting to find the addresses on poorly lit or sometimes unlit streets. With nothing more than a street map to follow, it was a navigational challenge.

I clearly recall the frustration my colleague Katrina Schiefer and I felt on the predawn morning of departure in 1999, when we were tasked with picking up two sisters and bringing them to the airport with us. We circled around the blocks but were unable to find the street or the girls' house number. We knew they and their mother were waiting for us—and probably getting anxious. There was no GPS, and neither of us owned one of the newly available but very expensive cell phones. Our work beepers were of no use to us.

I was crawling down a street at about five miles an hour when we saw two men with lit cigarettes sauntering toward our car. Katrina and I looked at each other, and without saying a word, communicated silently that we probably should not talk with them. However, nobody else was up and about at this hour except these guys, and we needed help. I made the decision to roll down my window halfway. One of the men peered in and suspiciously eyeballed Katrina and me. Before I could say anything, he asked, "What do you want? What are you looking for?" I told him we were having trouble finding an address.

"You don't want no drugs?" he asked.

"Oh, no, no!" Katrina and I blurted out in unison.

"Just directions, that's all," I said and stuck the piece of paper with the address on it out the half-open window. The man looked at it, thought for a second, pointed to the corner, and dispassionately told us to make two rights, and we'd find the street. We thanked them, I quickly rolled up the window, and we drove off, both of us holding in our laughter until we had turned the corner and the men were out of sight.

In a minute, we spotted the children's house. It stood out like a beacon of light in the darkness of the sleeping neighborhood. And there, indeed, were the two little girls standing silhouetted in the open doorway, their backpacked bodies illuminated by a lamp behind them in the living room. The girls began to yell and jump up and down with excitement when they saw our car. Their summer adventure was about to begin.

Then You Have to Get There by Plane(s)

The first year I accompanied our clinic kids to camp, everything went off without a hitch. They behaved like champions in the airport. The flight was uneventful, and the two-hour bus ride from the Houston airport to the camp in Burton was filled with happy chatter and the endless singing of "100 Bottles of Beer on the Wall." The trip we took the second year stands out vividly in my memory because of the things that did not go as planned.

Houston is the fourth largest city in the United States and a major hub for airlines. There are two large airports to accommodate all the air traffic: George Bush Intercontinental Airport and William P. Hobby Airport. We were supposed to have flown into George Bush Airport, but whoever booked the reservations made our destination Hobby Airport. I can only imagine the frantic response back at CFAP when the mistake was discovered shortly before we landed. Thank goodness, the day was saved and arrangements were hastily made for us to be flown in a small propeller plane from one airport to the other, where our bus was already waiting to take us to Camp Hope. It would be a short flight from Hobby, on the south side of Houston, over to Bush, on the northern edge of the city, but about thirty-five miles if we had to go by car. The children, many of whom had just flown for the first time in a commercial jet, were now going to be flying in a small commuter plane. It would be a monumentally different experience.

To our surprise, we had the entire plane to ourselves. This turned out to be a huge blessing. There was one flight attendant, and she appeared delighted to have on board this seemingly well-behaved group of kids, all neatly dressed in their matching white camp T-shirts. Once we settled into our seats, she took her microphone, introduced herself as Miss June, and welcomed us on board. Then, totally unexpectedly, she asked if any child would like to come up and take the microphone to give some very important instructions to the passengers. A dozen arms went into the air, followed by a cacophony of "Me! Me! Me! Pick me!"

Miss June made a random but good choice in twelve-year-old Jessica, known to CFAP staff as a lively and confident girl. Sighs and groans of disappointment came from the other children. Jessica proudly strutted down the aisle with a look of accomplishment and pride on her face as the kids cheered and whistled.

Miss June put her arm around Jessica's shoulders and swiveled her around so that they were both facing away from the rows of seats. Their faces now unseen, they huddled together up front, their heads almost touching. Miss June whispered the script to Jessica, and they both turned back to face the noisy passengers.

Softly and politely, Jessica spoke into the microphone. "All right, everyone. Now y'all please quiet down."

She waited a moment, and when she realized they weren't going to do as she'd asked, her voice exploded out of the speaker, "*Y'all quiet down, I said!*"

Completely startled, Miss June literally jumped back. All conversation on the plane stopped instantly and was replaced with giggles and laughter from the children and adults alike.

"I said *quiet down!*" Jessica said again, not as loudly as before but still deadly serious. This directive was accompanied by a look that could kill.

Behaving like a drill sergeant, Jessica spat out the orders, improvising only a bit from the script Miss June had given her.

"Now, fasten your seat belts. Watch Miss June do it, and then y'all do it. The whole time we're in the air, don't stand up! Don't get out of your seats! *Ever!* Y'all hear me?"

"Yes!" was shouted back, and seat belts were buckled in a chorus of clicks. All eyes were on Jessica. An awkward pause followed. Jessica looked up at Miss June, shrugged her shoulders and grimaced. She had forgotten what came next. Miss June bent down and whispered in Jessica's ear.

"It's a short trip and might be a little bumpy. But don't worry," she reassured "her" passengers. Miss June smiled broadly at her protégée and took back the microphone.

"Let's hear it for Jessica!" she called out. The plane erupted in whoops and hollers as Jessica returned to her seat all puffed up with happiness and pride in a job well done.

The flight from one airport to the other was indeed short: about twenty-five minutes. The takeoff was smooth, and we were up in the air quickly. The kids went back to chattering quietly with their seatmates. Those who didn't have window seats stretched their heads closer to their friends' windows, straining to see the huge city below them.

As we left the open airspace around the airport and began our flight over Houston, the little plane was suddenly buffeted by the updrafts and downdrafts caused by the skyscrapers. It bounced and bobbed in the air, causing the children to experience a kind of terror they had never known. Screaming and crying ensued. Prayers were shouted aloud. What may have started with one panicked child spread quickly like a four-alarm blaze.

"Save me, Jesus!"

"Grandma, help! Save me!"

"*H-e-l-p!* Oh, Lord God, help me!"

Miss June picked up her microphone and from her seat offered soothing words and reassurances that what everyone was feeling was perfectly normal. She explained that when a small plane flies over skyscrapers, it goes into what are called air currents. She assured us all, me included, that it would be over in a bit, and everyone would be perfectly safe. I, for one, genuinely appreciated her confidence and calm demeanor. I definitely was not alone.

Then You Get There by Bus

There were two big, luxurious buses waiting for us when we got to George Bush Interncontinental Airport. The kids were told to take anything they might want or need out of their backpacks and suitcases before they were stowed under the bus. We boarded and settled in for the two-hour ride to Camp Hope.

My seat assignment put me up front in the first row behind the bus driver. I had the aisle seat, and nine-year-old Latrice sat next to me at the window. As soon as instructions were given out and everyone's questions answered, Latrice spun around and talked animatedly for about twenty minutes with her friends in the seats behind her. She then sat back down and read her book for ten minutes or so. For the next ten minutes, she was content to stare out the window. And then, abruptly, she began to stare at me.

"Why are you staring at me?" I asked.

"I'm not really staring at *you*," she answered. "I'm staring at your hair."

"Why?"

"Can I cornrow it?"

"No, you can't. I'm sorry," I responded politely but firmly.

"But why? Why not?"

"Because I'd look ridiculous."

I had once taken a cruise to the Caribbean, and when we disembarked at one of the islands, I saw something that became imprinted on my brain. It was related directly to what Latrice was asking me to agree to. Local entrepreneurs had set up cornrowing "stations" on the dock where the tourist ships came in. In the few minutes it took me to exit the ship and walk the length of the dock, I noticed many White women with their hair in various stages of the cornrowing process. These women had paid good money for this, thinking it would be a great look for them. It truly wasn't. It looked, as I told Latrice, ridiculous.

"No, you'll look beautiful. Please let me do it! I'm good at it."

"No, but thank you."

"They said this was going to be a long ride, and we should all find things to do to occupy us. This will keep me busy and make the time go by fast—for me and you. Please? Please?" Latrice whined.

"I'd really rather not have you do this."

"I'll make a deal with you," she proposed. "I'll only do *this* much of your hair." She reached over and took hold of a big handful of my shoulder-length hair on the left side of my face.

"Just this side. Just this much. Puh-l-e-e-e-ease?"

I had given my best shot at declining her offer but sensed she would never stop asking. She was right about one thing: it *was* going to be a long ride. In the end, I relented. Latrice squealed in delight and turned her body to face me. She tucked her legs under her and with laser focus began to work on me. Tug. Pull. Tug. Pull.

"*Ow, ow, ow!*" I cried out. "That hurts!"

"Shush!"

Tug. Pull. Tug. Pull tighter.

"Please stop!" I begged. "This really, really hurts. You're pulling so tightly." It felt like my eyeballs were going to pop out of their sockets.

"I said shush, girl. Sit still and stop squirming," she scolded, repeating what her grandmother had no doubt told her dozens of times.

"I have to go through this all the time, all my whole life. You only have to put up with it once, so stop complaining."

So I shushed. My eyes watered, and I clenched my fists. I dug my nails into the flesh of my palms to distract myself from the intense pain. Latrice worked with (unintended) sadistic concentration. She had said that if I let her do this, it would make the time go faster. Well, it did not. It felt like an eternity, though, in real time, it probably lasted less than six minutes.

When she had finished, Latrice stood up, looked down the whole length of the bus aisle, and yelled out, "Anybody got a mirror?" One of my colleagues passed her a small mirror she had taken out of her makeup case.

"Look at how beautiful that is! You look really pretty," Latrice said, glowing with happiness at her own handiwork.

My scalp was throbbing, and I had the beginnings of a headache. There was a three-inch strip of cornrows on one side of my head. I thought I looked awful, but, of course, could not tell her that.

"I love it!" I said and threw my arms around her.

Fort Lauderdale Campers Arrive!

When we made our first trip to Camp Hope in 1998, none of the campers knew when the buses were getting close to our destination. This time, however, we had a good-sized group of returning campers, and they grew more excited and a lot noisier as they sensed we were getting close. All of them had been glancing out the windows, watching as the city turned into the suburbs, the suburbs turned into the countryside, the countryside into farmlands, and finally, the farmlands into wide-open spaces.

I was riding in the second bus. Our returning campers knew we had reached our destination when they saw the bus in front of us slow down, make a sharp right turn off the paved road, and begin to lumber up a dry dirt road. The huge tires on the first bus were churning up great beige clouds of dust and tumbleweed in front of us.

At this final turn, all the children rushed to the windows to see the welcoming committee of counselors and staff lined up on either side of the road, clapping and cheering for them. Happy pandemonium reigned inside the bus. The moment we stopped and the announcement was made that they could get out of their seats, the kids rushed the open door. They were almost falling over one another with eagerness to see their favorite counselors again. Old bonds were instantly rekindled and new ones formed in mere minutes.

Camp Hope is a unique and beautiful place staffed by devoted volunteers from around the country. No expense had been spared in its architectural design or interior furnishings for the unique populations it is intended to serve. Everything is wheelchair accessible. The bunkhouses are spacious and bright, with extremely comfortable beds and commodious bathrooms. There's a beautiful, well-stocked lake, an infirmary as well equipped as a small private clinic, and impressive arts and craft supplies. Plus, there are two beautiful pools, a small petting farm, gentle horses to ride, mountain bikes and trails through the woods, and great food. Yes, really good food! I'm talking chicken fried steak and barbecued ribs. It's Texas, after all.

The kids' days were filled with the usual camping activities everyone is familiar with: swimming, pedal boats on the lake, fishing, arts and crafts, archery, horseback riding, challenge courses, and so on. If you walked around the grounds or into the buildings and saw the kids engaging in only these activities, you would think there was nothing unusual about this camp—or about the kids. You had to enter the infirmary to realize this was an extraordinary place.

The Infirmary

The infirmary was where the doctors and nurses from Texas Children's Hospital and our clinic staff took shifts ministering to the sick campers. It was the place where counselors rocked anxious children on their laps to ease their fear or discomfort or held nebulizers in place over the children's noses and mouths to deliver airborne medication into their lungs to help them breathe better. It was where medical staff calmed and encouraged crying children who had to get injections or swallow foul-tasting medicines and where healthy campers held the hands of their sick friends curled up under blankets on the sofa. Every single camper walked through that infirmary door, even the ones who felt well had to be examined daily. Some children did it as often as three times a day to get treatments. But as soon as they could, they'd rejoin the fold to play and just be ordinary kids again.

The Wall

Lovey was ten, but looked much younger. She was painfully thin. Her cheeks were sunken in, and her arms and legs were like delicate sticks. Her smile was broad, and she had the spirit of a trickster and the heart of a champion. Lovey was one of a number of our patients whose determination to live was strengthened all year long by their treasured memories of attending Camp Hope—and by the desire to go back for one more summer.

On a monstrously hot afternoon, a small group of adults and campers were gathered at the bottom of the rock climbing wall. The adults were there to encourage the nervous kids to try to do the climb as well as to cheer on the confident ones who were eager to hoist themselves all the way to the top.

I could see how happy Lovey was while she was being strapped into her harness. She kept looking back at her friends and making silly faces. I was anxious for her, fearing she would never be able to do this. But that tiny speck of a child, girdled in belts and ropes, her head dwarfed by a big, shiny white helmet, demonstrated no hesitancy about making the climb. She followed the counselor's directions and placed one foot on the first rock and grabbed the dangling rope at her side. I watched her take a deep breath and try to pull herself up. There was no upward movement. She tried again … and again, but she didn't have the upper-body strength necessary to hoist herself up.

The climber has to face the wall in order to climb it. Because of this position, I wasn't able to see the disappointment I was sure had to be etched on Lovey's face. All the adults who had come to watch and encourage the kids seemed to be holding their breath. It was very quiet. No one wanted her to fail, but we realized she could never do this on her own.

One of the male counselors yelled, "Wait for me, Lovey! Don't go up yet!" He quickly strapped on a helmet, stepped into a harness, and clipped himself onto the line alongside the girl. Positioned next to her, he pulled on her rope, and she was hoisted up to the second rock.

"Put your foot on that rock there!" he called out while pointing. She didn't need to be told what to do next. The counselor pulled himself up. Next, he pulled on her rope, and up she went again. Her foot touched the third rock. He pulled himself, then he pulled her, pulled himself, then pulled her. Slowly, slowly up to the top of the wall they went, side by side, the big, strong man and the tiny, frail girl.

All of us below were looking up, our hands shielding our eyes from the blazing Texas sun, which seemed to hang suspended from an invisible thread above the top of the rock wall. Every last one of us had tears in our eyes as we watched this small, determined child rise up. This was what she had stayed alive for all year. This moment was the most important moment of her life right now.

Lovey and the counselor slid back down to earth amid raucous cheers and applause. The metaphor of this wall and of Lovey's life—and all the kids' lives—and their struggles to survive this disease was not lost on any of us.

Goodbye

A pall hung over breakfast on the last day of camp. Voices were quieter than usual, and the rare snippets of laughter felt inappropriate and quickly evaporated into the high ceiling of the cavernous dining room. No one wanted to believe it was over. The PA announcement telling us to walk outside to the buses was the undeniable signal that the week had come to an end. The staff walked solemnly hand in hand with the kids or carried them piggyback to the buses. Children and counselors alike cried openly. No one knew who would or would not be returning the next summer. The attachments made during this one week were small and exquisite miracles of devotion.

33

A New Way Forward

AFTER EIGHT AND A HALF years of working in the Comprehensive Family AIDS Program, first as a social worker and then as the program coordinator, I was offered a job in the executive offices of CDTC as manager of community relations and development. This position had never existed before. Historically, all of the center's major operating expenses had been covered by grants, but by mid 2003, that was no longer the case. Many more nonprofit organizations were vying for the same limited—actually, diminishing—pool of grant money. We needed to get serious about fundraising.

It was difficult to imagine myself not being physically close to the families I had worked with and equally difficult not being involved in helping to make their lives better. I didn't know if this new position could provide the same level of gratification I had experienced from my job in CFAP.

My CFAP colleagues and the staff of the medical team had all become very dear to me. Remarkably, our hard work was paying off in many positive ways for our clients and patients. What a wonderful thing! Could I give this up?

Deciding whether to move into something so different was similar to the decision I had to make twenty years earlier, when I went from classroom teaching to producing and directing special education television shows. Neither of these decisions came without some level of angst. The first time I faced this dilemma, I called my former NYU professor Dr. Mark Alter for his guidance. I now found my mind wandering back to that conversation.

He had juxtaposed the effect my work was having on the twelve children in my classroom with the effect a special education TV show would have when seen by maybe thousands of viewers. He said I would be finding another way to accomplish something important in my field.

I thought about the current equation. CFAP was a small program. Children's Diagnostic & Treatment Center served more than ten thousand children a year through all its programs. As manager of community relations and development, my efforts to raise awareness of us and, in turn, raise money, could dramatically improve the lives of many more families than I ever could reach if I stayed on as program coordinator, supervising our now seventeen social workers.

Although I had no experience soliciting large donations, I had often made presentations in the community about the work we did in CFAP. This type of outreach would be an important component of the new job and was definitely something I both enjoyed and was good at, but did I have the skills to convince people to open up their checkbooks?

When Dr. Widmayer offered me this position, I knew I'd be moving out of my professional comfort zone, and I expressed some insecurity to her about my ability to be a successful fundraiser. She countered that hesitancy by assuring me that she had great faith in my ability to do that part of the job extremely well. Then she sweetened the pot with a substantial raise. I accepted the offer.

As community relations and development manager, I worked directly under Dr. Widmayer and coordinated closely with the Sunflower Circle of Friends on major fundraising events as well as smaller projects. At the end of the fiscal year, when the tallying of monies raised by my individual and my

CDTC board members Judy Ambrose and Audrey Millsaps; Princess Diana's brother Charles, 9th Earl Spencer; Dr. Susan Widmayer; and the author.

shared fundraising efforts were disclosed, Dr. Widmayer and I were delighted. I was *really* successful.

In October 2004, eight months into my new position, the Sunflower Circle of Friends held its first large fundraiser, a gala at the Fort Lauderdale Museum of Art called "A Night of Royalty." During the months of preparation, my work focused on soliciting donations for the silent and live auctions, writing press releases, being interviewed on radio shows, and doing presentations about the event.

There were two huge draws for this fundraiser. The first was an extraordinary exhibit, *Diana: A Celebration,* celebrating the life and philanthropic work of the late Princess of Wales.

On display were some of her priceless personal memorabilia, including childhood home movies, private letters, family jewels, twenty-eight of her designer dresses, and her unforgettable royal wedding gown. The exhibit was making its way around the globe, and Fort Lauderdale had the distinction of being the second venue to receive this honor.

The other big draw was the guest of honor, Princess Diana's brother Charles Spencer. He addressed the gathering of 275 people and spoke about her life and philanthropic passions. The evening was an overwhelming success and contributed in large part to my own overwhelming success in this new job. The publicity brought lots of positive and much-deserved attention to Children's Diagnostic, Broward County's own "crown jewel" for children with special healthcare needs.

34

Finding Their Roots

If you don't know where you are from,
you will never know where you are heading.
—a saying in Sanda Village,
Sierra Leone, West Africa

DECADES BEFORE ORDINARY PEOPLE HAD access to their DNA genetic makeup through commercial genotyping and before Dr. Henry Louis Gates Jr.'s groundbreaking television show *Finding Your Roots* was imagined, one of our social workers, Jariatu Sesay, was working on an idea to help a group of clients possibly find their cultural roots.

I met Jariatu in 2003, when she started working in the Comprehensive Family AIDS Program. I learned she had immigrated to the United States by herself in 1989 from the Republic of Sierra Leone in West Africa. Her hope was to get settled in a welcoming community, further her education, and bring her family over here to be with her. While being a creative and energetic addition to our team, she accomplished all of these goals and more.

Jariatu told me that when clients met her for the first time, they were intrigued—puzzled, in fact—by her physical appearance and manner of speech. She was Black like them but had a different look and an unidentifiable accent. They could tell she wasn't African American, Jamaican, or Haitian, like most people of color they knew. Their curiosity always led them to ask her where she was from and what language she spoke, and some even asked which customs she practiced. The women were fascinated by Jariatu's background and heritage, and many expressed regret about not knowing anything about their own origins. Some believed they likely had relatives who had been slaves, but none of them could even guess about their African roots.

This troubled Jariatu enough that she decided to try doing something about it. She made a presentation to Dr. Widmayer about her idea for a new program she named the Women's Alternative Village of Empowerment (WAVE). It provided a uniquely designed Afrocentric curriculum, plus enrichment materials for cultural connections, life skills building, and self-empowerment. She spoke about how many of the clients had lost focus in their lives, due in part to traumatic events such as substance abuse, sexual abuse, poverty, unemployment, losing custody of their children, estrangement from family members, and of course the diagnosis of HIV or AIDS.

The overriding mission of WAVE was to help the participants refocus their lives and regain pride and confidence in who they are and what they could accomplish. Dr. Widmayer was fully supportive of going ahead with this program. It was originally intended for Jariatu's own clients, all of whom were struggling with addiction-related problems, but once WAVE's success became apparent, it was opened up to any client in CFAP wishing to participate.

To help them understand and embrace their history, Jariatu first taught the women about the African slave trade and the strength of their ancestors who had to endure the dehumanizing conditions of slavery. They took field trips to the African-American Research Library and Cultural Center, in Fort Lauderdale. On a subsequent outing, they toured the replica of the infamous slave ship *La Amistad* while it was temporarily docked in Fort Lauderdale. The women learned the history of the ship's slave revolt in 1839 and the eventual successful trial that granted freedom to the fifty-three enslaved Africans on board. The women were surprised to learn and impressed with the fact that the original schooner *La Amistad* sailed from Jariatu's own country of Sierra Leone.

The WAVE women learned about the power of imagery—how, for example, they could transform the likeness of a woven basket African women often carried on their heads into an imaginary tool kit they could "reach into" to fight off their demons.

They also learned about the African tradition of storytelling as a way to help people make sense of the world. Jariatu would frequently gather the women in a circle and ask them to share a story about a struggle or a success they had experienced recently. Here is an example of a WAVE woman's story that was shared with the group:

"I woke up this morning all sweaty because of the dream I had last night. I saw myself in the crack house, and my friend had the pipe all prepared for me. I turned around and saw the Monster on the floor, with one eye open. It was wagging its tail and waiting for me to reach out and grab the pipe. I panicked and felt myself frozen. Then I saw my own shadow by the Monster.

"'There you are,' I said to myself. 'You are carrying the WAVE basket on your head. Why don't you reach out and tranquilize that Monster before it carries you into the pit of this crack house?'

"I knew I had my respect, integrity, and dignity [acronym RID] hidden somewhere in the basket, and if I dug further into the basket, I would be able to grab it and throw it in the

Monster's direction. I closed my eyes and prayed like we always do in the WAVE group and put my faith in my higher power and reached out for my RID and got rid of that Monster and put it right back to sleep in the backyard where it is supposed to be. Then I walked to the bathroom and took a long bath before heading to group today. Ladies, I want you sisters to know that if I can fight my Monster, you can do it, too."[7]

These African concepts and techniques were useful in helping the women find the courage and strength from their ancestors. It helped guide them on their paths to sobriety, stability, and renewed health.

Jariatu invited me to observe two of the cultural empowerment classes. The first one was designed to help the women identify where their people may have come from. When I walked into the multipurpose room on my first visit, I saw a group of women seated around a long table, hunched over and poring through large books filled with photos of African women in native dress.

"Study their faces," Jariatu instructed. "Look at their bone structure, their body types, and their skin tones. Look at the shapes of their eyes, their noses, their cheekbones. See if you can see yourself in any of them."

The clients picked up hand mirrors that had been placed around the table and tried to match their own faces to those of the women in the books. From this exercise, and with information about different African ethnicities, they tried to determine where in Africa their ancestors might have originated.

---

7   Thanks go to the unnamed participant in the WAVE program who gave permission to share her story with Jariatu Sesay and have it appear in Techniques of Cultural Empowerment.

The women found the activity thrilling. As I sat among them, I noticed the noise level in the multipurpose room growing louder. Everyone was filled with the wonder of possibly discovering something about her unknown history. Their excitement was palpable. Exclamations flew around the table.

"She looks like me!" "Look at her cheekbones!" "That's my nose!"

One woman's comment elicited an explosion of laughter from everyone. She joked, "This one is fat and has a big butt. She could be my great-great-grandmother!" For perhaps the first time in their lives, these women were experiencing a connection to something all of them admitted they'd never thought much about before. But now it was becoming deeply important to them.

With Jariatu's guidance, each woman settled on an ethnicity, country, or geographical area from which she thought her people might have originated. The plan was to make these new connections to Africa real.

The second class covered the history, customs, and clothing of the countries. Everyone had arrived on time and sat around the table, but Jariatu was missing. This was unusual, as she always arrived early to welcome the women. Suddenly the door opened, and Jariatu made a dramatic entrance wearing a *lappa*, one of Sierra Leone's traditional dresses, and an elegant head wrap. Everyone broke into applause, whistles, and raucous cheering. With great aplomb, Jariatu executed a slow turn, took a bow, and then walked over to a covered clothes rack and lifted the sheet to reveal a row of brilliantly patterned hanging dresses. She conducted an amazing show-and-tell of her collection of traditional African apparel. To the women's delight, they were encouraged to choose a dress and try it on. In truth, they didn't need any encouragement. Once invited, they flew to the rack like a flock of hungry birds discovering a tree laden with ripe berries.

International Woman's Day was being celebrated the following week. With Dr. Widmayer's full support, a party and a parade were planned. The women, dressed in their boldly patterned *lappas* and head wraps, would parade throughout the building. Every employee, client, and patient there that day would get to see the elegant African dresses modeled by the beautiful, proud women of the WAVE program.

On parade day, Jariatu realized there were more dresses than there were models. A few phone calls were hastily made inviting people to participate in the procession and asking them to hurry over and choose one of the unadopted dresses. Staff volunteered eagerly, including me. With everyone now dressed in African garb, we wended our way through the building, passing every department, including the dental and therapy suites, the clinic, the administrative offices, and the reception area. All along the way, we were met with enthusiastic applause.

When we returned and opened the door to the multipurpose room, the air was pulsating with the drumbeats of African music. Dr. Widmayer had invited guests to witness this demonstration of newfound ethnic pride. Everyone, including clients, guests, and the staff volunteers was given the opportunity to learn original African dances. The room was filled with music, laughter, and the swirling colors of the dresses worn by the participants of the transformative Women's Alternative Village of Empowerment. It was a joyous celebration of newly found connectivity between themselves as modern African American women and their ancestral families.

My Last Eulogy

In my new administrative position, even though I no longer worked directly with our clients or their families, I continued to see and talk with them on a daily basis. Whenever I walked through the clinic, the waiting room, or into the CFAP division, I would see the people with whom I used to work. I loved it when a child or adult called out my name and came over to chat and bring me up to date on what was happening in their lives. They always had something interesting to tell me, and I was always so happy to listen.

One day in 2004, I learned that a former client of mine, Kimmie, had died. She was only seventeen years old. I'd been her social worker from the time she was nine years old until age thirteen. As a child with HIV, she was unique in one respect: she had no qualms about sharing her diagnosis and was unafraid of any possible negative responses. Kimmie told family members, friends, and even classmates about her HIV status.

After Kimmie's mother died of AIDS, Kimmie and her siblings went to live with their mom's sister Jean. The day Jean called and told me her niece was revealing her diagnosis to people, I immediately scheduled a home visit. I wanted to understand how she had reached this decision about something so many people were, understandably, not willing to reveal.

"I was born with this disease," she said matter-of-factly. "I didn't do anything to get it, and I'm not ashamed."

It was obvious to me that she had thought through what happened to her at birth and had made her peace with it.

I asked Kimmie to tell me how she believed the virus could be passed on to others. Her answers revealed that she had just a rudimentary understanding of the routes of transmission, but all the basic facts she knew were absolutely correct. She felt it was her responsibility to teach people about HIV and AIDS, to help keep others from becoming infected, and to give them emotional support if they were infected already. By disclosing her own diagnosis and wanting to help keep others safe, Kimmie proved herself to be brave and mature beyond her years.

Kimmie's aunt asked if I would deliver a eulogy at the funeral and told me that everyone coming knew Kimmie had died of AIDS. Knowing this, I was able to craft a different kind of eulogy from others I had written in the past. I didn't have to keep "the secret." I didn't have to limit myself to what a sweet, fun-loving child she had been or tell a few humorous stories about her. I could talk freely about Kimmie's fearlessness and truth-telling.

I knew this might well be the last time I would deliver a eulogy at Children's Diagnostic, and I wanted to do right by this young woman and her loving family. I needed to talk about them, too, because of their selfless acceptance of this terminally ill child and her siblings into their lives.

When it was my turn to speak at the funeral service, I rose from my seat in the front row and walked up the three steps to the stage. Standing behind the pulpit, I looked down and saw Kimmie's white coffin directly below me. It was flanked by lovely pink and white floral arrangements. I looked out at the large crowd of people who had come to the church for Kimmie's homegoing.

As I read the eulogy, the congregation vocalized their approval of Kimmie's actions and strength. The smiling faces of her relatives reflected their pride in her character. Even as a young child, she had displayed unusual compassion for others. Had she lived longer, she would have undoubtedly grown into a powerful voice for education about AIDS and acceptance of people with AIDS.

Because I am a saver of things, it was not difficult to find that eulogy written nineteen years ago. Here is the original eulogy remembering Kimmie, her family, her precocious courage, and her generosity of spirit.

Eulogy for Kimmie, 2004

"My relationship with Kimmie's family began in 1996 when I became her social worker. My job at Children's Diagnostic & Treatment Center allowed me to build wonderful relationships and meet many inspiring people. Kimmie will always stay in my memory as one of the most inspiring children I knew.

"She was part of a family that had experienced a tremendous amount of loss and grief. In spite of this, they never stopped taking care of each other. They cared for Kimmie's mother until her death, and then they continued to care for Kimmie until her passing.

"Kimmie's Aunt Jean made a deathbed promise to her sister that she would raise Kimmie and her siblings as best she could. She kept that promise. When Kimmie's older sister, Nikia, became a teenager, she, like the grownups, took on some of the responsibility for helping with Kimmie.

"Last night at the viewing in the funeral home, I told Nikia that she had done a beautiful job of caring for Kimmie. Nikia's eyes filled with tears as she answered me, her voice heavy with emotion.

"'Oh, but I wasn't finished taking care of her. I had so much more to give.'"

Nikia's words resonated with me. When I sat down to write this eulogy, I began to wonder where this family's wellspring of strength came from. How was it that Kimmie was so fearless and open about her illness at a time when few others were? How was it that Nikia, just a teenager at the time, made the decision to share in the caregiving responsibilities for her sister? Where did Kimmie's passion to teach others about HIV and AIDS come from?

"When Kimmie was thirteen, she told me she wanted to talk with a reporter from the *Sun-Sentinel*. She wanted to tell her story so that other children could read it and wouldn't feel alone if they were going through what she had to go through. Sadly, this never happened.

"I believe that until there's a cure for AIDS, it's up to all of us to reach out, offer support, and teach others *for* Kimmie, so that no one—child or adult—ever feels alone while battling this stigmatizing and terrifying disease. In this way, we will honor her short but beautiful life."

IV

Survivors

35

Becoming a Detective

I'VE PERSONALLY KNOWN AND LIVED with writers and am familiar with the euphoria they typically experience when they finish the last chapter of a book, complete the last act of a play, or send off a completed magazine or newspaper article to a publisher. After five years of working on this book, I, too, felt a sense of elation. However, it was quickly replaced by a nagging feeling that there were loose ends I should investigate and tie up.

Many years have passed since I had direct contact with my former clients and their family members. Writing about their long-ago lives made me deeply curious about their current lives and what might have happened to them. I imagined that readers, too, would be interested in knowing what the ensuing years held for some of these women and children. Who survived? What are they doing now? The children (now adults) who survived may well have children of their own. What are their lives like now?

It's important to clarify what I mean by *survivor*. I have taken the liberty of making the definition of that word more inclusive. As I see it, when it comes to being infected with the AIDS virus, you didn't have to live to be a senior citizen to be considered a survivor. Nor did you have to be infected with the AIDS virus. I regard any uninfected person living with someone with AIDS, be it a child, a sibling, or a caregiver, to be a survivor. Caregivers selflessly devoted their time and energy—maybe even sacrificed their own physical and emotional health—to nurse their loved ones. Children and siblings suffered monumentally as they watched helplessly as their parents, sisters, and brothers wasted away and died.

HIV/AIDS is no longer a forbidden topic. The stigma that used to surround it is greatly reduced thanks to the world now being much better educated and more accepting. We even see HIV medications advertised on television now, replete with images of HIV-positive men and women loving each other and happily going about their ordinary lives.

This sea change in attitude in no way guaranteed that any former clients I might find would agree to speak with me. Issues of privacy and confidentiality still had to be respected.

Since I was no longer employed by Children's Diagnostic & Treatment Center, I did not have access to my old documentation; nor could I ask anyone at the agency to give me information about my former clients. The best I could do was to rely on social media, historical newspapers, whitepages.com, and my original set of handwritten three-by-five-inch client index cards with very old phone numbers and addresses.

My search for survivors wasn't easy, and I couldn't locate many, but it most definitely turned out to be worth doing. I include nine poignant stories.

36

Tina and Janelle

I WAS ABLE TO FIND JANELLE, Tina's mother, with some unsophisticated detective work by using the website whitepages .com. It provides approximate ages of the person you're trying to locate, current and past phone numbers, and some names of likely relatives. Based on this information, I made my best guess and placed a call to the most probable phone number. I left a message with my name and number, plus a generic kind of greeting stating who I was looking for, but not why. I would explain that only if Janelle were interested enough to return my call.

My answer came back a day later in the form of a text message—"I received your message. Please give me a call"— accompanied by an animated red rose emoji on a sparkling background that read "Good Morning!" and six hearts with exclamation points. I was elated!

A second text message arrived soon after this with a smiling photograph of Janelle looking vibrant and healthy. Her message: "It's been years since I've seen u. Tina passed away in January 2017. My life hasn't been the same. But I'm staying strong [emoji of an arm with a big muscle] for me and my 3 grand kids."

Janelle attached two photographs, each one showing a beautiful young woman. The captions read, "Tina oldest daughter, she's 19 yrs. old" and "Tina baby girl, she's 15." I learned later that Tina had also adopted a two-month-old boy.

Now knowing Tina's date of passing, I calculated that she'd lived to be thirty-six years old. As an emotionally and physically vulnerable child, and then as a headstrong teenager with an AIDS diagnosis, she was always living on the edge of danger. I had imagined her lack of interest in taking HIV meds and her refusal to seek routine medical care would have contributed to a far shorter life; happily, I was wrong. She must have had an epiphany at some point and made the decision to take care of herself, or else she couldn't have lived twenty-two years beyond her original diagnosis. She was a survivor.

I was apprehensive, though, to hear the details of Tina's adult life from her mother. Janelle and I spoke the next day. True to the person I knew her to be so many years ago, she could still weave an absorbing story with an abundance of detail. She sketched a portrait of her adult daughter that was frequently heartbreaking in terms of the suffering that Tina continued to endure but also miraculously heartwarming in how admirably and heroically Tina had managed to survive. It became clear to me that, over time, some of Tina's understandably sharp edges had been filed smooth and transformed by the stability of family, friends, parenthood, love, and old-fashioned good times.

The best way for you to learn about Tina's life is to read Janelle's own words from my phone interview with her. Both mother and daughter went through unbelievably chaotic periods in their lives, experiencing the depths of sadness and witnessing genuine evil. Nevertheless, survivors they are and were.

"I'll tell you about myself first. Eight years ago, I stopped using drugs, and I have a good life now. I moved from Florida to the Bronx a few years ago to better myself. At first, I went from shelter to shelter, but then I qualified for a housing voucher and found a subsidized apartment in a high-rise building with a pool and exercise room. I love it! But I go to Florida as often as I can afford to, to see my mom and my *grands*.

"You knew that Carina's father raped Tina when she was fourteen and gave her HIV. Well, he spent eight years in prison for that, got out, and did it to another fourteen-year-old girl that me and my family knew well. Tina was subpoenaed to go to court. She brought her little sister's obituary with her and read it out loud to the judge. She told him her little sister's father infected her, and it was his fault that Carina was born with AIDS and died at four and a half years old. She cried when she said he took her little sister away from her. The judge sentenced him to eighteen years. He went to prison in 2003 and got out in April 2021.

"Tina enjoyed her life. She had a car, and she had good friends: three girlfriends and two men friends. They were all a lot older than her. She always liked older people. She took all of them grocery shopping. She loved to cook outside with the grill. She loved to sing and dance. She liked to drive family members to the beach.

"Even as an adult, she wouldn't always do what the doctor said. But when she got pregnant with her two girls, she took HIV meds the whole time. She loved her children, and she loved other people's children, too. She always had kids at her house.

"She had a three-bedroom apartment at first; then she got approved for a Section 8 house. She loved to sit outside with her girls, sometimes with a glass of wine in one hand and her weed in the other and watch what was going on. Tina didn't do cocaine, heroin, crack—none of that. Just weed. But she only had a chance to enjoy her house for three months before she died.

"When she was twenty-six, she was diagnosed with cancer. They found a spot on her brain, and she had it in her lungs, too. She got radiation and took medication for it. She lived with cancer for ten years, and you know what? She lived to thirty-six, and she enjoyed the good life until the end. Oh, yeah, she was grouchy some days, but she didn't let it get her down.

"And she was a good mother. She was excellent with her kids. She took her girls everywhere she went. She never left them with anybody. She said, 'Let me tell you something, Ma. I'm not going to let my girls spend nights with nobody. I don't want anybody to do anything to my babies. My girls stay with me.'

"And I'm real proud of her girls. Her older daughter works at a sub shop. She's a manager and makes twenty dollars an hour. She bought herself a new car, and she's going to hire her sister this summer. They live in their daddies' houses now. Her older daughter took the little boy Tina adopted to live with her and her daddy.

"When I'm in Florida, I keep expecting Tina to walk in the door. I miss her so much and cry like a baby. Tina was one character, and there'll never be another one like her."

37

Carla and Miriam

I WAS ABLE TO REACH CARLA's mother, Miriam, by calling the phone number I'd had for the family since 1996. Twenty-six years later, she still had the same number.

I was very fond of Miriam, and not just because at each home visit she would make me an old-fashioned-style robust cup of Cuban coffee brewed in a sock. She had great warmth and a delightful sense of humor. But there was always a tinge of sadness about her, which I attributed to the inherent difficulties of being an older single parent raising an adolescent with an all-too-often obstinate nature. When I spoke to Miriam for the first time in sixteen years, her voice sounded exactly the same in spite of the fact that she was now in her early eighties.

She was thrilled to hear from me after all these years, and we chatted for quite a while, a luxury I couldn't indulge in too often when I was working. She was eager to talk, and I was happy to listen.

I learned that shortly after I left Children's Diagnostic and moved back north, she and Carla moved, too. They went to live with Miriam's son and his family in a community outside of Orlando, Florida. She told me Carla passed away in 2007 at the age of twenty-four and that she still misses her terribly. I had hoped to hear that Carla lived longer, but, considering she had been living with AIDS since birth and rarely took her medication, I imagine twenty-four years was a kind of miracle.

I told Miriam I was writing a book about my time working with the families at the Comprehensive Family AIDS Program and that I had included a chapter about Carla. She laughed when I said this, saying that she didn't think Carla's life was interesting enough to put in a book. I respectfully disagreed and reminded her of a few things about Carla, including what had occurred after she'd made the decision to disclose her HIV status to her girlfriend, and how she handled that whole situation. Miriam recalled that immediately and commented that she was proud of Carla for going back to school to face everyone. However, she then bemoaned the never-ending difficulties of trying to reason with Carla throughout her life.

I asked what Carla's life had been like in the years leading up to her death. Miriam told me the following:

"Carla always lived at home with me and was basically unchanged from the time she was a teenager up until the day she passed away. She was always a happy person; happy and hardheaded. She did graduate high school, but her mental problems made it too difficult for her to hold a job. She liked babysitting for her girlfriends' children and taking long walks with her friends. Often, she would not come home when she was supposed to, and I was all the time looking for her and couldn't find her. It was hard on me.

"The day she passed away, it was almost like she knew she was going to die. She didn't come out of her room one morning, and when I went in to check on her, she complained that she wasn't feeling well. She thought she had eaten too much food the night before. But I knew this was more serious. I sat down on the side of her bed, and she continued talking. The last words she spoke to me were so touching. She said that I never reminded her that I wasn't her real mother. She told me she loved me so much and added, 'I've done so many bad things, and you never said nothing to me.'

"My son followed the ambulance to the hospital, but we had to turn around and go back home. I had forgotten some things Carla would need. Almost as soon as I walked into the house, the hospital called to say Carla was dying. I couldn't get back in time to be with her.

"Now I dream a lot that she's talking to me—and laughing like she used to."

38

Benita and Kimberly

I FOUND BENITA EASILY THROUGH WHITEPAGES.COM. She was very happy to talk with me and tell me about the many changes that have occurred since I last saw the family in 1997. Kimberly was nineteen when she became my client and was now forty-two. My interview with Benita revealed a woman who, in spite of decades-long battles with poverty, addiction, and mental health issues, saw a path for herself through education and her strong belief that God had set up opportunities for her. She felt it was up to her to recognize them and pursue them fearlessly. I asked Benita to talk first about herself and then about Kimberly.

"Do you remember that I had been studying computer programming at Broward Community College? I ended up getting an IT internship at Boca Raton Hospital; but, when Y2K was approaching, I put my résumé out there. Lots of companies were looking for IT specialists at that time. A headhunter found me and told me about a good job at R. J. Reynolds Tobacco Company in North Carolina. The kids and I moved there and stayed for two years.

"My contract with RJR expired, and Sprint called and offered me a contract to work in Texas. It was a fabulous job. They gave me an apartment, a company car, and even expenses for food. Unfortunately, I lost my job right after 9/11. I found a job at Time Warner Cable, and Kimberly worked at Kmart. When she used to live with me in California, she attended a retail school through a special program. She doesn't even need a job coach anymore!

"Off and on from 2014 to 2016, I served as a volunteer with the Red Cross, traveling up and down the East Coast from Florida to New York helping during disasters. I was also part of AmeriCorps under the Obama administration. I'm proud to say I was awarded a Volunteer Service Award.

"When I think about my life in Florida, I realize that everything down there was a crisis for me. I had to grow up a lot when I was living there. I had to learn self-determination.

"Life is a lot better now. I myself am a consumer of mental health services, and I got a wonderful job working for the Los Angeles County Department of Mental Health. I'm training to become a state peer support specialist. Evidence-based practices have shown that people with 'lived experience' have more success at connecting to people with similar issues.

"I also work with people with substance abuse and the homeless population. I sit in on support groups every week. I collaborate with peers, with people with mental illness. We get referrals from other organizations, and I do outreach at Santa Monica Pier and Venice Beach. The people I serve are on the road to becoming gravely disabled; their mental illness is impacting them so much that they no longer have the ability to seek housing, shelter, and medical attention. I feel great compassion and empathy for the homeless.

"There's so much joy in doing this kind of work, in helping those less fortunate. This is my life now. God has set all this up for me."

Benita had low expectations for what Kimberly would be able to accomplish as an adult and feared she would have to always "take care" of her daughter. But she was thrilled to report that she has been proven very, very wrong. This was such good news. Both their lives are now filled with professional and personal successes.

"Now I'll tell you about Kimberly. When we lived in North Carolina, she got into an excellent vocational rehab center and even got a Goodwill Section 8 apartment through them.

She was living on her own for the first time. With some help, she arranged for her medical records to be transferred from Florida to Wake Forest University, and it was then that we found out her HIV was undetectable. She never started any medication, and in fact, she's never been on any.

"Years ago, Kimberly wanted to move back to Florida. It's a better place for her. She wanted to be near her father and his family. She worked for three years at Burlington Coat Factory, and for the last six months she's been working for T.J. Maxx as a retail worker. They're training her to work on the cash register. They're starting her slow.

"I'm really happy to be able to tell you that she has a partner, and they have a nice apartment in a safe environment. She has many friends. She even got a driver's license! She's an amazing person. I did not think she would be productive in society, but she is just as productive as I am. Life for both of us is much better now."

39

S'marra

S'MARRA HAS A FACEBOOK PAGE. Like most people who are active on the social media site, she posts lots of pictures of herself, her friends, and family members; and she shares funny cartoons, jokes, and mouthwatering shots of holiday meals she's cooked. In every picture, she looks healthy and happy. Because she accepted my invitation to be Facebook "Friends" a couple of years ago, I have occasionally checked her page to see how she's doing. For the last couple of years, I've posted birthday greetings to her on her page, and in response, she has thanked me. But when I gave her my email address and asked if she would consider contacting me privately, she did not respond. I understood and did not pursue trying to interview her.

What I learned from her postings gave me a wide-open window into her life well after the loss of her baby daughter, Rosie (Sarita). Everything I saw filled me with happiness for her. When she and I shared time together, her baby was either sick or dying. S'marra was always super quiet—you could even say withdrawn. I never experienced one bit of the woman whose radiance now appears on her Facebook pages.

S'marra had a large extended family to support her, and they are still there, but she also has many friends, she has coworkers who admire her, and she seems to have a boyfriend. Best of all, in 2012 she gave birth to a son. All his pictures show a vigorous, handsome child highly likely born free of the virus.

From the moment of his birth, he became the center of her universe. Over time, she has used Facebook to convey a multitude of tender and loving messages to him and about him. He's a wonderful student, and S'marra posts some of his school report cards. You can tell she's immensely proud of him.

Although I would have loved to speak personally with S'marra, I am not deeply disappointed that I couldn't. She wrote so eloquently about her happiness with this child—her second opportunity to be a mother—that I truly believe an interview might not have yielded better results.

40

The Spencers

URING THE EARLY DECADES OF the AIDS epidemic, there were family members who were never infected yet whose lives were also upended by the disease. Some were caregivers who experienced both physical decline and feelings of despair as they exhausted themselves taking care of their loved ones. Like the people they were caring for, they, too, were often shunned when friends and even family members fell by the wayside and could no longer be counted on for support because of the stigma of AIDS.

A whole other category of uninfected victims of this virus were the children who experienced the trauma of losing a sibling or a parent, or in many cases, the unfathomable loss of both. In an article in *The New York Times* in 1989, Dr. Pauline Thomas of the New York City Health Department estimated that by 1995, twenty thousand orphans living in New York City would need either adoption or foster care. Around this same time, scientists from the CDC described a model that looked at this problem from a national perspective. Their prediction was that by 1991 there would be eighty thousand infected women in the United States, and "these women would have 125,000–150,000 children who could become orphans." For these heroic caregivers and family members, the poignancy of their memories of that time in their lives is indelible and lingers to this day. These people, too, must be considered survivors.

Now, having arrived at the end of the book, I want to introduce you to the Spencers, a resilient family that had to reinvent itself due to the AIDS-related deaths of two family members less than two years apart. You've already had a brief introduction to them through Linda Spencer's poem "You" in the beginning of the book, and in a later chapter about the Birch Family Camp that included her then fourteen-year-old son, Floyd, and his sick seven-year-old brother, Rayshawn. I met the three of them at camp in 1990. As with so many people I've met over the last thirty years who were either infected with or affected by AIDS, I often wondered about Linda, Floyd, and Rayshawn.

With some elementary sleuthing on Facebook in 2021, I found a Black man named Floyd Spencer from the Bronx and a White man named Floyd Spencer from the Bronx. The Black man's face was covered with a big beard. How could I be sure it was him? Months earlier, I had taken a screen grab of the fourteen-year-old Floyd from the camp video I'd produced and put the picture on my phone. I gazed into that fourteen-year-old's eyes, then into the eyes of the man on Facebook. The eyes were the same! It had to be him.

I wrote to the man through Facebook Messenger, explaining who I was and that I was searching for a Floyd Spencer who went to Birch Family Camp in Sussex, New Jersey, with his mother and little brother. I then told him the following:

"I produced a videotape called *A Week in the Country* and interviewed a Floyd Spencer who spoke about his little brother, Rayshawn. If you are that person, I think you might like to have a copy of that tape. I would be very happy to make one for you. Please contact me and let me know if you are the person I'm looking for. Thank you."

An answer came a few days later.

"It's me. I'm 44. Please, I need to see that tape."

I was thrilled. Phone numbers and email addresses were exchanged. I duplicated the videotape on a thumb drive, mailed it to him, and asked if I could interview him for my book.

He responded quickly.

"Hey Dale. I received the tape and seen the video. I appreciate you sooooo much! Thank you, thank you. I'm sooo grateful for your life. You are an amazing woman. I will love to do the interview with you."

Those beautiful words of gratitude were expressed because this video allowed Floyd, his grandmother, his daughters (who never met their grandmother Linda), and hopefully many other relatives to watch Linda and Rayshawn alive and having fun at camp. Perhaps naïvely, I'd like to think that the last sad images of Linda and Rayshawn that the Spencer family have been holding in their memories could possibly be replaced with those short, happy images.

Floyd is now forty-four and has three children of his own. His eighty-one-year-old grandmother, Mary, graciously agreed to let me interview her as well. She is no different from the tens of thousands of mothers, grandmothers, aunts, and great-aunts who stepped up to help care for dying children and grandchildren. Always partnering with her daughter Linda in raising her grandchildren, Mary had to finish the job of raising Floyd on her own after Linda's death. Both grandmother and grandson fought valiantly not to be crushed by AIDS. Mary and Floyd told me independently that for three decades, they had been silent about this period in their lives—but not anymore.

Floyd Spencer

"I was around eleven years old when my mother explained to me that she had HIV. My mother was a straightforward person. She never hid things from me, never sugarcoated things. When she told me about her having HIV and AIDS, she told me how it can happen. I didn't understand too much at the moment. I didn't realize it was as serious as it was. I thought it might be like the flu. She never talked about death but talked about how she was sick and she might get sicker as time went on. When I got older, I put the pieces together and understood.

"She told me my little brother, Rayshawn, was also sick, but he wasn't born with it. The doctors told my mother he got it through breastfeeding. He was eight years old when he died. He was a loving kid and very mature for his age. He knew how to save money so he could buy his own toys. I would take him and my little cousin, who was two years older than Rayshawn, outside to play Frisbee, go on the swings, or we'd play baseball and football. I was responsible for the two of them. I loved doing it. I taught Rayshawn how to ride a bike. We were very close.

"When he was in school, I was always hearing that he was very much loved. I'll tell you a story. My uncle used to work in a group home, and he seen a tattoo of a boy on one of the resident's arms. My uncle told the kid that the tattoo reminded him of his nephew. He asked the kid who it was, and he learned that *was* his nephew. It was Rayshawn! The kid told my uncle that they were best friends in elementary school and that he used to carry Rayshawn's book bag when he was getting weak.

"I didn't really think about losing my mother or my brother. I just felt like they would live with it and take meds, until I saw—with my brother—the weight loss. It seemed to me like Rayshawn went from being well one day, and then, *boom!* he was sick. It wasn't a gradual process. I was in high school when he was going through this. It was very hard for me. I really wanted to take some of what he was going through, and *me* experience it.

I wanted to take his pain. I wanted to help him and my mother when they were sick, but I didn't know what to do.

"I was sixteen when Rayshawn died and seventeen when my mother died. I was going to St. Raymond's Catholic School in the Bronx and playing a lot of basketball. That was a good distraction for me. It kept me very, very busy, and it helped me. But watching Rayshawn lose weight and be sick was always in the back of my mind. I dealt with it by the distraction of basketball.

"From 1977 to 1989, we all lived together with my grandma, and then we moved into an apartment on the other side of the Bronx for a few years. When Rayshawn and my mom got sick, we moved back with my grandmother so she could take care of them. She is a nurturer. I was a mother's boy, and when my mother died, I became a grandmother's boy. My grandmother provided so much security. She is a great woman. She was the head honcho. But after my mother died, I didn't actually know if I would be living with her. She went and got custody of me to protect me.

"While everything was going on, I didn't tell any of my friends what was happening. I'm good at hiding personal things about me or when something was wrong with me. The only person I told was my cousin Raymond. He's six months older than me. He knew everything from the beginning. Also, Albert Einstein Hospital created a group for kids my age who went to that camp, and I would go to those meetings. We were a tight-knit group of about eight kids. It brought relief because it helped me understand that I'm not in this by myself. We shared, we cried, and we laughed. Some of the kids' parents had passed before mine did. The counselors helped console us.

"After my brother and mother died, I went through a bad period. I questioned God—a kind of 'Why me?' situation. I acted out. I behaved really badly, cursed, and was quick-tempered. I never used to be like that, but if one little thing went wrong, I would make it a big deal. I showed a lot of aggression and anger.

"I was acting out because, you know, when you have a family tree, there are branches on that tree. My uncle had his two kids and his family tree. My mother had her two kids, and we had our family tree. But the branches of my tree were suddenly gone. We always had each other, but suddenly I felt abandoned. Even though my grandmother was there—and I give her a lot of credit and feel she kept me stable—I felt that my family core was gone. For a daughter or son to lose their mother and their brother is heartbreaking. It took me maybe until my thirties to heal.

"You know, I could have gone the other way and got off the tracks and become the person who got into serious trouble. But when I was eighteen, my son, Joanquin, was born. He was an angel, a blessing. I still got into minor troubles, but, in the back of my mind, I always knew I had my son to live for. I lost my first two angels back-to-back in '92 and '94, but I gained another one. My son filled a lot of that void. He was the sunshine in my darkness. I looked at life differently. When I graduated St. Raymond's, the church gave me a job working in their cemetery. I was there for twelve years. I could 'visit' with my mother and brother all the time when I was working at the cemetery.

"I never forgot what happened. I learned to cope with the ordeal, but you can never get over it. It's like if you have a pain in your arm that always comes at certain times, you get kind of immune to the pain, but it's still a pain. You learn how to fight through it. The pain is never going nowhere. In the beginning, I was always crying, angry, but as the years went by, the anger simmered down, and now the crying is only now and then. But I still cry about it at forty-four years old.

"In 2002 my daughter Lynda was born. She's named after my mother. She's now nineteen. Ten years after that, my second daughter, Skye, was born. She's now nine. I am so grateful for my grandmother and my kids. That's my family now, and we are all very tight. They uplift me."

Mary Spencer

"For years, my daughter, Linda, and her two children lived on the fourteenth floor of this building, and I lived on the twenty-sixth floor. I still live in the same apartment. We were always together.

"My grandson Rayshawn was born in 1984; that's when Linda was diagnosed with AIDS. She didn't tell me anything about it. I learned it from the doctors at Montefiore Hospital after Rayshawn was born. They took me into the conference room and sat me down and told me. They didn't really know much about what was wrong with her. Rayshawn was born healthy. His blood work was okay, but Linda breastfed him for about two months. Nobody knew anything about that in those days.

"He was a very happy baby, an excellent grandchild. He was so smart and always joyful. Other kids loved him. He loved school. If he didn't make one hundred in his studies, he would get very upset and always wanted to do his work again to get a better grade. I still have his books. He loved to write stories about his family and draw pictures of them.

"Floyd was seven years older than Rayshawn. They had a very close relationship. Rayshawn always thought he was the boss and was always telling Floyd what to do. He was a little man with everyone. He used to save any money he was given, and he would loan money to family members. But you had to give him back more money than he loaned you!

"Rayshawn and I were very close. He was something. He was funny and smart and very brave for a little boy. He knew he was sick, but he didn't know why. If he had to go to the doctor and maybe get a shot, he never screamed or hollered. He would say to the doctor or the nurse, 'Just give me the shot.' Even when he was sick, he never had a sad moment. He never exhibited anger or screamed or hollered. He was only eight years old, just a baby, and he was so brave.

"He went to a camp for families with AIDS. The brothers and sisters who weren't sick could go, too. Floyd and Rayshawn went to camp for a week for two summers. When he came home and got off the bus the second year, he was sick, but he was really happy. They treated him so nice. He told me he caught a fish. They took a picture of him with the fish. I still have it.

"When he got really sick, I knew I had to do what I had to do for him. I could not show sadness. I just kept on moving forward. I was there when he went into the hospital. Anywhere he was, I was always there. Before he was heavily sedated, I would sit down next to his bed, and we would talk and watch *Family Feud* together. That was his favorite show. And we would drink Pepsi. That was his favorite soda. When he was sedated all of the time, he couldn't talk anymore, but he could sometimes shake his head to answer my questions.

"I was glad I was there to spend the last hours with Rayshawn when he passed. I was there when he was born, and I was there when he left. He was dealt a very bad hand. If he had lived, he would have been something, been somebody.

"After he died, it was a very difficult time for me, a real trauma. It took a long, long time for me to accept his loss. I couldn't feel anything for a long time or show any emotion. I didn't want to talk to no one. I didn't want to have no one here. It took me almost two years to talk to anyone about it. People said the pain will go away, and that really got me upset because the pain doesn't really go away. I prayed a lot, and I went to church. I had a social worker, like a therapist, and I saw her twice a week to help me get through this.

"And then, less than two years later, Linda died. One thing about Linda, you would never know she was sick, because she was always helping someone else. I'd get to her hospital room, and she was usually four or five doors down, helping someone. She was very brave. No matter how sick she was, she would help the next person and then the next person. She was always talking to everyone on the floor, and then when she saw me, sometimes she'd send me home. She'd say, 'Go home, Mommy. It's snowing outside. Go home.'

"The terrible thing was not one of her friends came to visit her, or even called. AIDS was a taboo. All these people thought if you touched somebody, you could get it. It never crossed my mind that I shouldn't be touching Rayshawn or Linda. I didn't care what they thought. They never supported her or me, and I shut down from them. Linda was a forgiving person and never wanted me to say anything to them about not visiting or calling her. She would tell me, 'No, Mommy, don't do that.'

"At some point, I realized I would be raising Floyd on my own. I spoke to my daughter about me getting full legal custody of Floyd. I said to her, 'I just want you to know that I'll take full responsibility for Floyd if anything happens to you.' She said she thinks she'll be okay. A little while after she said that, she got real sick, and we had to do that paperwork fast. Thankfully, I had help doing the custody paperwork. Even with a social worker helping me, it took about three months to go to court.

"In 1993 Linda got really sick, and the doctors and social workers from the hospital wanted to move her into hospice care. But I wanted her and Floyd here with me in my home. They brought the bed and all the machines. I cared for her in my apartment until she died in 1994.

"My whole life was involved around those two. I look back at it now and say, 'Wow, by the grace of God, I got through it.' My faith kept me going. I think I did a very good job. It was about ten years from Linda's and Rayshawn's diagnosis and going through everything we had to go through.

"I got a lot of support from the people at Albert Einstein [College of Medicine]. If it wasn't for them, I wouldn't have been able to get through everything. Montefiore Hospital has a wonderful group of people. They tried their best. Every medication that came out, they got it for Linda. She was on AZT and a lot of other medications. I had them all set up here, and I would give her her meds. I couldn't have handled all that without them.

"By the time Linda passed, I didn't have any of my friends left, either. People shied away from me. A lot of people didn't want to talk to me. You know, they were afraid of AIDS. When she passed, all I had was my family.

"I was having a difficult time, and Floyd was also having problems. He was acting out and getting into trouble. I tried to console him, but he was trying to be a big man and say that he was okay. I couldn't help him as much as I wanted to. I also had my two sons to support him. The night she passed, he disappeared, and we couldn't find him. My sons went out looking for him and finally found him. I know he was in a lot of pain. His mom was his whole life. It was very tough.

Linda Spencer with Rayshawn on her lap.

"Floyd didn't want to go to school anymore. We went to St. Raymond's and explained the situation, and they helped us. We would tell him, 'Your mother wants you to graduate,' and that's what he did, with a lot of help and support from the school and the church. After graduation, the pastor gave him a job at St. Raymond's cemetery, and he worked there for many years. He's always worked.

"Before you located and talked to Floyd, I didn't think nobody knew or thought about Linda or Rayshawn except my family. I was overjoyed to talk with you. I had periods of a kind of depression, thinking I was all alone. I couldn't even talk to my mom or my sisters about it. No one in the building knew. No one at my job knew. I was shocked when I learned that you had met Linda and Rayshawn. You know what I went through. It's helping me to cope with it now. It's been so long, but I look at her picture, and I'm keeping her alive now by talking about it. I've been silent for thirty years, but I don't have to be quiet about it anymore."

Afterword

EARLY IN THE PROCESS OF writing this book, I learned that one of the first things many people wanted to know is what genre it fit into. An acquaintance suggested it might be called a "witness memoir." That made sense to me because this book is a memoir and I was, indeed, a witness to a largely ignored chapter in the early history of the AIDS epidemic in America. But my CFAP colleagues and I were so much more than witnesses. Like journalists embedded in an army during a protracted war, we were embedded for years in a community of marginalized people, fighting an intense battle against the virus, stigma, misinformation, misogyny, and the unrestrained discrimination that existed at the height of the AIDS epidemic.

Many of my clients with HIV or AIDS had short lives and endured great physical and emotional suffering. With the passage of time, there were life-saving pharmaceutical advances and an increase in the number of HIV/AIDS specialists offering advanced health care. This made it possible for people to survive beyond anyone's expectations, many even to the present day.

Although I left Children's Diagnostic & Treatment Center in 2005 to move back north to be near my daughter and her growing family, the voices of the people I accompanied through their children's births, daily lives, and untimely deaths continue to resonate deeply with me to this day. Just as I advocated and spoke up for them in the past, I found myself compelled to do so again. Writing this book has given me the chance, as the expression goes, "to speak truth to power." After all these decades, the people you have read about in these pages deserve nothing less.

Made in United States
North Haven, CT
07 August 2023

40044912R00202